PRAISE FOR
MANNERS WILL TAKE YOU WHERE BRAINS AND MONEY WON'T

"'It is not what you know, but how you treat people that matters.' You don't need to be related to Emily Post to understand that the best manners, and books on manners, focus on people and not rules.

Donald James has written a book of wisdom, integrity, and kindness. In his hands, the topic of manners serves to take you into a world of motherly care and hard-earned lessons from a career at NASA. Somewhere along the way you start to realize the whole of this book is more than the sum of its parts and offers remarkable lessons.

Written with warmth and understanding—like a firm handshake, a well-received compliment, or walking through the door on time—this book leaves you with the feeling that doing what is right and being at ease in the world of human relationships is not complicated and is completely attainable for anyone."

—Daniel Post Senning, Emily Post Institute

"*Manners* . . . is a powerful must-read. Donald G. James is a master storyteller, a wordsmith interweaving personal stories of achievement while giving his account of success at NASA. His 'Momma's Rules' are timeless, a real blueprint for success. Every page is filled with literary joy—a brilliant triumph."

—Skip Jennings, minister, author, speaker, coach, and founder of Mind Body Spirit Solution LLC

"Reading *Manners* is like sitting down with your favorite uncle, whom you trust and admire, and hearing how getting ahead really works. Having manners, as Donald says, is 'more than behaving civilly—it is a way to walk in the world with integrity, respect, mindfulness and compassion.'

During a time when the world desperately needs to be reminded of these values, *Manners* is an elegant yet practical story that is probably the best book on how to become a conscious, compassionate leader. Donald doesn't give you models or theories, he shows you how to lead through his life's work in breezy, readable stories.

This is a must read for all those who strive to do great things in life and want the world to throw open its doors. Momma, I approve."

—Libby Robinson, MA, master certified coach, managing partner at Integral, a global leadership consultancy

MANNERS

WILL TAKE YOU WHERE
BRAINS AND MONEY WON'T

Donald B. James

Pleasanton, CA

9/2021

MANNERS

WILL TAKE YOU WHERE
BRAINS AND MONEY WON'T

WISDOM FROM MOMMA AND 35 YEARS AT NASA

DONALD G. JAMES

WITH CAPTAIN DENNIS D. JAMES

Pink Suit
·PRESS·

Published by Pink Suit Press, Pleasanton, California
www.donaldgregoryjames.com

Edited and designed by Girl Friday Productions
www.girlfridayproductions.com

Cover design: Paul Barrett
Project management: Sara Spees Addicott
Editorial: Michael Trudeau

All photos courtesy of the author except: Page 148 and
261 (Donald G. James), NASA/Aubrey Gemignani; 148
(Charles F. Bolden), NASA/Bill Ingalls; 148 (President Barack
Obama), Official White House Photo by Pete Souza

ISBN (paperback): 978-1-7356740-0-1
ISBN (ebook): 978-1-7356740-1-8
Library of Congress Control Number: 2020922773

First edition

Printed in the United States of America

In loving memory of our mother,
Muriel Yvonne Gassett James

CONTENTS

FOREWORD

My friend Donald James seems like a man from another, better time.

He's a man of science, of education, of service, and of course, of manners. Since the day we met, I've been deeply impressed and inspired by the leadership he shows and the life he leads. NASA was lucky to have his expertise and leadership for so long; I wish Congress had more people like him.

Donald and his brother Dennis argue here that manners are much more than etiquette, politeness, civility, and protocol. Rather, they write, manners are the authentic and genuine way in which one shows up in the world for good, a foundation for fulfillment and meaning. For them, manners are a moral dimension and a virtue.

From its inception, NASA has been a nexus of our nation's innovation and a sort of civic telescope for seeing mankind's future. As the education director at the Ames Research Center and then as NASA's associate administrator for education, Donald led the effort to inspire the next generation of scientists, engineers, and explorers.

In this book, he imparts the wisdom he gained during his long and distinguished career. He hopes to inspire even more young people to attain fulfillment and meaning by finding their own "NASAs" through which to make the world a better place. And he hopes to inspire parents to consider the wisdom that was imparted to him and his brother by their late mother, Muriel Yvonne Gassett James: Give the people around you nothing but reasons to help you.

Don't mistake this for some milquetoast, go-along-to-get-along philosophy. Being consistently genuine, polite, and principled is a learned skill and hard work. It requires you to step outside your comfort zone, to subvert your reflexive impulse to hit back, and to constantly think about how to stay on the higher ground. It is in many ways a spiritual undertaking and a journey that never ends.

So as you read this book, try to think about how its lessons fit into your daily life. How do you present yourself to your colleagues? To your ideological allies and adversaries? To the myriad people you meet in your daily life? How do the words you speak and the actions you take reflect upon you and advance your goals? There's some element of the Golden Rule at play here: Are you being the kind of person with whom you would want to live and work?

I'm grateful that my parents taught me as Donald and Dennis's momma taught them—that being kind and honest is never wrong, and that unless rules apply to all of us, they're not really rules at all. As a father of two young kids, I believe we all owe the same to our children, and I'm glad there are people like Donald and Dennis writing books like this to help us along.

Today's America too often feels like a perpetual shouting match in which opponents face off with no respect for each other's knowledge or motive, and with no regard for truth and facts. Too many strive only to gain and to win, not for what's right and just. Too many principled disagreements are turned into unprincipled all-or-nothing showdowns.

There's an oft-used exhortation to "be the change you want to see in the world." That's Donald James to a T, and the truth is, America needs more Donald Jameses. That he lives in the congressional district I represent is a source of pride; that he lives in our nation is a source of hope. I have every confidence that this quiet hero's book will help inspire others to follow his example for a more civil and honest country in which principled public service toward a greater good receives the praise it so richly deserves.

Congressman Eric Swalwell

PREFACE

COVID-19

After I finished the draft of this book in early 2020, the world experienced an unprecedented event: the coronavirus, or COVID-19 pandemic. As you read these words, I suspect the pandemic is still being felt. My heart is heavy over the loss of life and the life-changing impact it has had on so many people worldwide.

The pandemic changed our behavior overnight, from "physical distancing" to quarantining to enhanced hygienic measures, not to mention the cessation of a vast portion of the economy. The pandemic, as well as more recent social unrest, inspired me to rethink the relevance of this book's message. As you read these words, you may know some of the answers to the questions I currently have: Will a vaccine save the day? Will we all go back to business as usual? Will the economy, ravaged by this virus, recover? How will our interactions with each other change? Will exposed societal inequities and social justice matters be addressed?

Though I don't yet know the answers to these questions, after much consideration, I still believe that the messages and principles in this book apply. Only you can determine how the principles might apply to you for today, tomorrow, and beyond.

In chapter 4, "Pink Suits," I talk about stepping out of our comfort zone and trying on a (metaphorical) "pink suit" as a new way to approach an issue. The coronavirus has forced the entire world to put on one big bright-pink suit. For me, maintaining a six-foot distance from those I love and wearing surgical gloves and a face mask in public while hunting for toilet paper and hand sanitizer—while essentially remaining under quarantine for a few months—is a whole closetful of pink suits. The virus is like the wind. We can't see it, but we experience its impact.

Another significant change is the near ubiquitous use of online or virtual gatherings, whether for business, education, or social activities. This includes interviewing for a job. Chapter 8, "Am I Being Interviewed?" focuses on the job interview but is biased toward the face-to-face interview. During our shelter-in-place edicts to thwart the spread of the virus, if an interview is taking place, it's probably on the phone or via the computer.

How could the environment of a virtual meeting impact the outcome of an interview? Well, for starters, it's more challenging to read someone's body language—and impossible if it's a phone interview. The quality of the audio and video may be poor and include lag times and distortions. The interviewee may need to be extra mindful to look naturally into their computer's camera (versus off to the side at their screen) and to ensure there are no visual or auditory distractions.

After adjusting to my new reality during the shelter-in-place period, I was struck—hard—and embarrassed when I finally comprehended the pandemic's devastation. Tens of thousands of lives lost; tens of millions unemployed; families crushed; no loved ones allowed at a dying relative's bedside; virtual funerals, weddings, and religious services, not to mention distance education and widespread teleworking; travel all but stopped; businesses shuttered, many of which may never come back. I often equate the enormity of the situation to the proverbial asteroid that has smashed into Earth. Fear, anxiety, and helplessness dominate the emotions of many. How will humanity adapt and cope?

I asked myself during the most sobering moments of COVID-19, which parts of *Manners* are still relevant? My instincts led me to the story I share in chapter 12, "Money, Brains, and Success," about the "magic money exercise," which invites us to take a second look at money and what it means to us.

During the time of the shelter-in-place, while taking a walk alone in the park and enjoying the quiet sounds of the living earth, I often meditated on the rules my late momma, Muriel James, taught me. And with a deep inhalation of clean air, I rejoice that I have another day to give.

Donald G. James
Pleasanton, California

INTRODUCTION

MY NASA CAREER— THE BEGINNING

"Phone, Don," my dad shouted from upstairs, waking me up. The blackout curtains made it easy for me to sleep late, never knowing if the sun was out or not. It was another hot, muggy summer day in Bethesda, Maryland. I went to the den to get the phone, still a bit foggy.

"Hi, Donald. This is James, James Snyder from Goddard."

I'd met James the day before at my interview at NASA's Goddard Space Flight Center in Greenbelt, Maryland. It was 1982, and I was fresh out of graduate school and still living with my dad, my stepmother, and their two children. I was a newly minted Presidential Management Intern, and Goddard had sent me a letter asking me to apply. NASA was not my first choice for where I wanted to work in the federal government. I had just earned a master's degree in international development and wanted to save the world from the scourges of poverty and economic destitution.

To this day, I do not know why NASA plucked my résumé out of the pile of PMIs, as we were known. Perhaps they had dug deep into my academic history to learn that I'd studied aerospace engineering in college, but that seemed improbable. I'd majored in aero for only a year before switching to international relations in my sophomore year.

My father had convinced me to do the interview even if I didn't plan to work at NASA. He said practicing interviewing was *important* and that "the best way to learn is to do." So, I did. I had been honest with the NASA interviewers. I'd shared my desire to secure a position with the US Agency for International Development or the US Department of State. I said I would definitely keep NASA in mind. I was sincere about that.

"Donald, I'm pleased to let you know that we are extending you a job offer. Our interview team was pretty impressed," James announced.

I considered my response carefully, still clearing cobwebs after a long night's sleep. I thanked James for the call and the offer. I said I was honored. I told him that I wanted to think about it, as I was still looking at working in the international development field. I probably said, "I will get back to you"—a cliché phrase often heard as code for "He isn't calling back."

The next morning, James called again, asking me if I had thought about it. I gave the same answer as the day before. This went on for three days straight. On day four, my father said, in his usual diplomatic way (after all, he was a diplomat), "Son, you may want to consider taking this offer. It is an actual job, you know." His suggestion included a not-so-subtle reminder that my efforts to take my newly earned PMI badge of honor to the United States Agency for International Development or the State Department was not bearing fruit. I had nothing, and NASA was offering.

"You can always work at NASA for three to five years, get some solid experience, and then try to transfer to do what you want to do." It was a reasonable strategy and good advice.

I called James that day to accept. I didn't reveal my strategy to do this for three to five years and then move on to save the world from the scourges of poverty and economic destitution. I had a plan. Or so I thought.

Several months later, I received some interesting feedback from James about my job interview. Apparently, I had done everything properly. He commented on how I'd dressed compared to one of the other interviewees. I'd worn a dark suit, a red tie, and a white shirt. My shoes were polished, and I sported a fresh, clean haircut. In the profound words of Tyler Perry's Madea character from the movie Madea's Family Reunion, I was "casket sharp."

James confided that another interviewee had arrived with a bit of a swagger, sporting sunglasses, an open-collared shirt, a blazer, and a gold chain around his neck. I got the impression that his attire alone may have doomed his interview.

James also talked about my responses to their questions. He said it was both what I said and how I'd said it. He implied that I was responsive to the questions, to the point, and sufficiently self-deprecating to inoculate myself against arrogance. He went on to share what the Goddard interviewers, including him, had thought about my overall performance in their postinterview assessment, after I'd left the office. What amazed me were the things they apparently noticed. It didn't seem to matter that I couldn't calculate aspect ratios or delta-Vs or solve a differential equation to save my life. What *did* matter? Well, that is the point of this book. I believe manners made the difference. I ended up working at NASA for thirty-five years, ascending to the highest level a United States federal government civil servant can reach.

I began as a midlevel civil servant, working in procurement at NASA's Goddard Space Flight Center, and I ended my career as a senior executive, serving as the associate administrator for education at NASA Headquarters. In between I moved back to California and worked in public affairs and education at NASA's Ames Research Center. I enjoyed challenging and fascinating projects and worked with and for incredibly smart people. My career launch upward began in 2004, when I was accepted into the Senior Executive Service Candidate Development Program. This program was the way NASA trained its next generation of senior leaders. With the support of many, some perseverance, and guidance from the universe's gracious power, I managed to rise to the top rung of NASA leadership. At the end of my career, there was only one person separating me from the president of the United States. How was this possible for a man with a B average, modest SAT scores, and degrees in international relations and economics?

I want to emphasize something that I strongly believe. A former boss and someone I consider a mentor and key to my growth at NASA once said, "There are many paths to the throne." I didn't appreciate his wisdom at first, but the words stuck with me. Here's what I believe about that statement: there is no one right way to a fulfilling career and life. There is no one answer, but good manners can hold a significant place in the journey.

The domain of "manners" can be viewed similarly to the domain of "space exploration." Space exploration can include a lot of things, and it has many subsets and overlaps: examples include human exploration, space science, planetary geology, astronomy, astrobiology, and exobiology. There's a lot inside the box. Manners are like that. Manners reflect the way people show up to others and to themselves. They are the way in which we exist.

NASA

Without the lessons my momma taught me, I wouldn't have made it as far as I did in my NASA career, which culminated in my dream job as associate administrator for education. Manners and proper English, both verbally and in writing, were a big deal for Momma. As an English and French teacher, Momma insisted on proper, respectful conventions. She taught at a school that had many immigrant students, particularly from Vietnam, Cambodia, and Laos. She insisted on calling her students by their birth names and pronouncing them correctly. She was also convinced that a dangling participle, an uncombed Afro, or an unacknowledged gift were life's debris. "It's your neighborhood," she would say. "Keep it clean and right, so they can't use it against you." What she meant by "they" were people who could help you or harm you. "Do not give anyone a reason to harm you," she would say. "Give them a reason to help you."

Momma believed the key to success lies *not* in how "book smart" you are, or how rich, but in how you treat people and how you show up in the world. Our prisons are populated with smart people. The world is full of unhappy people who have a lot of money. Momma didn't lecture; she just showed up in her truth and let her wisdom ooze out over time.

As a young, naive NASA hire, if I wasn't the smartest guy in the room (and I certainly was not) or the most experienced (for certain), I did know how to engage people and carry myself in a way that usually engendered cordiality, respect, and trust. *I had good manners*, albeit with occasional lapses in judgment. Doors opened that may have remained shut had I shown poor manners (which often equal poor judgment). Opportunities presented themselves that may have been mysteriously absent had I assumed that my knowledge, skills, abilities, or credentials alone would carry the day. People were willing, at some risk to their own reputation, to help, endorse, or support me along the way, enabling me to reach my dream job at NASA, a job for which I competed against more than eighty candidates.

Toward the end of my career, I became interested in sharing what I'd learned from my NASA and non-NASA trainings. During a question-and-answer session, a young man asked me how I might advise my twenty-five-year-old self if I could go back in time, knowing what I know now.

"Great question," I replied. After some thought, I answered, "I would tell young Donald to say 'yes' more to opportunities and to *really* work on his manners."

What do I mean by manners? I'm speaking of more than just civility, etiquette, or politeness. Though manners encompass a broad range of skills, manners are actually more than simply learned skills. Manners are a way of being that is rooted in one's essence.

Everyone has a view about the "right" way to be, what good behavior is, or what's acceptable in the home, school, or workplace. The dynamics and values of human interaction evolve. Rules, policies, standards, and conventions of what is acceptable change. Manners can be situational, and they can also shift over time. What may have been bad manners when I began my career (not wearing a tie to work) may be acceptable now. What might have been tolerated then (jokes of a racial or sexual nature) isn't now. When I speak about manners, I'm not talking about "please" and "thank you." I'm talking about good or appropriate manners *for our time*—the second and third decade of the third millennium. My view of manners is quite broad, as I hope this book reveals.

THE BOOK'S ORGANIZATION: STORY AS TEACHING

Because of my experience as a former NASA leader, early-career professionals have sought my advice about advancement and "making it" in the work world, particularly at a place like NASA. Invariably, the talks and speeches I offer include lessons from Momma, especially the lesson that became the title of this book: "Manners will take you where brains and money won't."

Although I've written this book primarily for early-career professionals, it is my hope that it will also inspire and support high school students and college students on their journeys. My intention is that this book will benefit anyone who reads it, whether they fit those target audience categories or not. Perhaps just viewing the world through the lens of manners will open new possibilities for opportunity, fulfillment, and meaning.

In this book, I draw on stories, both personal and from my experiences at NASA, that serve to illustrate a manners point or one of Momma's Rules. These rules are listed at the start of chapter 1, and we will delve into them throughout the book. Each chapter opens with a story that illustrates to some degree the point of that chapter. This is not a scholarly book. I will simply strive to point out where I've been directly influenced by others. My messages emerge from the synthesis of my experience, training, and learning. My training was not limited to NASA. I've always been and continue to be a "learning junkie." In my twenties and early thirties, I was introduced to two deeply impactful and personally meaningful trainings. The first was the "est" training seminar, created by Werner Erhard, and the second was an intense gathering called the "Men's Weekend," created by A. Justin Sterling. Both were somewhat controversial. My experience with them was powerful and life-affirming, and they profoundly shaped my worldview and my manners.

A note about some of the book's conventions: I use pseudonyms in most stories and references. Actual names are not critical for the story's purpose. In some cases, I use actual names because the reader could easily learn an identity. For example, it would be silly for me to not use the names of the NASA administrator or deputy administrator because anyone can find that out.

I refer to Black people as "Black" instead of "African American." This is just my preference. It reveals when I came of age and when I became more conscious of my race. Once upon a time, Black people were referred to as "Colored," then "Negroes," then "Afro-American," then "Black," then "African American." We were called other things, too, throughout history, mostly derogatory. I prefer "Black" because Black is what I was in my formative years, and that is how I now identify. I am Black because much of society sees me as Black. I am Black because I like being Black, even though I am lighter complexioned than my dad and darker complexioned than my children.

And, for transparency, please note that Momma wasn't the original author of many of her rules about how to live in the world. I know, for example, that Rule #8 came from either Dr. Seuss or Colombian writer Gabriel García Márquez. I'm certain I have come across some of her other rules in my readings. Many aphorisms are timeless, universal kernels of wisdom that have long been repeated in the general culture.

It is my intention that by the time you finish reading this book, you might have discovered a few nuggets of wisdom that are actionable for your journey. Some of the topics we'll cover include the following:

- Manners: an appreciation of manners as much more than being polite and behaving civilly— but as a way to walk in the world with integrity, respect, mindfulness, and compassion.

- Pink Suits: the importance of considering ideas, behaviors, or actions that fall outside your comfort zone—long enough to see if they make a positive difference.
- Money, Possessions, Success, and Achievement: greater awareness of what matters to you beyond these concepts.
- Momma's Rules: not only understanding what they are, but how they may apply to you and how you can develop your own rules that serve your specific journey.
- Interviewing: being prepared for the interview you didn't know you were having. Appreciating that, in a way, you're always being interviewed.
- Building Your Team: the value of having a team in your life to support you.
- Decisions and Consequences: becoming better prepared to handle injustices that may invade your life.

With a cacophony of voices and libraries of books telling you what you should do to be successful, why on earth should this book be any different? Perhaps something I write about or the way I say it will resonate with you. If we connect on just one thing, then this book will have been worth it.

CHAPTER 1

MOMMA'S RULES

MURIEL'S EIGHT CARDINAL RULES OF LIFE

#1: Make peace with your past, so it won't screw up the present.

#2: What others think of you is none of your business.

#3: Time heals almost everything; give it time.

#4: Don't compare your life to others, and don't judge others. You have no idea what their journey is about.

#5: Stop thinking too much. It's all right not to know the answers. They will come to you when you least expect it.

#6: No one is in charge of your happiness except you.

#7: Smile. You don't own all the problems in the world.

#8: Don't cry because it's over; smile because it happened.

One day Momma, a child of the Great Depression and ever the frugal person, drove herself to her neighborhood Dollar Tree store. To Momma, the next depression was always around the corner. At the time of this particular outing, she was about eighty-five and getting feebler, although she was still able to get around pretty well. But on this day, as she got out of her car, she was blindsided by a man who grabbed her purse, forcing her to fall to the ground. As people rushed to help her, including workers from the Dollar Tree, the man darted away with her purse and all its contents. Thank God she wasn't badly hurt, although paramedics and the police were called to look after her and take a report. As Momma recounted the incident, she said, "You know, all the brother had to do was ask me for money, and I would have given him some." Momma was saying, without saying it, that she understood the plight of a "lost" young man. She understood that his crime had roots far deeper than the decision he'd made in that parking lot. She also understood that for many reasons, he probably hadn't learned much from his parents. Perhaps he had role models who believed life is a zero-sum game—you get yours however you can. Or perhaps he had a drug problem he needed to finance, or a hungry young mouth to feed. Momma was an easy target. Never mind that he could have seriously hurt an innocent, vulnerable human being. Above all, Momma recognized that her assailant *did not have good manners.*

In order for you to fully understand Momma's reaction to her attacker, you need to know something about how she developed her set of rules to live by—that is, the *manners* to take her through anything—and the profound, lifelong effect that her teachings had on my brother, American Airlines captain Dennis D. James, and me, a former associate administrator for the NASA Office of Education. Let's start with some insight into Momma. I'll drop in relevant morsels of my own story and use "hard" lessons from my NASA career, as well as my accomplishments, to illustrate my points.

MOMMA

Momma was born on May 13, 1929, in Atlanta, Georgia, five months before the beginning of the Great Depression, the only child of Ralph and Isabel Gassett. She spent her childhood, teenage, and young adult years living through the Depression and World War II. She was a light-complexioned Black woman born into the Jim Crow segregated South, and as such, she was automatically thrust into one of the most insidious manifestations of racism—the complicated distinctions between different-complexioned Black people. It was well understood that slave owners gave preference to lighter-skinned slaves, who were "privileged" to work in the master's house instead of in the fields, generating one of the most incendiary terms in the racist lexicon—that of the "house (N-word)" versus the "field (N-word)."

Fortunately, for our mother and other Black people in the South, this racist distinction didn't prevent people of different complexions from gathering in solidarity to work together, worship together, socialize together, march together, and learn together—not just because they had to due to segregation, but because they wanted to.

When our parents migrated to California in the early 1950s, they immediately sought out the Black communities in Stockton, where my brother and I were born, and Sacramento, where we were mostly reared. Our community—my parents' contemporaries and their children—was our social network. It wasn't until we befriended some of our street neighbors and got to know kids at our local elementary school that our world became more integrated. The Sacramento Black community was an indelible part of who I became; my identity as a Black man, and the way I was supposed to comport myself, was established during that time. The men, all professional and with advanced degrees, were the paradigm of my educational and professional aspirations. The women, mostly professional, represented the epitome of who to consider for a future spouse.

Momma was a product of her times. As an only child, she learned to entertain herself as well as to play with other children her age. I recall her telling us that she used to play with this young boy named Martin in Atlanta. This was not any old "Martin." He was Martin Luther King Jr., who became a minister, a PhD-educated man, and later America's most celebrated civil rights leader. You never know who you know.

Momma was also influenced by her church. Her spiritual nourishment came from the First Congregational Church in Atlanta and several prominent Black families who regularly attended. She sang in the choir, as did some of my cousins, one of whom became a celebrated international opera singer— Mattiwilda Dobbs. The Dobbs family, my grandmother's family, sat near the Westmoreland family, whose patriarch was Isaac Owen Westmoreland, a former slave and cofounder of the First Congregational Church. Westmoreland's granddaughter, Eva Elsie Neal, and her husband, William G. Rutland, or Mista Rutland, as he was known to us kids, were very close family friends dating back to their Atlanta days and then in California, where both families migrated. We shared many Thanksgiving and Christmas dinners together for as long as I can remember. Momma babysat Eva and Bill's kids; their children in turn babysat Dennis and me, and then Dennis and I babysat Bill and Eva's grandkids. In a fitting tribute to our enduring, lifelong friendship with the Rutland family, we buried Momma right next to Eva and Bill's plot at the Masonic Lawn Cemetery in Sacramento.

My brother's and my existence perhaps had its genesis in Momma's singing. While attending Middlebury College in Vermont for graduate school, Momma sang in the choir. As one of the few Black women on campus, she caught the eye of one Charles A. James. One day Momma, studying French and under strict requirements to speak no English, emerged from practice at Mead Chapel to find a gentleman waiting for her on the steps. In halting French, Charles introduced himself to Momma. Later, she received permission from the dean to speak English to Charles. Dad joked later that he believed the Middlebury administrators felt sorry for the two "coloreds" and thought they should have a chance to get to know each other. Well, they did just that.

As the saying goes, the rest is history. In 1999 Dad wanted to attend his fiftieth reunion at Middlebury. I agreed to take him. One of the things I asked Dad to do was recreate the moment when he first met Momma on the steps of Mead Chapel. He did so, and I captured it on video. I remember thinking at the time that I would not be here if that encounter had not turned out well. I mused about going back in time to that moment to warn Momma about the way things would turn out. On the one hand, she would endure the pain of losing her first child when he was three and the painful dissolution of her marriage, and on the other hand, she would have Dennis and me. We always knew that Momma regarded our coming into her life as her greatest gift and joy, especially compared to the hardships she endured.

We also felt grateful for her sacrifices, both before and after we were born. Our gratitude toward her fueled our desire to be the best version of ourselves. Perhaps this is why Momma's Rule #1 is so important:

> "Make peace with your past, so it won't screw
> up the present."

Momma made her peace with her past so she could focus her energies and love on us. At least this is what I believed until much later in life when I realized, sadly, that she'd shoved her past to the recesses of her mind through the strength of her commitment to us.

As she aged, Momma's anger and sadness over much of her past would trickle out. It became clear to me that she had issues with an overbearing mother. She never remarried or had a serious relationship with another man, and, truthfully, I suspect she longed for that. She expressed disgust over what happened to her body from the scourge of radical breast cancer surgery, asking, in what I can only guess to be her sense of feeling mutilated, *"What man would want a woman with a body like mine?"* It hurt me deeply to hear her express this, yet I couldn't help but just be grateful that, as radical as her cancer surgery was, at least she was alive and cancer-free, and she remained so until she died.

I suspect that the most painful episode of her life was losing her first son, Charles. Momma rarely spoke of Charles, though she reluctantly would, if we asked questions. I never knew if she had been able to grieve deeply over the loss of her firstborn. I was born just three months after Charles died. I cannot fathom the emotional roller coaster she endured. Among the many things Dennis and I found while going through Momma's files was a manila folder dedicated to Charles, with more details and photos of him than I had previously seen. Before I even opened the envelope, I cried as I read the line from John Greenleaf Whittier that she had written on the front: *"For of all sad words of tongue or pen, / The saddest are these: 'It might have been!'"* I felt the strong sense of deep sadness from her as I toured this most delicate part of her past.

Perhaps the peace she made with her past was her unwillingness to allow her despair to control her life openly. She did not believe in pity parties. Many of her friends probably did not fully appreciate her painful past. I suspect that there were hurts she kept private all the way to her grave. Her privacy was very important to her. Current research tells us that there is a cost to harboring unresolved issues, whether this is manifested in one's health, family relationships, marriages, or work. I believe Momma fully endorsed Rule #6:

"No one is in charge of your happiness except you."

Dennis and I internalized this message and have carried it through our lives. Dennis recalls being in Niger and seeing a man with only one leg, which was severely crippled, and one arm. The man was lying in the shade of a tree on a dusty piece of cardboard, smoking a cigarette, and laughing with a friend. "I didn't understand them because they were speaking, I believe, Hausa, but the joke they shared had them laughing almost to tears in the stifling heat of summer. This man was fully in charge of his happiness despite enormous challenges."

As Momma's suffering began to reveal itself later in life, she never publicly blamed any of her unhappiness on the traumatic events of her life. They were simply events that happened. She was hurt, angered, saddened, abused, or marginalized, for sure. But these events only caused her unhappiness to the extent that she gave them permission. From this I learned there is not a "happiness switch" that you can flick to dissolve the hurt. But you can take ownership for how you express your feelings. You do not have to blame anyone or anything for those feelings. Assigning causality for how you turned out—good, bad, or indifferent—is risky because you could be wrong or only partially right. The story is probably more complex.

As the son of Muriel and Charles James, and having grown up Black in the US, I cannot pretend that race doesn't matter. However, this isn't a book about race relations. It's a book about career and life navigation. As one who has maneuvered through, and since retired from, the National Aeronautics and Space Administration (NASA), I know a little—though not everything—about careers, interviewing, and effective behaviors. I'm using my own stories and some of Dennis's to illustrate points that I hope will resonate with you, and more importantly, I hope you will be able to extrapolate relevant meaning that fits your background, culture, and economic situation. So, when you read Black man/white world, you may substitute trans woman/straight world, or gay man/straight world, or Hispanic person/white world, or immigrant/native, or privileged/not-so-privileged, and so forth. I equate gender and race only for the sake of pointing out that the nature of prejudice is similar across all groups that are considered, in one way or another. A common denominator of prejudice is the "other"—those that fall outside our own "tribe" or the so-called mainstream culture. Whatever your self-description and personal identity, I'm speaking to you—in spite of our differences. If our differences are the colorful mosaic of diverse tiles, then manners are the grout that binds us as humans. That is my hypothesis.

This seems like the perfect place for me to say more about Mista Rutland, one of the icons of my youth.

MISTA RUTLAND

We called Mista Rutland "*the* Hamburger." He called us hamburgers, too. I was "big burg" and Dennis was "little burg." I don't recall where that term of endearment came from. Probably from when he reacted to what he thought of as a stupid play by a sports figure. He'd follow it up by saying, "Ah, datsa hamburger right there." The comment was usually well seasoned with the swear words that were the hallmark of his vocabulary. "Hamburger" just stuck.

William G. Rutland, Eva, and their four children lived in a house not far from ours on Thirty-Fifth Avenue in South Sacramento. The Hamburger was as much an influential male fixture in my life as my own father and other prominent Black men I had the good fortune of growing up around. I cannot do justice to explaining the type of person Mista Rutland was. He was a colorful and incredibly funny character whose generous use of the N-word was legendary. Somehow, my brother and I learned early on that just because *he* liberally used the word, it did not give us license to invoke the same, at least not carelessly. We were too young to understand how a person could appropriate or "take back" a word originally used as a slur and rework it into one's own vocabulary to spice up a "dish of smack talk."

To me, Mista Rutland was a master of manners. He possessed a quality that endeared him to many, even to those who were offended by his language. He was genuine, authentic, present, and funny. He was his own man, and yet he knew how to navigate a world that was often hostile to him simply because he was Black.

Mista Rutland, my parents, and others of their generation fought to change America's laws, rules, and ordinances to make our country more just and aligned with the principles of our Constitution and Bill of Rights. I am grateful for their struggle and sacrifice because I am the beneficiary. Changing laws and rules doesn't always translate into changed attitudes or beliefs, however. Race in America is a complex, difficult, and challenging topic to address, as are other distinctions. Whether consciously or unconsciously, our feelings, beliefs, and personal history impact our view of the world, and they can also impact our manners, regardless of our race, gender, religion, or socioeconomic status.

BE AWARE OF HOW OTHERS SEE YOU

As a Black man, I am aware that my race may impact the dynamics of my interactions. Sadly, some of those impacts are negative and hurtful. The challenge is knowing whether race is playing a role when I see the clutched purses or the locked doors, or when I hear the myriad comments, such as "You don't seem Black to me," or "You people," or "No offense, Donald, but . . ." or "Now, we have to make sure we hire based on merit and qualification," the latter coming after my advocacy for increased diversity in the workplace. Even when I think I'm *certain* that race is at play, I am not. And I am not sure it matters if I am right or wrong in my assessment. What I do think matters to me is how I act and react. I have a choice, and that choice is rooted in the core belief that my manner of showing up will carry me forward and, as Momma said, "take me where brains and money won't."

I still get bewildered when I'm walking alone and I approach a Caucasian woman who, after noticing me, tightens her grip on her purse or heads in a different direction. This is often subtle, but I notice it and feel it. I don't actually know what's going on in this woman's head, but I make up an entire story about what's happening. And I'm offended. I am convinced that if she *really* knew me, we could easily be friends. Of course, not all Caucasian women do this in my presence, and some of the women who clutch their purses tighter as I pass by are not Caucasian.

Once, in Los Angeles, I was walking across a street in a crosswalk just as a car came to a stop. As I got closer to the car, I glanced at the driver to make sure we made eye contact so I knew that she knew I was there. The driver was a lone woman, I'd say in her thirties. When she noticed me, she surreptitiously reached over to lock her door. Cars in those days had a small rod-shaped device on the inside of the door, near the window, that when pushed down would lock the door mechanically. I caught her pushing the lock button down, and I heard the click. *That's weird,* I thought. *She must perceive me as a threat.* Well, I was determined to demonstrate that I wasn't a threat to her, so when I approached the front of her car, I stopped in the middle of the crosswalk, turned to face her straight on, bent my knees a little, and raised both arms above my head while wiggling all my fingers and pretended to be a mean, growly monster. We both burst out laughing as I proceeded to finish crossing the street. I wondered what data she had that made her conclude, *Threat—lock car door?*

I believe some Black people know that when they engage the "white world," they don't have the freedom to represent themselves as individuals. This has been my experience, so I will just speak for myself. I think, reluctantly, that I am representing *all* Black people. Why? Because the world typically sees me as Black first and as an individual second.

I make gross generalities here to make a couple of points. Yes, it is unfair to be judged by one's skin color rather than one's character. I admit I've made this mistake, too. I'm not immune. I see a bald-headed, heavily tattooed white dude—and I'm immediately thinking neo-Nazi skinhead. I don't care if I see a hundred of them. It's not fair to prejudge the 101st bald-headed, heavily tattooed white guy. This is why I cringe every time I see a news story about a Black man who has murdered someone, especially a white person or, God forbid, a white cop, or even worse, a Black man who has attacked a white woman. I know, as a Black man, there will be some who will encounter me and raise their shields a little higher. Threat. Lock the car door. That said, Black men should not be held responsible for the irrational fears of others.

My point is this: *being aware of how others may see you is wise, practical, and reasonable.* This wisdom may help you act and react intelligently. It may even save your life. This doesn't mean you're selling yourself (and others) out. You have to know where to draw your line and what the consequences may be when someone crosses your line.

* * *

Let's return to Momma's trip to the Dollar Tree store. For Dennis and me, the idea that someone would brazenly attack our mother and steal from her crossed a bright-red line. We were ready to hunt him down and, at the very least, get Momma's possessions back and get him thrown in jail, where anyone perpetrating crimes against the elderly belonged. But Momma couldn't identify the perpetrator because he had run away just as she lost her balance and was falling. She knew only that he was Black. In my outrage and protectiveness toward my mother, I drove to the Dollar Tree the next day to see if I could find anyone who even remotely looked like the person she had described. Momma taught us that vigilante justice was never justified, but I was seething mad and didn't let Momma know I was heading out to look for the culprit who'd harmed her. She would have also objected because she wouldn't want me to get into trouble by taking matters into my own hands. It didn't take me long to realize that my own anger at what had happened was clouding my judgment and that I ran the risk of accosting a young Black man, only to be wrong. *How many times had I seen this happen?* After scanning the parking lot, I soon came to my senses and left. I was still mad, but I knew I was doing the right thing by leaving and not making a difficult situation worse.

What I believe is that somewhere in that young man's history, something went astray. I do not believe he was genetically predisposed to a life of crime the day he was born. Life's deck probably was stacked against him. I submit that if he'd had the opportunity to learn the lessons we'd learned from our momma, he would not have sunk to the depths he did—knocking down a helpless elderly woman, risking her life, to get an unknown amount of money and valuables. Can I wager something with you right now? He stole less than one hundred dollars in cash. Momma immediately canceled her credit cards. As I write, I will wager a year's salary that he is still poor and probably still stealing. If he is a drug addict, he may have gotten one or two hits to satisfy his craving. He is not better off because he took that money. He is worse off.

I am not arguing that manners would have guided that young man away from a life of crime. I am certain there are polite and well-mannered prisoners who deserve to be incarcerated. Manners won't inoculate you from wrongdoing unless your definition of good manners includes a notion of right (versus wrong), lawful (versus unlawful) behavior. Even if the perpetrator thought about this, he could have concluded that because he'd been screwed over in life, it was only "right" that he stole to counter what life had taken from him. That is an ethics matter at least, and it's still morally wrong.

My purpose was not to find and beat up the perpetrator who hurt my mother. Had I done that, I would have dishonored my mother's lessons and legacy. My job is to do my part, however small, to ensure that other elderly women do not suffer the indignities and potential life-threatening circumstances that Momma did.

* * *

When Momma died, Dennis and I had the difficult task of going through her belongings. In this process, we discovered things we had not seen before. Momma always wrote detailed notes to us because she was continually preparing us for the time when she would no longer be here. Among the things we discovered was a box containing several articles and many of those notes, which she had saved over the years. We discovered collections of her favorite sayings, many of which we'd heard her espouse over the years. One list was titled "Eight Cardinal Rules of Life."

Now you have some insight into how and why Momma developed those rules. Some existed to keep her safe; some to keep her in good stead with others; all to support her with clean, clear communication in relationships. With hindsight, Dennis and I know that she created her list knowing that she was raising two sons in a challenging and unfair world. She wanted to give us all the tools we'd need to make it—to live the life we wanted to live and not be like that young man who stole and ran, leaving an elderly woman on the ground, all because he had no knowledge of how to maneuver through his life to get what he really wanted.

Momma did not always fully abide by her own rules. On a continuum, I would say she was pretty close, though. When it came to certain manners and etiquette behaviors and practices, she was 100 percent. If you gifted her, you would receive a handwritten thank-you note in her elegant penmanship. Her requests included "please" and her appreciations "thank you." She respected you fully on the outside even if she took issue with you on the inside. She was a thoughtful conversationalist who rarely dominated a discussion with her own stories. She did not raise her voice. She did not use profanity unless it was with her inner circle of friends. Her grammar and penmanship were old-school elegant. She smiled and was gracious. She had presence. She was a southern lady.

Now Dennis and I, two fortunate sons who have enjoyed what to us have been our "dream jobs," want to pay it forward. We want to show others that something that perhaps has been labeled and misunderstood as old-fashioned or out of style can, in fact, be the building block of personal and career success. I am convinced that learning and cultivating good manners is like installing a train's track switch—just when you might go off track, the reset switches you back to the direction you desire. Switched to the wrong direction, or not switched at all, means you're heading for a collision, a cliff, or a rocky, unknown future. Dennis and I, channeling our mother, are offering our humble, long-developed and cultivated insights on how to install the correct switch.

At the end of the day, your manners will govern how you act and how you react. Your manners shape the decisions and choices you make, as well as the actions you take, including what you say and how you say it. Your manners determine the results generated from your actions, and those results have consequences. I have used this strategic thinking to stop myself from saying or doing something that I realized wasn't going to take me where I wanted to go. I've also used this thinking to govern how I carry myself in the world. Momma always said good manners are not only the key to making it in life, but they are important because they are the right way to show up in the world. Good manners are not about developing a skill just to get something. Good manners are just the right way to be. Manners are a virtue. Behaving with well-developed manners usually does reap immense benefits—and it is simply the right thing to do.

CHAPTER 2

KNOW THYSELF

One of the first working relationships in my very first job at NASA didn't start off well—and, unfortunately, it was with my boss. I felt an immediate distance between us—it was all business, with little warmth. She supervised me appropriately, but it was clear I was not a part of her inner "club." I wasn't sure why. After weeks of analyzing our conversations and interactions, I still couldn't figure it out. Eventually, a couple of my colleagues confided in me, and I was able to conclude, to my chagrin, that from the moment we first met, she'd been seeing me through the lens of her experiences with a former subordinate. Though I didn't know the details, I learned that he hadn't worked out, and she had to dismiss him—not an easy thing to do in the federal government. I understood their relationship hadn't been a healthy one. *But what did this have to do with me?* Those same colleagues confided that this person, like me, was a young Black male. The inference was that my boss worried I might be like him. To make matters worse, she hadn't selected me for the position, but she had to accept me because I was on a job rotation, and senior leadership had unilaterally assigned me to her organization. Wow. This didn't seem fair.

To be honest, there was at least one other man who was not a part of her "club" either, though he was Caucasian and of a different generation. This confused me even more. Perhaps I was being overly sensitive. I recall thinking that my boss just didn't know me. If she did, she would know I was not at all like her previous subordinate. If she *really* knew me, she'd know that *I'm wonderful! Why couldn't she see that?* I wanted this to work, and I wanted her to see *Donald* when she looked in my direction; I jumped through every hoop that came along and then some. I was determined that she see the "real me." Why did I care so much? We both knew that my job in her organization would last only three months, and then I'd move on. Yet I had a strong desire to show her I was worthy of being in her inner circle. I wanted to be accepted for who I was and not the person I thought *she* thought I was. I kept trying, and eventually my perseverance began to pay off; our relationship improved. When the time came for me to leave, to my surprise, she planned a farewell party for me *at her home.* It was a wonderful send-off. I was adorned with gifts and accolades, many from her. I felt I'd finally made it. I was no longer "like that other young Black man." I was Donald G. James. She had seen the "real me."

At the time of my farewell party, when I felt my boss had a clearer sense of who I was, I couldn't have described the evolution of my feelings. I couldn't even describe the Donald James that I wanted her to know. I had sensed I was being judged, and I later learned that the judgment wasn't even about me, but about a "manner" of character she saw when she looked at me. The Reverend Dr. Martin Luther King Jr. described this in his famous "I Have a Dream" speech, when he spoke of judging people not by the color of their skin (or by a person you reminded them of) but by the content of their character.

Let's review what happened in this situation: My boss prejudged me, based on someone I reminded her of. She projected negative past experiences onto me and was blind to the real Donald. Let's call this "unconscious prejudice." I then tried to show her the "real" Donald, and in doing so, I realized I wasn't exactly sure myself who the real Donald was. Let's call this "lack of self-knowledge."

Both unconscious prejudice and lack of self-knowledge can follow you into your job interview and that dream job, wreaking havoc on your professional life if you aren't at least somewhat acquainted with them. Let's start with self-knowledge because it encompasses the unconscious prejudice that can reside in all of us, no matter how free of judgment we think we are. For those at the beginning of their career search, as well as those who have started their careers, there are three essential processes that I recommend you consider in order to better prepare yourself for your professional life. Skipping over any of them can set you up for a bumpy ride.

- Take the time to gain a deeper awareness of who you are.
- Figure out what you really think about yourself, based on how you think *others* view you.
- Gather insight into someone else's idea of who you are.

THE THREE DONALDS (TRANSLATION: GET TO KNOW YOUR *SELVES*)

You already know that Momma taught me to pay attention, to observe, and to improve myself by learning from my experiences. Here's what I learned from that boss: there are three of me!

1. There is the **real** me: authentic Donald.
2. There is the me **someone else** sees and experiences.
3. There is the me **I think** someone else sees and experiences.

They are not always the same. Sound confusing? I'll break it down, using examples from my personal life and my work life at NASA.

THE REAL ME: AUTHENTIC DONALD

The "real me" is the me I *want* others to see—mostly. There are some parts I wouldn't want an interviewer to see, for example, because they're part of my private life and not appropriate to share. Revealing those parts would be in the category of TMI or "too much information." Revealing those parts could backfire. The skill is in knowing where the line is between showing up as an authentic person or revealing information that isn't appropriate.

The real me doesn't pretend, put on an act, or try hard to look good. This is the authentic me. The one so comfortable in his own skin that he can acknowledge his strengths and his weaknesses and be okay knowing he isn't perfect. He's on the "journey of life" and will screw up sometimes and do a praiseworthy job at other times, all the while growing, learning, and getting better. Don't we all wish we could be this 24/7? But it *is* a journey. Once we know we're on a journey and we're willing to remove the shields we place around ourselves, we can accept ourselves and be more available to others—authentically.

THE ME SOMEONE ELSE SEES AND EXPERIENCES

BEWARE OF UNCONSCIOUS PREJUDICE

The second "me" is someone else's beliefs, judgments, and stories about me. This is the narrative I do not hear because it's happening between others, to my exclusion. Have you ever gossiped about someone or talked behind their back, or said things you would never say to their face? Or maybe you did not verbalize your beliefs and judgments about someone. You just quietly held on to them. Here's an example of mine.

Around 1987, I met an elderly German man with a distinct accent, and he had an air about him that I labeled as guarded, cool, distant. I put him at about seventy-five. A quick calculation revealed that he would have been in his thirties during World War II. In my head, I was thinking, *Hmm, eye vonder vat ver hiz rezponzibeeleetees during za var?* There is a word for this. It's called *prejudice.* I saw "Nazi" when I looked at this stranger, about whom I knew nothing. I projected on him all my stereotypes about Germans and Nazis. In reality, he may have been a retired professor, a truck driver, an insurance salesman. But my prejudice blinded me from taking a further step and finding out more about him. To me, he was a Nazi— pretty much "dead to me," cut off at the knees without a chance. Imagine my surprise had I discovered that he was the head of the local food bank? Or a caretaker for the elderly? Imagine if I found out that he had protected Jews in Nazi Germany? But with my judgments, I never discovered who this human being really was. Can you imagine if he'd come to me for a job? Without my even realizing it, I might have ruled him out—all the while patting myself on the back for my righteous decision!

I still struggle with prejudice. I cannot meet an elderly Caucasian male with a heavy southern accent without wondering if he was holding the fire hose against Black civil rights marchers or yelling venom at those young Black students integrating an all-white school—or, worse, wearing a KKK hood. Did the German man and the southern man experience the same thing I experience when I notice clutched purses or locked car doors? Are you getting my drift? That early boss of mine wasn't the only one who could look you directly in the eye without seeing the real you. We're all capable of this! Becoming aware of our prejudices not only helps us see others more clearly—and gives them a chance to be their authentic selves—but it helps liberate us from our own snap judgments.

THE ME I *THINK* SOMEONE ELSE SEES AND EXPERIENCES

Let's begin by remembering Momma's Rule #2:

> "What others think of you is none of your business."

The third "me" is the me I *believe* someone else sees. In actuality, this is the cumulation of all my beliefs, opinions, and judgments—about *myself.* What I believe others think of me isn't necessarily the *actual* truth because, unless you have some superpowerful ability to read others' minds, you don't really know "the you someone else sees." What you can conclude is what you *think* they think about you. "My boss thinks I am stupid . . . My partner does not love me anymore . . . My best friend thinks I am arrogant . . . People think I am fat." In this case, I don't *know* something to be true; I just *believe* it to be true. This is an important distinction and one that drives our manners.

Think of it this way: What you think someone else thinks about you is *your story.* It's what you think and believe, and *it's all in your head.* You may be right, and what you think may be true, as determined by a thousand independent observers, including your own observations, but it does not matter. It's still the story you created and tell yourself. I have learned that the more I take complete ownership and responsibility for my stories, the more powerful I feel. I will catch myself with a story in my head about what someone must be thinking about me. When I do, I will often chuckle and say, sometimes out loud, "Ha, you just made that up." This is liberating. It helps to prevent me from spending mental energy worrying about whether I'm liked, appreciated, or loved. I don't care if some woman thinks I'm a thief. I mean, she is the one walking around in fear; why do I care about that? Well, actually, I do care. I care that we live in a society where some people walk in fear of others for whatever reason, fairly or not. I care because I could be killed by someone who believes that I'm a criminal. It happens and, sadly, it happens to many Black men.

The difference is that what others think about me isn't personal. It's *their* thoughts, so it's on (and in) them. That said, someone's thoughts can have deadly consequences. The purse-clutching woman probably is not afraid of *me*, as in the literal actual *Donald*. I am symbolic of something that triggers her fear, in a similar way that "Mr. German" and "Mr. Southern" were symbols in the stories in my head about Nazis and the Klan.

I noticed in my career that when I am in tune with my "stories" about a person or a group, and when I recognize what is going on with me, I can manage my prejudices and check them. I can ask myself, *Is this really true about this person?* Maybe I do not really know that person. I am then able to engage the person as a human being and not as my *story* about them. *This is good manners.* Understanding your own three "me's" begets good manners on a grand scale. It not only keeps you from operating from a place of unconscious prejudice and lack of self-knowledge, but specifically, it helps prevent misunderstandings, unfounded judgments, or even bad hiring decisions.

HOW DO I CHECK MYSELF AGAINST MY UNCONSCIOUS PREJUDICE?

Another of my personal examples of unconscious prejudice involves one of those older white southern men I referenced. I met him at a function at our NASA facility in Alabama, the home of Wernher von Braun, the German rocket engineer the Americans appropriated after World War II. After some brief pleasantries, I made up a whole story about this person. I was on a roll. I mean, after all, I was in "the South." After I talked to him and probed a bit, it turns out my story was 100 percent complete fiction. *He was a fictional story in my head.* You never know when you may be reacting to the person in the story in your head instead of to the actual person in front of you.

One way of checking yourself is to talk to the person about whom you have constructed a story and probe a bit to see what you learn. Pay close attention to the attributes about the person that caused you to construct your story. You must be brutally honest with yourself here. "He's German. About seventy. Has an accent. He doesn't talk a lot. Aha! He *must* be a Nazi." Can you consider the attributes and characteristics you may have missed? Look for the data that may be hiding in plain sight.

SELF-AWARENESS AND THE JOB MARKET: *KNOW THYSELF*

What are the stories you've constructed about people? I am not inviting you to negate your stories or come up with different ones. They're still your stories. I'm inviting you to choose one story you have constructed about one of "them" and now go and get to know this person as best as you can. See their humanity, learn their history, experience their heart. Find out what they are passionate about, or what they fear. Just listen deeply. Thank them for their time.

In my experience, I have learned that deepening my awareness of who I am is as important as developing a deeper awareness of others. Perfecting this skill may be more important than specific technical skills you develop. I use the word "deepening" purposefully. At a shallow level, you may know the basics: "name, rank, and serial number," as the cliché goes. When I was in a social setting and someone asked, "So, tell me about yourself," or, more likely, "So, what do you do?" I used to respond with basic information, such as my name, where I'm from, what I do for a living. I may mention that I'm married and have two children. I call this the "no duh" level of information sharing. Anyone who has known me for even a short while would know these facts.

If you were applying for a job and this was the only information you conveyed to your interviewer, that person would not have a sense of who you really are and probably would not make a hiring decision based on such simplistic information, especially if your manner was robotic and cold. This is obvious, right? You could be a real jerk, a loner, a whatever, and if the interviewer *really* knew you, their decision might be easy. Or you could be the most amazing person on the planet, and if they knew only the real you, you'd be signed up immediately.

SO, TELL ME ABOUT YOURSELF

You walk into an interview and the first question you're asked is, "So, tell me about yourself." Pause for a minute, and think about that question. What is it you are really being asked? Do you really know? Who is the "self" in "your*self*"? Which of your three me's are you planning to speak from? The interviewer is asking you to tell them about somebody they don't know. What do you talk about? Equally as important, how do you talk about it?

I have asked this question many times in job interviews and informal discussions. Even if I know the person's name and they know that I know their name, they will usually begin with their name. "Well, as you know, my name is Devin." It turns out that people tend to self-identify first and foremost with their name and appreciate hearing it spoken.

Try this exercise. If you're comfortable, and if the conditions are right, introduce yourself to two people you haven't formally met.

- For person #1, say, "Hi, I don't believe we've met before. My name is (state your name). How are you?"
- Then for person #2, do the exact same thing, except instead of saying, "My name is (state your name)," say, "I am a loving, giving person."

Which version feels normal and which feels weird? I am guessing the second one feels weird. Yet, isn't it true that at your funeral, your family and friends will say (hopefully) that you were a loving, giving person? Our birth names are simply a label for something much more complex—a complicated, multidimensional sentient being. A "loving, giving person" speaks to that something. Not the whole something, but a good part of it. Allow me to play the funeral metaphor further. If you go to a person's funeral and the deceased's name is never spoken, I wager you will still learn a great deal about that person.

When I interview someone, I'm really looking to learn more about that "something." I can read that person's name in a file, and of course I will look forward to hearing that person speak it aloud. But when I ask you to tell me about yourself, I'm *inviting you to open a window for me to see inside,* to actually "get" who you are. I'm interested in your name and, more importantly, how to pronounce it correctly. I may even want to learn why you were so named. I have asked a person to share with me the etymology of their name if it's one I haven't heard, but I'm more interested in your character, what makes you tick, where you struggle, where you soar, what you are curious about. I'm paying attention to more than the words that come out of your mouth. I'm watching your body language, especially your hands and feet. I'm noticing your eyes and where they go. I'm observing how you dress. I'm sensing how well you listen and how sincerely interested you are in me. I want your authenticity and a bit of vulnerability. I want to know if you are putting on a show for me—an act—or is this the real you?

How do you discover who "you" are—the person you describe when you're asked, "Tell me about yourself"? Do you really know? During a training class at NASA, we were asked to write down three things:

- what we thought of others in our class
- what we thought of ourselves—like a self-assessment
- what we thought others would say about us

Turns out that what I thought others would say about me didn't match what I thought about myself. It took me a while to see the trick in this exercise. You see, as Momma said, *What others think about you is none of your business.*

What I thought others thought about me was more about what I *really* thought of myself. It turns out that my regard for myself was much more critical and negative when I assigned my beliefs about me to others. In some cases, we know that we fool people. I may say, for example, that my friends think I really have my you-know-what together. That's what I *think* they would say about me. But my own assessment is more negative. I *know* I am just full of you-know-what. This is known as the "imposter syndrome." I don't feel authentic because I either know for certain or I *think* I'm fooling people. It's the old, "If you *really* knew me . . ."

Remember: all these thoughts and beliefs are just that—thoughts and beliefs. And they are *your* thoughts and beliefs unless you have developed some superpowers that permit you to read others' minds. Your thoughts and beliefs are *not* necessarily true. They can be chatter in your head—as my wife says, "It's your 'committee' having a good ol' tea party up there."

Our behaviors and our manners are influenced by this "committee." I don't enjoy walking on the beach without a shirt because I'm self-conscious about my body shape. My committee is critical of my body, and they're whispering to me that others are surely noticing, too—both women and men, but for different reasons. My committee tells me that real men look strong and powerful to women. And that men see other men as potential competition. If you're out of shape, old, and weak, then you are lower on the totem pole, pal. My committee also manages to dictate different manners depending on who I am with and where I am. I often wonder what my chameleon mannerisms are all about.

It's true: I want to be liked, admired, powerful, coveted, and validated. My committee is a very powerful bunch. The good news is that my committee is *not* the real me, nor is your committee the real you. The "you" that most interviewers want to know isn't necessarily the same one your committee commands of you. The gap between the committee's commandments and your authentic self reveals the proportion of the act you're putting on. People noticing the gap may label you as phony.

I didn't invite my committee to set up camp in my head. How they got there and how to change their membership is beyond the scope of this book and better left for psychologists and therapists, *but*—I'm asking you to try the committee theory on. You're not your committee, and you *can* change the committee's membership. I have developed an understanding with my committee. If they ever get out of hand up there, I just turn the light on and say, "Hey people. Listen up. What you're talking about is not on today's agenda. Ain't showing up that way today." For me, what my committee wants me to do is put my ego front and center. Not a helpful strategy.

CONVEYING AUTHENTICITY

Our challenge is to convey who we really are and not what the committee decrees. Conveying who you are is much more than what you say verbally. One of my all-time favorite artists was the soul singer James Brown. James Brown was tagged as "the hardest working man in show business." That people said that about James didn't make it true. All you have to do is watch one of his performances to know that it was true. Go to YouTube, find a James Brown performance, turn off the sound, and you'll see what I mean.

Think more deeply about the question, "Who are you?" How do you answer that question for yourself? How could you answer it in an interview? You're not just your name, your race, your religion, the number of Twitter followers you have, your GPA, or the number of times you made the honor roll. Don't just tell me (as one interviewee did) that you're "a Christian." Martin Luther King Jr. and Adolph Hitler both said they were Christians. Can you *show* me your faith without using those terms? Show me the way your religion works through you and serves your purpose, and, I trust, for good. Terms will be heard differently by different people. I'm the first to admit that I have judged people based on the terms they use to describe themselves. It's unfair because I don't know all that goes on beneath those terms. The terms are the proverbial tip of the iceberg. It's what lies beneath that matters. That's what I want. I want the clothes, not the label.

CHAPTER 3

THE SUCCESS ILLUSION

I don't remember many of the gifts I gave my mother as a child, but there is one I'll always remember—I made my mom "worms." They were made from egg cartons, cut in half lengthwise and flipped over so the egg holder parts became worm segments. I recall carefully painting each segment in bright colors. When the paint dried, I used pipe cleaners for the legs and buttons for the eyes. As you might guess, this was a gift my mom *never* forgot. She always joked that whenever I was mad at her, I would say, "Well, I'm not going to make you any more worms." Clearly, I had made my mom the supreme gift, whether she understood its value or not. This was my belief, and I knew I was right—I had the *best* gift.

Have you ever come across a righteous person who always knows the best way to do just about anything—and believes they are absolutely right? I remember meeting an incredibly knowledgeable engineer when I did a six-month detail at

NASA's Johnson Space Center in Houston, Texas. He always seemed to have the right answer about spacecraft and knew the right way to do something. Data rolled out of his mouth like sweat pouring off an athlete's forehead. He clearly was smart. He certainly sounded smart. He was confident and had a lot of experience.

Yet something about him struck me as odd. His world seemed just a little too "black or white." No gray, no alternative points of view possible, just what he knew to be "right." I certainly was not knowledgeable enough or trained enough to ever consider questioning his views, and I never did. But I always had a nagging feeling that his inability to entertain different perspectives could cause problems for the project. Forceful people who have strong intellect, broad knowledge, and street cred, and who don't suffer fools, often get their way. However, I find these people can be susceptible to blind spots. In the space business, *blind spots can be fatal.*

PROTOCOL, ETIQUETTE, AND MANNERS

Communication problems can arise from how people interpret concepts and even specific words. Two people may hear the exact same word and have a different sense or perspective on it. Take protocol, etiquette, and manners, for example. What is the difference between these three related topics?

Protocol will tell you how to properly handle a diplomatic function, such as who gets invited, what the dress code is, or the seating arrangement at a formal NASA event or a wedding reception. The United States Department of State has a whole office dedicated to protocol. (Shirley Temple Black was the chief of protocol for President Ford, and she was the person who swore my dad in as a US ambassador.)

Etiquette will instruct you on how to set the table properly; how to manage introductions; whether or not to high-five the Queen; when to turn your cell phone off; when to handwrite thank-you notes; when you can start eating at a dinner party; or when and when not to text. Etiquette and manners are often viewed synonymously, but I believe there is a distinction.

Manners encompasses all these skills and more. You can navigate protocol perfectly, execute your etiquette impeccably, and still fall short in manners. Remember that when we speak of manners, we're channeling Momma. Her "manners" or rules for life are about the way we walk in the world, not about which fork to use (etiquette). They're about being grounded in values that are so deep that, with practice, they become second nature to us. They're about the way we present ourselves to the world, not just at our jobs. They're about living with integrity, respecting ourselves and others.

There's a benefit to exploring concepts like success and terms like manners and etiquette, and that is to discover, through critical thinking, why you would do *anything*. A common understanding of terminology—and appreciating the distinctions between concepts, such as manners versus etiquette, or success versus fulfillment—helps clarify what we want to accomplish and how we want to accomplish it. But how can we know if we're all on the same page, hearing (and reacting to) the same thing? How, if we're on a team, or in an interview, or planning a wedding dinner, can we be successful if we don't share the same understanding of what our mutual interests might look like?

SUCCESS: IS THIS WHAT WE REALLY WANT?

Most people want to be successful, right? But what does success really mean? The term itself can be complicated and nuanced.

What I think of as success may not be the same thing that you envision success to be. Is success binary, as in, we are either successful or not? Perhaps it is more realistic to say that "it depends," as in, "I'm a successful entrepreneur, but not a successful tennis player," or "I was successful in completing the half-marathon, but I failed my calculus test." How can we ever say we're successful unless we are specific about its relational meaning?

Success can mean the criminal who successfully robbed the bank—because he got the money, which was his intention—or the student who successfully aced her final exam. Success, conceptually, is often confused with "accomplishment" or "achieving goals." NASA was successful at landing a man on the moon and returning him safely to Earth within the decade, just as President Kennedy had declared as America's goal. Rosa Parks was successful in bending the arc of justice with her defiance by refusing to yield her seat on the bus.

I believe that because success is dependent on so many variables, it's more an illusion. As I see it, chasing success for the sake of appearing to be successful, or even for the emotional high of being successful, is a waste of time. It's like chasing your shadow. But figuring out what success means for *you* is crucial. Once you nail this, you're free to plan, prepare, and envision your own success.

Here's a short exercise about success. I call it a "thought" exercise because I expect that most readers will try it "in their heads." I recommend you write it down, though, because you engage your brain and your emotional sense better when you write. But written down or not, please do it.

First: Identify three or four things in which you want to be successful. Your categories may include health, profession, school, financial, relationship, service, or parenting. You may have other categories. Choose topics that are important for you.

Second: Assume that *you will achieve success* at some point in the future.

Third: Spend five (preferably ten) minutes "seeing" yourself as successful. Spend time visualizing and experiencing the feeling of success in the areas in which you most desire success. Examples are:

If you're thinking about your health, see the blood pressure you desire or the number you want on the scale; imagine feeling great, having energy, and being in no pain.

If you're thinking about your profession, see yourself as powerful (and in a position that pays you very well!). You command respect and give tremendous value to your company. Visualize and experience this success. If it's financial success, imagine being debt-free, with enough financial resources to buy all of what you need and most of what you want—when you want it.

Do this for every area of success that is important to you.

Fourth: Now, describe *in detail* what you see and how you feel when you see yourself as successful in the areas that you care about. Go for the deeper feeling, and do your best to capture it in writing, or verbally, by saying it out loud to yourself. What is that feeling? Are you happy? Are you proud? Are you fulfilled? Life is good, right? Someday, when you're successful, this is how you're going to feel. That "aah, success" feeling! Sweet success.

Take a deep breath. Now exhale.

Let's consider the two American icons that I mentioned— President Kennedy and Rosa Parks. I think we'd all agree they were successful. Kennedy wanted to beat the Soviets at something technologically challenging to demonstrate that American democracy (and capitalism) was a superior way of life compared to Soviet communism. Rosa Parks wanted to see a better, more just, and fairer world for Black people. But had they done the exercise I just invited you to do, I believe they would have seen their actions as an important step, among many, to something *bigger*.

Had Rosa Parks succeeded in changing laws about where Black people could sit on a bus, but not much else changed, I doubt she would have argued that she was successful. I had the high honor and privilege to meet Mrs. Parks at NASA's Dryden Flight Research Center near the Edwards Air Force Base in Southern California[1] when she attended a Black History Month celebration in 1993. Mrs. Parks argued that we are a long way from the "promised land." For her to say she was successful would have suggested that her work was complete. It is anything but. I believe that Kennedy and Parks, if pressed about what success meant, might have said something like their *desire for change* resulted in their actions, which led them closer to a "vision" being realized. Some might label that success.

Why have I spent time trying to characterize success and suggest its limitations as a concept? Because I think the kind of success that many of us chase is illusory. Most of us can imagine being considered successful by our peers or colleagues while simultaneously (and probably privately) feeling unhappy or unfulfilled. Conversely, we know we can be happy and fulfilled but not considered successful. Doesn't it come back to your definition of what success means?

What is your purpose, your mission, your calling; what is the point of what you "do" to live your life? Now, you may not be aware of your purpose at any given moment. You could be going through the motions, on autopilot. The clearer I am about *what I am doing* at any given moment, and the clearer

---

1. NASA's Dryden Flight Research Center was renamed the NASA Armstrong Flight Research Center on March 1, 2014, in honor of the late Neil A. Armstrong, a research test pilot at the center prior to his joining the NASA astronaut corps and becoming the first man to set foot on the moon during the Apollo 11 mission in 1969.

I am about what the *purpose* is of what I am doing, the closer I am to a sense of fulfillment. I use "fulfillment" loosely. For you it could be contentment or tranquility or another desirable feeling. The absence of this awareness is what my wise young cousin Brandon Outlaw calls "sleepwalking." My background predisposes me to enjoying charts, so here's one for those of you who can relate:

WHAT YOU ACTUALLY DO	WHY YOU DO IT (PURPOSE)	HOW YOU FEEL DOING IT	WHAT IS THE DEEPER FEELING?
30 minutes of physical exercise	To be healthier. To lose weight.	Accomplished. Energetic. Proud.	Blessed. Self-esteem. Fortunate. Grateful. Happy.
Write a term paper	It's required.	"Into it." Tired. Checking a box.	Satisfaction. Pride. Relief. Energized.
Meditate	Reduce stress. Lower blood pressure.	Peaceful. Content. Calmer. Less mental chatter.	Connected to heart. Grace.

What I have found is that having "purpose"—and aligning my thoughts, actions, behaviors, efforts, and sacrifices to that purpose—feels wonderful. Articulating one's purpose versus "living/being/doing" one's purpose is a distinction worth clarifying. You can live your purpose—the thoughts, actions, behaviors, efforts, and sacrifices—without needing to articulate it. (Full disclosure: I'm guilty of articulating and thinking about my purpose more than *living* my purpose.) If you are truly living your purpose, people will know. If I told you that my purpose is to be a good father, does that mean I'm a good father? It does not. It just means that I articulated my desire. I don't recall a lot of speeches Dr. Martin Luther King Jr. made in which he talked specifically about his life's purpose. He *did* talk about his intentions and vision—reread his "I Have a

Dream" speech. He lived, preached, and ultimately gave his life for his vision. His life was his purpose.

Discovering my purpose and living it is liberating. I can more easily choose activities I will do each day that are consistent with my purpose. I can be honest with myself about things I'll consider doing that aren't consistent. Sometimes, I will make those activities fit my purpose. Or, after careful thought, I will not do something that clearly isn't aligned. Remembering my purpose allows me to make meaningful decisions and choices. Here's an example:

At this stage in my life, I have come to see that my purpose is "to give." Giving suggests doing something for people, causes, or community. I've learned to include myself on the list as one of the people worthy of giving to—from myself to myself, not just from me to others. Some people express this as "receiving." I view the idea of *giving* to oneself and *receiving* from oneself as closely related, but with this distinction— giving tends to be an active, conscious, mindful and loving behavior, whereas receiving is more passive. The giver controls the initiation and execution of the transaction. The receiver benefits from someone else's action and is not in charge of initiating what is received or determining the result of what is received. The receiver is only in charge of how they react to that which is received.

Giving to myself is also distinct from taking something for myself. Again, the distinction is subtle. For example, I may say to someone, "I am taking a yoga class." But if I reframe this as, "I'm giving myself the gift of health by being in a yoga class," this helps me relate to the class as a gift—my purpose—more than just something I do. The student takes a math class but is giving herself the gift of education. The notion of giving adds meaning and purpose to the engagement. There is caring, generosity, and love in a gift.

I'm asking you to think about the concepts of giving and receiving. Test your thoughts. Think about what it means to give. Consider that giving to yourself means something different than taking something for yourself or receiving something. Consider that the act of giving is purposeful, thoughtful, meaningful, and has loving power. Can you identify what you have given to yourself at the end of the day? Were the things you gave yourself something you intended? If you worked your butt off today, did you "give" yourself a break or did you "take" a break?

Here's the catch. If you are giving yourself fun and adventure, I say it's important to do just that. Give. And be mindful of the moments that you are in "fun and adventure mode." I say this because I've been guilty of believing that I am in fun and adventure mode, while checking my work email every ten minutes or taking that one important call or doing something that isn't in the fun and adventure bucket. This is a variation of sleepwalking—theoretically doing one thing but actually doing something else, usually in zombie mode.

Perhaps you view these distinctions as silly semantics. That's okay. Indulge me. Just try shifting your language, and see how it feels. Importantly, see if the shift impacts your manners.

HOW TO LIVE A "SMART" LIFE

In today's culture, our relationship with our smart electronic devices has evolved to being as necessary to life as air and water. As I write this sentence, I pause and look around the coffee shop in which I am sitting. Every single person is staring into a smart device. I started to write the words "with one exception." At the table in front of me, there is a young man sitting with, I assume, his young daughter. His back faces me, so

I can't see in front of him, other than his squirming daughter, who is enjoying her bagel. I feel delight that this young man in a beanie cap, skin decorated with tattoos, appears to be completely engaged with his daughter. *Yes!* I get up to toss out some trash and just as I do, I see that he is, in fact, on his smartphone while his daughter eats, fidgets, and talks to him.

Bad manners! He's teaching his child during their precious time together that what's on his phone is more important to him than she is. He continues to talk on his phone while wrapping up her leftover food. She's still talking to him. Okay, I confess I have violated these standards. My wife and I implemented a no-texting rule at the table, which I have often violated. Amazingly, our children will now call us out if we slip up and break this family rule. It's hard, I know. You might as well tell a drug addict to "just say no."

Getting too accustomed to texting or taking a call just because the phone rang can have significant consequences. I read a story about a man who flew to Chicago to interview for an executive position with another man who flew in from a different city. The interview was taking place at O'Hare Airport. Clearly, this was a high-level position for which the expenditure of flying in for a face-to-face interview was deemed critical. About five minutes into the interview, the interviewee's phone rang. He excused himself, took out his phone, then said to the interviewer, "Oh, so sorry, this is important. I need to take this. Won't take but a second."

Do you think he got the job? Not only did he not get the job, but within seconds of the interviewee hanging up and apologizing again, the interviewer held his hand up, stopped the interview, and firmly but politely ended it, adding that they wouldn't be making him an offer. The interviewer walked away, probably with the prospect's mouth still gaping in shock near his phone. This may be an obvious and extreme example of "no duh—bad manners." And it is. My caution is about being caught in sleepwalking mode where you forget your manners.

WHAT ABOUT "THE BEST"?

As a senior official in NASA Education, I was often asked by parents what the "best" universities were for their children who were interested in an aerospace career. "What do you mean by 'best'?" I would ask. The answers varied, but it was usually that their child was interested in engineering and aspired to work for NASA. They wondered which schools their child should attend, and some of them, with a whiff of embarrassment, would confess their child wasn't really "MIT material." They still wanted the "best" school for them. This is an understandable desire, one that I appreciated as a parent.

This term "the best" is used frequently, especially when referring to the medical profession; everyone wants to be treated by the "best" doctors, naturally. I haven't met anyone who was delighted to have surgery by the third-best surgeon. Where I live in Northern California, Stanford Hospital is considered "the best" at just about anything medical. But think about it. What constitutes "the best" in your mind? How does one *know* that a doctor or a hospital or a university is "the best"? What are the attributes, measures, validated research, and data to back up a belief that one university, hospital, doctor, or anything else is better than all others? Are those attributes and measures valid? Or are you simply going on rumor or untested consensus? In the case of something as serious as the right school for your kids or the right surgeon for your operation, critical thinking, research, and homework matter. Otherwise, you can end up in the quicksand around the desire for "the best" by enrolling your child in a school that isn't a good fit for them.

And by fit, I don't mean only intellectual fit—I mean a fit for who they are and what their purpose in the world might be. These are not easy things to know, especially about their purpose. I had no idea what my purpose in life was before I went to college. I thought I did, until I discovered that I didn't know myself that well. I'll get to that.

Many parents are guilty of pushing their kids to attend schools that may not be the right fit, simply because they believe a particular school is the *best*. When talking with parents, I carefully attempt to steer their thinking away from this notion of the "best" to the notion of the "best fit" for their child. I tell them that I believe it is critical that their child is *actively engaged* in choosing a college.

The challenge with the concept of "the best" is that it may mask something important. Like the idea of success, "the best" is elusive. The best for Jamal may not be the best for Gerard. The best for Esmeralda may not be the best for Esther. I get it, though. No parent wants what's worst for their child. I believe it's important to help parents remember that what they're really after is *what's right for their child*. Harvard or Spelman may not be the right school for your child. It's easy to assume that just because the 2020 astronaut class attended MIT, Stanford, University of Denver, UC San Diego, or UC Berkeley, these schools are the best because your child wants to be an astronaut.

I thought the best way to be an airline pilot was to join the Reserve Officers' Training Corps (ROTC). Easy. Check that box and fly away I go! There was only one problem. I didn't relate to military culture well. My brother Dennis, who also had flying aspirations, took a different path. After college, with a journalism degree, he went into Officer Candidates School with the United States Marine Corps to eventually learn how to fly. You don't get more military culture than the Marines. For Dennis, the Marine Corps was a great place to serve our country and a means to an end—to fly. I was naive about what resonated with me at the time. I didn't understand what inspired me or what mattered to me most. I hadn't envisioned my success because I didn't really understand my purpose. I didn't know that means and process were as important to me as ends and results. Dennis didn't care if he had to eat snakes and take heat from the drill sergeants. For Dennis, the ends justified the means. Me? Snakes? I don't *do* snakes.

MANNERS ON THE JOB: NASA EXAMPLES

Let's take a quick look at real-life situations that show us how clear communication and Momma's good manners, in the form of doing the right thing, can play out on the job. These two NASA examples reveal that manners are vitally alive and incorporated into the values of the daily work structure at one of the world's most notable institutions. Not an old-fashioned thing about it.

One of the more gratifying responsibilities I had at NASA Ames was serving on our Diversity and Equal Opportunity Board (DEOB). As stated in the DEOB charter:

> Members are to maintain current knowledge and engage in continuous learning on diversity and equal opportunity issues and trends at the national level and at Ames. They must closely monitor the effects of such trends and issues at Ames and they must promote diversity and equal opportunity policies and help to demonstrate commitment to such policies

in all NASA programs, processes and practices at all levels throughout the center.[2]

Example One: Diversity. Diversity at NASA is important,
as you can see from the DEOB guidelines. Every employee is
responsible for advancing diversity and looking for practices
and processes that hinder the cause. For example, in the early
days, we learned that our scientists and engineers, when asked
to support recruiting opportunities, were more inclined to
visit their alma mater. There's nothing wrong with that on
the surface, but upon review, this meant we weren't reaching
historically Black colleges and universities, Hispanic institutions, or the tribal colleges, because most of our scientists and
engineers had not attended those schools. We also weren't
recruiting at community colleges. Eventually, we adjusted our
practices to be more inclusive in our recruiting.

Example Two: Disability. An observation brought to the
Diversity and Equal Opportunity Board concerned parking
spaces for our disabled personnel. People noticed that occasionally, when they tried to park in a handicapped space, they
found a delivery truck or other vehicle in the space or blocking access to the space. Trucks usually had their flashers on,
suggesting they were there temporarily. Technically, this was
against code, but violators treated the infraction like a driver
might treat a stop sign or a speed limit—a rule that can be
broken occasionally. For those who used handicapped parking,
this was an offense that was personal and contrary to the center's diversity and inclusion policies. A small committee was
formed to address the issue. I was proud to participate and add
my voice to rectify this.

---

2. From the January 2007 Office of Equal Opportunity and Diversity policy
statement. Note: This may not reflect the current NASA policy on diversity
and equal opportunity.

Make no mistake about it, Momma would say that both examples were manners problems. Insensitive, yes. Inappropriate, yes. Traffic violation, yes. Bad manners, no question about it. In an ideal world, without prejudice, bias, or any of the "isms" that poison our culture, cultivating our manners is like preparing fertile ground. The soil would be perfect and weather conditions ideal to sow and reap abundance. But perfect conditions are not present in our society. Distinctions are never clear. There are no easy quick answers.

Yet it's clear that communication, including the language we use daily, can lead us closer to our goals or push us astray. We often aren't clear about each other's definitions of frequently used terms and concepts. My sense of success may be entirely different than yours. What can we learn from this?

- Success isn't the litmus test for fulfillment and happiness.
- The "best" may not be what's best for an individual.

As you practice and improve your awareness of relationship dynamics, especially the terms and concepts we use, and as you become exceedingly self-aware, you can see more clearly what is happening around you—in an interview, on a job, in your personal relationships. As we asked in NASA when communications got fuzzy, "What problem are we trying to solve here?"

CHAPTER 4

PINK SUITS

I have never had a pink suit, nor do I imagine trying one on or buying one—but if I did, I'd certainly get my own attention as well as that of my friends and colleagues. I use the "pink suit" as a metaphor. It is an invitation to suspend judgment toward that which you are, proverbially speaking, *trying on*. Obviously, people do wear pink clothes that don't phase them or others. The term "pink suits" is an analogy that suggests a difficult or unusual thing for someone to consider "trying on," such as an idea, a political position, a religious point of view, a new job, a new love, or anything that doesn't suggest the typical direction of someone's behavior, thoughts, or direction. You *always have a choice* about what to do with a pink suit.

When we explore the idea of trying on something we may not otherwise wear, we're pulling that pink suit out and trying on something that may be so different from who we are that it scares us or pushes us outside our comfort zone. Examples of our pink suits may be test-driving *completely new behaviors or practices* with the end goal of improving our manners. We may try these pink suits on for a month or two just to see what they're like and how we feel about the experience. We may discover that we look pretty good in pink—or that our personal status quo is fine just as it is. At least we tried, right?

Let me illustrate this with a personal example. As I write this, the federal civil service General Schedule (GS) system uses "grades" from GS-1 to GS-15. After that there is the Senior Executive Service (SES), in which there are five levels. I began my career at NASA as a GS-9. I once had a boss who flat out told me that my promotion potential was capped at a GS-12. I was an 11 at the time. Still somewhat new to NASA and "the system," I didn't comprehend that what he probably meant was that the job series for my position as a public affairs specialist only went as high as a GS-12. It was still possible for me to rise beyond a GS-12, but he didn't explain that to me, nor did I push him on how to get promoted to a higher grade. I assumed I'd gotten as far as I was going to get—forever—in my NASA career. I was dismayed. My fellow public affairs colleagues also felt disturbed. Our boss didn't seem interested in advancing our careers.

My colleagues and I would meet outside of work, secretly, to talk about how to cope. The little things bothered us most. For example, we took issue with how our boss supervised us around punctuality. If we came to a staff meeting even a few minutes late, he would make a point of looking at his watch conspicuously. He was letting us know that *he* knew we were late. Sometimes he would acknowledge our lateness publicly, and sometimes in our performance review, he would state the exact number of times we'd been late. Golly, were we back in elementary school? Punctuality is expected, as are good manners, in a professional environment. But we felt that the way he handled our occasional tardiness was petty.

Things didn't improve. Around this time, I reconnected with a friend in my professional circle who was the vice president of communications at Lockheed Martin's Sunnyvale campus. I thought the world of this person and still do. I considered her a mentor and a trailblazer. You see, leadership in the corporate aerospace world was, and still is today (though improving glacially), dominated by Caucasian males and is disproportionate compared to gender and race demographics in the United States. (I should note, however, that as of the spring of 2020, the CEO of the Lockheed Martin Corporation, the largest defense contractor in the United States, is a woman.) To see a Black woman, my friend, as the vice president of communications in a company like Lockheed was inspiring. She was smart, savvy, and extremely personable. She excelled at rapport. When she spoke, you felt as if you were the most important person in the world.

We scheduled a lunch, something I valued, since she was far busier than I was at the time. We exchanged pleasantries. Then she surprised me by asking if I wanted to work for her. She reminded me that she'd made a similar offer previously, and I had declined. Now, she said with a smile, this was the last time she would ask. My feelings about my NASA Ames boss added to my enthusiasm about my Lockheed friend and the chance to work under her wing was a perfect storm. This was a career pink suit that I was ready to try on.

Why was it a pink suit? Because I'd worked at NASA since right out of graduate school. Most Presidential Management Intern positions went to the Department of Defense due to President Reagan's massive defense buildup. I wasn't interested in the Defense Department. Lockheed Martin was one of the biggest defense contractors in the United States; I would be making a significant change by going from an agency that took us to the moon to a large company that built defensive and offensive weapons, among other systems and products. As a public relations person, there would be times when I couldn't discuss Lockheed matters due to the classified nature of some of the work.

This was not a muted pink suit; it was a bright, neon-pink suit. I said yes before I could talk myself out of it. First, I felt the excitement, then the fear; then I thought about the millions of things I needed to do to make this happen. I was going to return to Ames wearing a bright-pink suit! I needed to move quickly to tell people before they noticed something was up. It's hard to hide a pink suit, even a metaphorical one. Little did I know at the time that this wasn't the only pink suit I would be invited to wear.

I returned to my office and continued with my responsibilities. Ironically, nothing my boss said or did from that moment forward caused me angst. I was already free. I was liberated. I was moving on. Good manners dictated that I needed to take the high road in the communication of my intention to resign. This was new territory—I had never resigned from a job. Good manners and professional etiquette, in addition to your organization's personnel rules, prescribe proper protocols. If you choose to quit a job, please know your organization's rules regarding the separation process. Your timing and your own financial well-being could be impacted. When in doubt, talk to your friendly human resources person in confidence. *The way you leave an organization may well be one of the most significant things you do at that job.* People will remember how you handled yourself. It's like a comet that passes close enough to be observed by telescopes. There is usually a long tail behind it. Astrophysicists love to study comets as they get closer to Earth and as they move further away. People will notice how you exit. Did you leave with good manners, or did you leave a trail of litter?

"Don't burn your bridges" means don't resign or quit and then say or do anything that may cause your employer or your former colleagues to think negatively of you. Even if you depart on not-so-great terms, be gracious in your exit. Thank the company, your colleagues, and your boss for the opportunity. Finally, express your appreciation to the company in writing, stating some of the *positive experiences you had and things you learned.* Doing this gives your employer a couple of positive things to say about you if ever asked, and that's what you want. Cultivate the narrative you want your former colleagues to have about you after you are gone.

Not long ago, I found the resignation letter I had submitted to my boss. It was short, to the point, and expressed gratitude for working for a great agency. Little did I know that my life at that career turning point was going to be anything but tranquil.

I calmly walked my resignation letter to my boss's door, knocked, and asked if I could speak to him. He rose from behind his desk and walked toward me (good manners). After brief pleasantries, I said in a measured cadence that I was resigning from NASA. I handed him my letter. He shook my hand and said something nice; I don't recall exactly what. Then he did something odd. He pivoted back toward his desk with alacrity, reached for his sweater, and told me he had to get to human resources right away so he could quickly get an announcement out to replace me. He said something like "I'd better strike while I can. You never know when they might impose a hiring freeze."

As the saying goes, "I may have been born at night, but I wasn't born *last* night." While still feeling the breeze of the wake he left in his hasty departure, I received the clear message: "Don't let the door hit you in the butt on the way out." I'd been hoping to score a little pushback, such as "Are you sure? Will you reconsider?" Nope. But my roller-coaster ride was just beginning.

I sauntered back to my office, remembering that resigning for something better was what I wanted. My self-pity dissolved as I thought more about my new future with Lockheed and my friend and soon-to-be new boss. I started sharing the news with my colleagues. Word spread quickly: I was leaving NASA. Two weeks until the end of my NASA career.

The next day, I was summoned to my boss's boss's office. Let's call him William. He was about my age—younger than my current boss, the man so eager to replace me. A young, quick, entrepreneurial type who'd ingratiated himself with Ames leadership, William couldn't have been more different than my immediate supervisor. When I got to his office, he closed the door, held up my resignation letter, and asked, "So what is this all about?"

I told him the truth. I was resigning from NASA to explore new opportunities at Lockheed Martin. I was grateful for my time at NASA, but now it was time for me to move on. It took me a while to understand what he meant by the question, "So what is this all about?" He repeated the question but then threw in a curveball: "What is it that you want, Donald?" I started connecting the dots.

William thought my resignation was a negotiating tactic to get something. That was so far from my motive that it took me a while to understand his question. Then he made it perfectly clear. William said that he'd "done this same thing" in his career to get a promotion or a job he wanted. He would work hard to make himself indispensable and then threaten to resign or quit to extract something he wanted, like a promotion.

I was emphatic—this was *not* why I was resigning. My integrity wouldn't allow me to play that game. I repeated unequivocally that this was not my reason for resigning. I told William about the person I greatly admired at Lockheed and recounted how she'd asked me to come and work for her before. I told him that I believed that now was a good time. William leaned forward, locked eyes with mine as if penetrating deep into my brain, and as if he could read my mind, asked, "It's (my boss's name) isn't it? You're leaving because of (my boss's name)." I'm sure my facial expression revealed the truth before the words came out, so I confessed that he was part of the reason, *yes*.

MANNERS

Let's pause the story for a minute to consider the manners implications, starting with my motivation to leave. Choosing to quit a job in order to take one that pays more money can be legitimate. Using a decision to quit to extract a pay raise concession is troubling. It's a mild form of extortion. Prior to quitting, you may have diligently and diplomatically explored your options to get a higher salary, a better position, or a better boss. Perhaps you discovered you aren't being paid as equally as peers doing the same work. In that circumstance, it's not only correct to make your case for a higher salary, but obligatory in the name of justice. A note of caution, however, regarding the way you handle yourself in challenging a discrepancy of this nature. If you threaten to quit unless they meet your demands, *you must be prepared for them to call your bluff*. You may be in the right, but you may be in the job market, too.

Threatening isn't exactly good manners and could establish a narrative about your character that will follow you wherever you go in your career. I've heard about a potential new hire whose reputation preceded him because of the way he left a previous position. The watercooler talk went like this: "He's only here for the money and not the company." Or, "We should be careful about this person because he might walk if we don't adhere to his demands." "High maintenance" or "a trouble-maker" are code for "I suggest you don't hire that person."

Pay attention to the character traits you want others to believe about you. Their beliefs about you will turn into their narratives about you, meaning you may never know with whom they will share these views, including people in the company or organization where you want to work next. You never know "who knows whom" in your circles.

The second manners point concerns my decision to tell William one of my motivations for leaving. As a rule, *tell the truth*. It's too hard to remember a lie, even a mild one. One's body language can often reveal an unspoken truth or an overt lie, so if your mouth tells a lie and your body tells the truth, many people can pick up on the discrepancy. In my case, I told William that, yes, my boss was part of the reason I was leaving. My goal was to take full responsibility for my decision. My goal was not to, as the saying goes, "throw my boss under the bus" by barfing out my complaints, judgments, and evaluations and declaring him the evil one. What I wished I had said to William was, "I couldn't figure out how to make my relationship with my boss work. This job opportunity arose, and I chose to accept it." That's taking responsibility for my decision while keeping my judgments to myself.

William then opened up with his own opinion, confessing that he wasn't a fan of my boss, either. Here comes pink suit #2. William said, "Why don't you go back to your office and write down all the things you would need from this center in order to reconsider your decision." I wasn't stunned by the offer because it didn't matter. I was resigning and going to work for Lockheed. I was certain that no matter what I proposed, the center's leadership wouldn't approve. I knew enough about bureaucracy, rules, and regulations to know that, unlike in private industry, a government official isn't Captain Picard, who can command, "Make it so." Or so I thought.

Sitting at my desk with a blank piece of paper in front of me, I recall vividly thinking, *What the hell? This won't happen anyway, so I'll just list everything I want.* And I did. My ego took over. I walked back to William's office and gave him the list. He took a quick look, thanked me, and said, "I'll get back to you." Just like that.

Toward the end of the day, William leaned into the door of my office and said, "They agreed to all your demands." Now *I* was stunned, though I didn't appreciate the term "demands" because I hadn't been "demanding" anything. I was going to work for Lockheed Martin. I'd indulged William with my list because he'd insisted on it.

After realizing what he'd just said, I responded with, "Well, a deal is a deal. I'll reconsider my decision." William asked for my answer in three days. Those were the most agonizing three days of my early career. I was putting on yet another pink suit while just getting used to the first one.

Before continuing the story, I want to pause here and reflect on the importance of recognizing what manners have to do with a pink suit situation. For starters, I see many pink suit opportunities as a "fork in the road." You know that the decisions and choices you make when presented with a pink suit will change the course of your future. You'll be going from a predictable trajectory—*I will continue to work for NASA*—to an unknown one. The unknown can increase anxiety—even those unknowns we want, such as getting married, or getting into college, or having a baby. What if it doesn't work out? Learning how to recognize when you're in a pink suit moment helps you prepare for the outcome. You become more mindful in the moment. You give yourself an opportunity to be deliberate in trying on the pink suit, evaluating its fit, and contemplating your new relationship with it, whatever "it" represents.

A pink suit opportunity forces a decision. Some decisions and choices can have significant consequences, whether good or bad, helpful or not. Declining to accept the suit, just as agreeing to put it on, is in fact a decision. That decision, too, will have consequences.

Pink suit opportunities tend to bring excitement, energy, and vitality. There's a disturbance in your universe that now has your attention. The opportunity may not always feel good. Getting fired from a job, flunking a class, or being rejected in love are all pink suit moments. Regardless of the way you classify your pink suit, the real opportunity isn't so much in the suit itself as a *thing*, but in your noticing the suit in the first place, your process of trying it on, your evaluation of it, and your disposition of the suit.

Why is this important? Because when you step into a pink suit opportunity, those around you are observing how you handle the change. This matters if you're a person of influence and someone others look up to, like a manager and a leader. It *really* matters if you're a parent. Your children are paying attention to you more than you know. *And* your peers, friends, teachers, and potential future employers are also paying attention to you more than you know. Reverend Dr. Martin Luther King Jr. said it best: "The ultimate measure of a man is not where he stands in moments of comfort and convenience, but where he stands at times of challenge and controversy." A pink suit opportunity can be a time of challenge and controversy. Consider that how you handle a pink suit is a "tell" about your manners.

Getting back to my story, I often wondered whether my decision to provide my requirements list was appropriate. I was not *demanding* something in exchange for something else. I don't believe in playing games as a negotiating strategy. I could simply have told William that I appreciated his desire to keep me, but I had made up my mind. Perhaps I was just being nice and accommodating? He'd wanted my list, so I obliged. I recall clearly that I felt I had nothing to lose. I remember reading a story of a woman in a similar situation. When her company agreed to her "demands," she said later that she wished she had asked for more. She also saw the truth of the adage, "Be careful what you ask for, because you just might get it." Momma used to say this, as well. There really is power in an ask. Good manners are about *how* you ask and *why* you're asking.

I kept my word. I said I would reconsider my resignation. But before I got too involved in my reconsideration with NASA, I called my friend and soon-to-be new boss at Lockheed to let her know what had transpired. I didn't want this to be a secret. I wanted to assure her that I was committed to working for her, and I suspect I needed to assure myself that I was still committed. Her response to my news affirmed my desire to work for her. She told me that she wasn't surprised. She said I was a capable person and NASA knew that. "They would be remiss if they didn't try to keep you."

I was impressed. Her sincerity and compassion for what I was going through made me want to work for her even more. Just when I thought this pink suit could not get any pinker, I received a phone call from Lockheed's HR department. I had spoken to a man there about the process of starting employment with the aerospace giant. I assumed he was calling to let me know what forms I had to fill out or what I had to do for a security clearance. What he said surprised me. My Lockheed friend and new boss had apparently told him about NASA's desire to keep me. He'd called to, let's just say, sweeten the deal. The most challenging thing for me at that very moment was to muzzle the shouts from my ego about what appeared to be a bidding war over me. I dismissed my ego, and in that very moment, I felt powerful, honest, and grounded in integrity.

I told the HR person that I appreciated Lockheed's generous offer. I said that my original decision to resign from NASA and work for Lockheed was not about extracting concessions from NASA, as William had suggested. I hadn't expected NASA to "counter," and now Lockheed was countering the counter with cash on the table. I told him, respectfully, that this was not about money and that I planned to spend the next couple of days reconsidering my decision, as I'd agreed. I said, "Thank you for your generous offer, but no thank you." *Manners will take you where brains and money won't.* Lockheed's money was not going to take me where I needed to go, even if I was uncertain of that destination.

You know how this movie ended. You know which pink suit I kept. Over the next two days, I did a detailed cost-benefit analysis to help me reach my decision. I listed the pros and cons of working for Lockheed. I listed the pros and cons of staying with NASA. I gave a numerical score to each item, weighting them based on my assessment of their relative value. This was all subjective, but I endeavored to be as honest as possible. For example, one pro for staying with NASA was the stability of working for the government. One con was the risk that NASA could not keep their end of the bargain.

This was also personal. We had lived in several countries while I was growing up because Dad was in the foreign service. Although my brother and I lived with Momma most of the time, the agreement our parents had made when they divorced was that we would also live with our dad from time to time. That was an exciting time—a real adventure. We lived and went to school in Thailand and Kenya and traveled to Europe and other African countries. However, instinctively, I knew I didn't want to move frequently as a professional or even as a family man. Stability in a career was important to me.

Prior to finishing the cost-benefit analysis, I searched my heart to see what my instincts were telling me. I didn't get a clear answer. I was at an impasse. I had a team of men in my life who supported me around my most difficult challenges. Their support wasn't, "Well, just pick door #1, Donald." My men's team was my safe place to openly grapple with my challenges. They were not my crutch and wouldn't tell me which direction to go. They knew I needed to struggle through this question on my own. They were there to listen and give me a safe space in which to struggle.

The cost-benefit analysis became my inductive reasoning science project, where I started with known details about my current NASA situation and what I thought I knew about the new Lockheed opportunity. I then looked to see where the data led me. A funny aside: I saw a sign above a door of someone's office at NASA's Johnson Space Center that read, "In God we Trust—all others bring data." NASA is a data-driven science, technology, and engineering organization. No astronaut will set foot in a spacecraft designed by an engineer who says, "Well, my gut tells me it will work. Trust me."

If you saw the movie Hidden Figures, you'll recall the scene when astronaut John Glenn is waiting for the final "go" to board Friendship 7 for his historic orbital launch, the first by an American astronaut. The wait was due to concern over the trajectory analysis of his flight. This *had* to be perfect. The wrong analysis could mean Glenn's spacecraft would, at best, land in the ocean way off target or, at worst, he and his spacecraft would disintegrate on reentry. In the movie, you see Glenn talking to the flight controllers at Cape Canaveral and asking them what "that girl" says about the analysis. That "girl" he was referring to is Katherine Johnson, the lead character of the movie, who was one of several "human computers" whose job it was to do the math needed for a successful spaceflight. John Glenn was asking what her analysis showed. When the flight controllers confirmed that her calculations confirmed the trajectory, Glenn said, "That's good enough for me."[3]

My preference to rely on data to understand, believe, or conclude something had not yet fully developed at the time

---

3. The movie, though based on a true story, took some liberties with the actual facts. It is true, however, that John Glenn asked for confirmation of the data from Ms. Johnson.

of my decision of whether to stay with NASA or go work for Lockheed. Later, surrounded by data-oriented scientists and engineers, I would become much more comfortable with a conclusion about almost anything if I had data. There had to be some science behind it.

Once my cost-benefit analysis was complete, it was time to crunch the numbers in the computer. The "computer" was a twenty-dollar calculator from RadioShack. Once crunched, the numbers spoke: *Stay with NASA*. I double-checked to make sure I hadn't missed anything. Then I looked at the parameters and the data to try to make sense of the results.

First, I realized that I'd never wanted to leave NASA. I'd felt compelled to because I had a boss I didn't care for, and I believed my career was at a dead-end. I loved NASA and NASA's mission. It was and remains the best place in the federal government to work, and I know why. NASA has smart, driven, curious people and a unique mission, with the coolest facilities in the world.

Second, the only pull to Lockheed was my friend and mentor. I wasn't drawn to Lockheed's defense contractor mission. My analysis revealed that working for her was not a sufficient reason to leave NASA, especially since NASA Ames leadership was willing to meet my requirements for staying.

Third, since Ames Research Center agreed to my requirements, I concluded that staying was a risk (meaning that things might not go as planned) worth taking. I trusted William and Ames leadership to keep their promise. Deep down, though, I felt that the probability that my requirements couldn't be met was high. I'd put my cards on the table. One requirement was that I no longer work for that boss. The other requirement was to be on track for promotion beyond the GS-12. If neither of those things occurred, I would be back to square one, with my Lockheed option gone. I was gambling with my professional future.

Magnifying that risk, within two months after I rescinded my resignation letter and told Lockheed that I would decline their offer, William, the man who persuaded me to rethink my plans and "secured" the agreement from Ames leadership— nothing in writing, by the way—announced he was leaving. The person with whom I had the handshake on our deal was leaving—the one person who could go to bat for me. What were the chances now that I would get what I'd asked for?

In the end, the Ames leadership kept their side of the bargain. Everything I requested, they made happen. When I'd originally created my list of requirements, I hadn't cared, so I'd thrown everything in except the kitchen sink. I did take some requirements off the table because they were either frivolous or just not right. But the biggies—yes. They made those happen.

This largely explains why I am so fiercely loyal to NASA. They didn't have to handle the situation as they did. They could have said, "Enjoy your career at Lockheed." They could have shined me on about the deal—bureaucracy has an amazing ability to gum up just about anything. But that didn't happen. And because that didn't happen, my career shifted to a new path. One that would eventually lead me to the highest echelons of NASA leadership.

I worked my butt off to make sure I was worthy of the deal. I will let others judge my success on that. I have no regrets about how I handled those pink suit moments. I am sure that had I decided to leave NASA and work for Lockheed, it would have turned out just fine. But this I also know—had I chosen that path, I might not have met my wife and become the father of my two incredible children. I thank the universe that guided me through that time and for giving me the greatest gifts I've ever received. And I thank my mother for giving me the wisdom to understand the importance of considering my pink suits with integrity, character, and good manners. Don't be afraid to try on a pink suit, and then see what bubbles up regarding its usefulness in your life. If it works, wear it proudly. If it doesn't, hang it in the back of the closet. You never know when you might need to wear it.

CHAPTER 5

WHAT ELEPHANT
IN THE ROOM?

Soon after becoming a new manager, I needed to have one of those uncomfortable discussions with a subordinate; I had an issue with one area of her performance, and I wanted to address it before it went further and jeopardized her job. I didn't beat around the bush. I sat up tall, looked her in the eyes, leaned in, and delivered a clear, focused, strong message. I was giving it to her straight. I was being a good supervisor, I thought, delivering a little tough love while remaining professional. I felt proud of how I handled the meeting.

A few days later, my boss summoned me to his office. I was about to learn that my tough love may have been more toughness and less love and respect. My boss informed me that after our meeting, Alicia (not her real name), my subordinate, came to him in tears. I hadn't a clue she was upset when she left my office, but she'd told him about her *horrible* experience with me.

"*What?*" I asked incredulously. "How is that possible?" I was surprised—shocked—that what I had said could have caused anyone to break down. I defended my behavior, explaining that I hadn't raised my voice, used profane language, or threatened her in any way. I argued that I was measured, clear, direct, and pointed. Apparently, though, I hadn't considered one little matter—there had been a six-foot-four elephant in the room with Alicia and me. *What?*

My boss then said something to me that was incredibly courageous but supremely risky. You see, he's a Caucasian man. With his feet on his desk, leaning back, arms in the cobra position, he smiled and said, "Donald, you're a six-foot-four *Black* man (his emphasis). You may want to be aware of your presence with people. You cannot just present big, square off, and be too in-your-face when making your point to those who report to you. You presented in a threatening manner, especially when you slapped the desk." At this point, he took his feet down, leaned closer to me while making his upper torso as big as possible, and slapped his own hand hard on the desk to demonstrate. "This physical expression of your point of view can be unnerving and highly intimidating to some people. Unfortunately, right or wrong, that's the way it is for some. I suggest you consider this."

My internal CPU (central processing unit, a metaphor for brain) was humming and confused. My immediate, deep, private thought was, *Who da hell is dis white boy to tell me to de-Black myself so I don't "threaten" some little white girl? I should storm out and go right to the EEO* (the Equal Opportunity and Employment office, which handles discrimination complaints). His comment scraped at the core of what psychiatrists William H. Grier and Price M. Cobbs called "black rage" in their 1968 book of the same name.

Pause.

Inhale.

I was profoundly hurt. I had been misunderstood. Besides, Alicia and I were on good terms, or so I thought. *I just can't believe she would react that way.*

Pause.

Lean back.

I'm crushed and a failure. I did my job the only way I knew how, and now I can't even be myself. Did I really slap my hand on my desk? I don't even remember. Wow.

I struggled to remain respectful in my discussion with my boss, after being initially defiant and defensive. I calmed down and listened to what he had to say. It wasn't until sometime later, reflecting on my discussions with him, that the epiphany of that experience hit me.

First, I appreciated that he was so committed to helping me professionally that he was willing to risk extreme consequences by shining a light on the proverbial race card. This was gutsy. He probably trusted that I wouldn't act on first instincts and would understand that he was coming from a genuine desire to help me. He didn't want me to unconsciously wear the "angry Black man" label. He understood the historical racial context of this. *He was trying to help me.*

Second, I understood that the way I'd experienced the encounter with Alicia wasn't the way she'd experienced it. Neither of our experiences were the only way to see things. The point was that people will experience and recall situations differently. I thought I was being a good supervisor. She thought she'd received an unnecessarily harsh reprimand from her boss *along with* an unspoken threat in the shape of an imposing six-foot-four "scary Black man" who slapped his hand hard on the desk.

Third, I remembered that I always have a choice about the way I behave. My goal hadn't been to be "right" with my boss and defend my behavior (my choice of words, my body language, or slapping the table). My goal with Alicia had been to communicate my displeasure at an unprofessional handling of an incident on the job and to persuade her to do things differently the next time. I believed my intentions were in the best interest of her career. My goal was *not* to present my largess or my power, or to intimidate or threaten. This was my first lesson on how my goal and my actual behavior in a personnel situation could be completely out of sync. It was a difficult lesson but one that helped me see things I may not have seen before.

* * *

Most of us are familiar with the "elephant in the room" metaphor, which refers to an unpleasant presence that everyone senses, but no one feels comfortable or brave enough to admit is there. This usually large—and always disturbing—presence or situation is one that we feel is in the room but decide to keep to ourselves. Everyone bonds together in silent agreement to ignore the elephant. Yet it sits right there among us, taking up space, draining our mental and emotional energy—and often keeping us from being present to the real reason for our gathering. But make no mistake about it, when one of these creatures is present, there is a disturbance in the universe, and you and others feel it. These colossal mammoths can be so uncomfortable that they can cause us to do or say things (or *not* do or say things) we may regret. They're like mold. If the environment is right for them, they'll show up for a visit—sometimes a herd of them, all having a big comfy party at your expense.

There's a lot to learn, however, from these uninvited pachyderms. They can teach us how to best confront an unmentionable problem that is controlling us.

In the early days of my NASA career, when I first became aware—the hard way—of the existence of elephants in the room, I learned a few things that I hope will help you when you run into your own—and you *will*. I'll focus on three things:

- *Practicing Awareness of the Elephant:* Hone your skills of recognizing (and trusting yourself) when there's a woolly mammoth in the room. (Note: they invade personal as well as professional relationships.)
- *Acknowledging the Elephant:* Admit the presence of that strange trunk in the room. Don't pretend it's not there. It ain't goin' away unless you first admit it's there. Trust me, sooner is better. You might let it sit in the corner for a while, though, if you must, as you plot on how you're going to persuade it to leave.
- *Dealing with the Elephant:* What's your strategy? Learn how to invite it to come out of the corner, let everyone see it for what it is, and then dismiss it.

IS AN ELEPHANT IN THE ROOM?
PRACTICING AWARENESS

At times in my NASA career, before I knew about the metaphor of elephants in the room, I'd find myself running a meeting in which something seemed not quite right. There was a "funk" in the air, a sense that something was amiss. I wasn't sure what it was. No one was saying a word about it. *Was* there a thing? I now know that half the battle, if not more, of addressing the elephant is recognizing that something is amiss. Practice raising your level of awareness—catching the smell of the elephant on the breeze in the room. If you don't, you'll be frustrated and left to wonder why your meetings and gatherings aren't as effective as you want them to be.

As managers and leaders, and even friends and partners—which many of you are and many of you will go on to be—we must develop and strengthen multiple senses when communication is not overt. Elephants don't sit in the corner with a big sign around their trunks, screaming, "Look at me. I need to be noticed and talked about *now!*" We often notice the more obvious ones, but sometimes we just have a nagging feeling that something strange is present. Maybe it's just you. Awareness. That's the key to keeping these larger-than-life photobombs out of the picture. Developing an ability to see the elephant and the strength to call it out will help you be more effective as a friend, colleague, manager, leader, or partner. I'm suggesting you develop a deliberate, practiced awareness of the existence of elephants. Awareness allows us the time to carefully consider our response versus being completely clueless or overreacting in a way that we may regret or be embarrassed about later.

OKAY, NOW I SEE IT! ACKNOWLEDGMENT

When an elephant makes an appearance in the workplace, it's important to get to the bottom of things, and promptly, before it grows larger than life. Once we realize that elephants can show up in all areas of our lives, then we have a chance to sharpen our skills to appropriately address the situation. An effective leader must be prepared to break this kind of troubling, loud silence. But we often try to pretend it's not there. We ignore it, just like our staff does. *Why would we ignore these huge signals that all is not well?*

As a manager, I may be afraid I'm imagining things or concerned I'm wrong. I may fear that if I say "elephant," I may be ridiculed or chastised for my audacity. I may not trust myself to avoid making the topic too personal—*is it about me?* What if it *is* about me? Or I may believe that acknowledging it won't make a difference, so why bother? Regardless of what real issue the elephant represents, even if the elephant isn't named or called out, it *will* dominate emotions, feelings, and behavior. And it *will* drive manners.

IT'S JUST SITTING THERE IN THE CORNER: DEAL WITH IT

In my work experience and studies, I have learned that effective team members, managers, or leaders become highly attuned to the presence of elephants, and they develop strategies for addressing them. When I was first learning, I'd often hit it head-on with a direct, "It seems there's an elephant in this room. What's up?"

Interestingly, just acknowledging what people feel is true can be enough to open the floodgates: uncommunicated feelings; frustrations not acknowledged; personality conflicts; not being heard; concerns not shared; retaliatory feelings; old wounds unhealed; a sudden new boss; a fear of organizational change. These are some of the indicators that an elephant has joined your space.

An elephant exposed is usually the tip of the iceberg. Sometimes it can be a serious, unconscious projection that lives not just in the office but in our heads, as a beastly prejudice that can influence our behaviors, shape our opinions, and run our lives. It's like the imaginary boogeyman that causes us to be scared out of our wits. When we give it power, it will influence our manners. I ask you to consider the danger of judgments, beliefs, and uncommunicated feelings or concerns and how these impact behaviors and manners.

Let's say an elephant exists between two people, Maria Elena and Derrick. Everyone else in the meeting can feel the tension between them even though they may not understand what's causing it. Nothing can really move forward effectively in the group until the leader determines how best to address the situation. Maria Elena probably isn't mad at Derrick because he interrupts all the time. There's likely more to the story. We may not know their full history. Maybe she doesn't feel her views are being taken seriously, and one interruption sets her off. She may have insecurities about her capabilities, or Derrick reminds her of someone else who always discounted her value. Maybe Derrick interrupts because, in his family, it was the only way he could be heard. Perhaps he doesn't respect the views of others, especially women. He just knows he's right. The point is that you may not know the complete history and context of the elephant that exists between two particular people.

Managers have a responsibility to manage a situation skillfully when an elephant is present. It takes courage to stop a conversation from disintegrating by saying, "I think there's more going on here, and I completely get that. What we need to accomplish now is a respectful discussion of this matter, and I really need all of you to give honest input. I ask that we each work harder to listen deeply to others before offering our own viewpoints. I'd like to take offline the more sensitive challenges that we see right now. Thanks."

Okay, this sounds good, right? But, unfortunately, it's only a Band-Aid approach. This doesn't slay the elephant. It shines a little light on its existence and keeps it in the corner, instead of letting it dance all over the room, disrupting everything.

Some elephants are more like mirages than the full-grown pachyderms you see in the zoo. You walk into a room and sense something, a twitch or a whiff in the universe. You aren't sure. You pick up body language nuances that you couldn't describe if asked. This kind of elephant is the worst. Here are some clues to tip you off that an unwanted guest has joined your meeting or gathering. You enter the conference room, and here's what you see:

- little to no chatter
- heads buried in smartphones (a leader at NASA once described this to me as the "iPhone prayer"—arms folded, no eye contact)
- the type of eye contact that lets you know people are actively communicating (stealing glances), but not verbalizing a single word

I have strengthened my peripheral vision to spot these signs. Ignore the elusive elephant at your peril. When you encounter one, you may think your antennae are receiving meaningless noise. What do you do? *Keep paying attention.* Gently probe. Look for any uncharacteristic behaviors, stilted conversations, or icy looks. Trying to call it out with "Are we good here?" may elicit some variation of "Oh, we're good," or no reaction at all. You, and only you, may be the one sensing danger.

Sometimes just being aware that "something" is going on is enough to avoid land mines. If you have a trusting relationship with your team and have developed strong rapport, you can usually get clues that something is amiss *before* the meeting. If you're close to your team members and check in with them frequently, you likely know when a train wreck may be in the works. Another strategy, postmeeting, is to carefully poll the team one-on-one to see what may be hiding below the surface.

* * *

In a new position as a NASA manager, in meetings I noticed subtle behaviors that I would label as passive-aggressive. There was some undercurrent of discontent and irritation. My colleagues were not vocalizing the real issue—no one was calling out the elephant. They were just reflecting their angst in subtle, yet noticeable, and at times unprofessional ways: interruptions, poor listening, inappropriate criticism, curt conversations. I clearly saw an elephant, and I'm pretty sure everyone else did, too. What to do?

My training and instincts told me that unless we dealt with the elephant, our ability to address work challenges, solve problems, and enhance our mission would be jeopardized. The difficult part was distinguishing between legitimate professional disagreements and deeper uncommunicated feelings. I would be the first to admit that my track record at guiding a meeting to *honestly* address the elephant was mixed. Most of the time, I was able to bring the elephant to light only to fail at actually getting it out of the room. For instance, in the above example, the problem was poor listening skills fueled by deeper mistrust between staff members. Additionally, I felt that the pressure of our workload and ongoing external threats to the organization exacerbated the situation. It's rarely just one thing. While we could honestly discuss some of the issues and work on better active listening, I was mostly ineffective at getting the core behavior to change. I'm more convinced now than I was then that the blame lay with me for not addressing the underlying dynamics sooner and more effectively, including seeking external help.

It is hard to clearly show what works, but here's a scenario that does not work:

"Hey, Joe, it's obvious to me and everyone that you're just not listening to Sally. You need to be a better listener; it's preventing us from addressing the budget issues we have."

What's wrong with calling it as you see it? You may be a "no BS" person and really busy, so you want to cut to the chase, stop the poor behavior, and get on with it. Well, first, you made an assumption about Joe's behavior. You may be right, but it's possible you are not. Saying it's "obvious" sounds arrogant, as in "even an idiot can see your behavior." Second, the statement places sole blame on Joe, as if no one else has any responsibility for what's happening. Third, there's likely more going on than meets the eye.

Remember that what you see or directly experience with elephants is often the first hint that something deeper is at work. Though you don't want to turn your meeting into a group therapy session, there are ways you can tame the elephant and still move forward. One technique, if you are the manager and are leading the meeting, is to take responsibility. Make sure you aren't blaming anyone for what's happening. It isn't about your people, anyway; it's about their behavior and what's behind it. This is a subtle and important distinction.

Here's how I've learned, after many frustrating failures, to handle the situation:

"I feel that we're not allowing everyone to have their full say, and I get lost in the discussion when I hear two or three voices simultaneously. This doesn't work for me. What recommendations do you have to help us move forward, and what can I do to help with that?"

This statement includes you, as a manager—"I feel that *we* . . ."—and doesn't cast blame on one individual for the problem. You're taking responsibility for *your* experience—"I get lost in the discussion . . ."—and by handling the elephant in this manner, you don't *impose* a solution, but rather, you ask your staff to come up with a solution. My training and studies have taught me that the best solutions are those that people come up with themselves, versus having a solution imposed on them, as in, "You need to be a better listener." The latter isn't even a solution, but a judgment and opinion with no guidance on how to be a better listener and why it's important. Even if you know exactly how Joe should be a better listener, you run the risk of embarrassing and shaming Joe in front of his peers.

He's likely to feel blamed and become angry. You probably just compounded the problem instead of mitigating it.

With the second approach, you're also stating that what you're experiencing doesn't work for you. If you happen to be the manager or leader of the group, the message will be clear without you having to call anyone out. You're saying, "We have to fix this and do better." You're asking your team what you can do together to make things work. You're taking responsibility for your experience, and you're asking for support to help fix the problem.

The autocratic approach to addressing elephants may get you short-term results, but you'll sacrifice long-term goodwill. Issues that are below the surface? They'll be shoved deeper into the abyss only to rear their big heads later. It's like a parent telling their child to stop crying. "Stop your crying, or I will give you something to cry about." The child may stop out of fear of further punishment, but the root cause of the child's crying won't be addressed or acknowledged.

HERDING THOSE ELEPHANTS

Practice awareness. Notice and try to understand those thick-skinned elephants. Tread carefully as you tame them and excuse them from the room. The hardest part of working on a solution may be failing to notice that *you* are part of the problem. *You* may have invited the elephant to the party without knowing it. Over time I made it a rule, especially when I was a senior leader: if there was a problem in my organization, *it was my fault*, my responsibility. It was easier to work on a solution from the premise that I was to blame for the elephant in the room, rather than coming from a place in which I had to "fix" something or somebody else. As the saying goes, "You can delegate authority, but you cannot delegate responsibility." You own the elephant.

Reacting to elephants is a manners matter. React improperly and the consequences may be uncomfortable or catastrophic. When you notice that you're in one of these situations, the first reaction is to take a deep breath, exhale slowly, and consider how you can serve those around you. Do everything you can to get rid of that elephant. That's good manners. After that, listen to Momma's Rule #5, which says it best:

"Stop thinking too much. It's all right not to know the answers. They will come to you when you least expect it."

Elephant in the room? Sit still, observe, breathe deeply for a while. What's really going on? The answers will come eventually because you're "sensing" in a deep way. Practice awareness. Consider taking it personally when you discover elephants have crashed your party. *You've got this.*

And did I mention? Elephants don't always represent "bad" or "negative" situations. When I was in elementary school, I had a crush on a girl named Teresa. Of course, I didn't tell her. That would have been worse than death. What I did do was pick on her, sort of. Not like a bad bully thing, but just little things. I made it seem like I didn't like her when in fact, I did. I'm sure others saw right through my antics and knew that my childish taunts were a cover for my real feelings. I never was outed in elementary school, but I did get busted in ninth grade over another crush. I guess my personal elephants were obvious to everyone but me. My "bad behavior elephant" was the only way I knew to handle my young, burgeoning feelings.

CHAPTER 6

MY TWO-THOUSAND-DOLLAR SUIT

Picture this: I'm taking my first international business trip as NASA's associate administrator for education. The NASA administrator and other senior NASA leaders will be at this important international function.

Destination: Toronto, Canada

Decision: I'll get a ride to Dulles Airport because I don't have a car.

Choice: I choose Uber and request a 9:00 a.m. pickup for my 11:00 a.m. flight.

Action: I leave my apartment and stand at the usual spot, near the Metro entrance. Uber can't find me. We connect. I get picked up at 9:15 a.m.

Result: I arrive at Dulles at 10:10 a.m. I get to the airline check-in counter at 10:17 a.m. I'm told I missed the forty-five-minute required cutoff time to check my luggage for the 11:00 a.m. international flight. I'm ignorant of the forty-five-minute standard. "Huh?" I confidently inform the agent that I will make the flight. She takes my bag, saying she can't guarantee it will make it. I tell her I believe it will. I make the flight. I arrive in Toronto, but my bag doesn't, nor does it arrive that night or by nine the next morning, the day of the international event.

Consequences: I don't have my dress clothes for the evening event, at which the administrator (my boss) will be in attendance, along with other senior NASA leaders *and* international dignitaries. My *first* international business trip in my new capacity. I will *not* look good. I am so screwed.

Now what?

New decisions, new choices based on poor decisions, and not-so-great consequences: I decide I must be dressed properly, no matter what. I buy a new suit, two dress shirts, and two ties from the amazing people at the Harry Rosen menswear store in the Toronto Eaton Centre mall, who promise to have my suit altered and pressed by 4:30 p.m., just in time for the event. Incredibly, a shoe store in the same mall has a pair of size 15 dress shoes. I buy extra ties and dress shirts for the remainder of the trip in case I never see my bag. My final bill? About two thousand dollars. You with me? *Being two minutes late cost me two thousand dollars.* Wow!

Hindsight is happy to inform us that the simple moral to this story is this: don't be late to your flight, or, make sure you understand the travel rules, or, as we say at NASA, build in a sufficient schedule margin. I see a deeper lesson here, and that is what I want to discuss—decisions, choices, and their consequences. Oh, and what manners has to do with these.

Stephen Covey, in his seminal book *The 7 Habits of Highly Effective People,* recommended this for Habit #2: "Begin with the end in mind." This is perfect as part of your decision-making strategy. What was my end? I'd wanted to be at the special event on time and dressed as a senior NASA executive should be dressed, representing not only myself but also my administrator and my agency. I worked for the man who worked for the president of the United States. And this was my first international trip in my new high-level job. You remember the saying "You only get one chance to make a good first impression"? Exactly what kind of impression would I have made showing up in jeans, tennis shoes, and a casual shirt? That would have been unprofessional and the height of disrespect. I probably would have made an excuse about my bag not arriving, but it would have been embarrassing to admit that it was my fault for being late to the airport—by two minutes—and my ignorance of the forty-five-minute rule.

Here's a playful example of making good decisions based on working toward the result you absolutely want: Imagine you're in Vail, Colorado, in the middle of the winter. You get a call that your rich Uncle Joe died in Scotland and left you five million dollars. In order to get your money, you must be at the magistrate's office in Paisley, Scotland, precisely at 4:00 p.m.—in three days. If you're late, no five million. Period. This is not a trick. What would you do? I'm willing to bet that you'd move heaven and earth to be there *early*. You may even charter a plane, spending twenty-five thousand dollars to take you directly to Scotland. You'd probably even work with the plane company to make *sure* the aircraft is in tip-top condition. You'd double-check that the pilots know when to arrive and allow ample schedule margin in case of weather or delays. You'd book a commercial flight as a backup, costing you, say, five thousand. That's a thirty-thousand-dollar insurance policy to get you five million. This is a loopy scenario, but you get my point.

DECISIONS AND CHOICES

What is a decision? Are decisions the same as choices? I think there are subtle differences worth exploring. I'll use a classic example from NASA. When President Kennedy made a decision that the United States would send a man to the moon and return him safely to Earth, the NASA engineers debated how this would be accomplished. There were several engineering choices and subchoices. Grossly oversimplifying this analogy, one choice was to build one gigantic rocket that would lift off and head straight to the moon. This turned out not to be feasible. Another choice was to send spacecraft in stages or segments, with the latter being the preferred strategy.[4]

At NASA we sometimes categorize decisions or "requirements" into levels. For example:

Level 1: Send a man to the moon and bring him back safely.

Level 2: The choices made to accomplish the Level 1 goal—the staged or segmented strategy.

Level 3: The actual actions and behaviors taken to achieve that choice.

In NASA's case, there were tens of thousands of actions taken to accomplish the mission. Infrastructure had to be built, testing had to be performed, and astronauts had to be chosen. Of course, in this moon mission example, even at the action level, one can imagine hundreds of additional decisions and choices.

What about all those personal decisions that we're faced with every day? For example, you decide you want to go to graduate school, and you even know what you want to study. Your choices are the multiple schools and their programs. Or,

---

4. There were many variations of the strategy that ultimately led to Apollo. For further reading, see *Project Apollo: A Selective Bibliography of Books*, by Roger D. Launius and J. D. Hunley, NASA, https://history.nasa.gov/ap11ann/booksbiblio.htm.

even more personal, you may decide to lose weight, and you choose to follow a paleo eating strategy versus a vegan strategy. Your best friend makes the exact same decision to lose weight but chooses the Whole30 strategy. Your actions probably include choosing recipes, making the food, and eating it, in addition to other actions required to accomplish your Level 1 requirement, lose weight, via your Level 2 choice, eating vegan.

Making a decision and making choices first happens *in your head.* It's not until there's an action or behavior—when you *do* something—that your decisions and choices are realized. Of course, many decisions and choices can be undone or changed even after you've started to act. You can decide to fly to Europe, choose to take United Airlines on March 16, and take all the actions necessary to realize that trip. However, you can change your mind about flying, probably right up to the time the door closes.

The decisions and choices you make, followed by your actions or behaviors, generate results and consequences. There's a lot in this, so let's examine it. This concept is important to understand in order to appreciate the relationship between what actually happened—the results and consequences—and your role in making it happen. *Your* decisions and choices, and *your* actions and behaviors, determined the results and the consequences. This is about the decision-making process, not about assigning judgment to the decision. This isn't about "good or bad" decisions, "right or wrong" choices, "desirable or undesirable" results, or "negative or positive" consequences.

There are cases where the action that results from a decision happens so quickly after the event or stimulus that it's difficult to imagine you thought about your action first. Slamming the brakes to avoid a fast-moving animal crossing the street in front of you, for example. Moving your hand from a burning hot pan. I have done this. I assure you that I did not ponder if I should jerk my hand away. Perhaps the decision to avoid killing an animal or avoid pain is already preloaded in our brains. I am not addressing these types of decisions.

RESULTS AND CONSEQUENCES

Results and consequences are closely related. The distinction is this:

Results are what actually happened—the facts of an event.

Consequences are how we or others feel about what actually happened.

Consequences are the impact, usually on a good/bad, right/wrong, satisfied/disappointed, joyful/angry continuum. Consequences are the effects of an action—the aftermath. Hurricane-force winds are the result of meteorological conditions. Downed trees, ripped roofs on houses, or flooding can have the consequence of ruined or lost lives. However, it's important to note that consequences are *in the eye of the beholder.* Consequences are the judgments, evaluations, opinions, and emotions that emanate from the result. As such, two people may experience the exact same result differently. Therefore, we must be careful. You make a joke in one interview and experience a great response, establishing rapport and showing yourself to be someone with a good sense of humor. You try the same joke in another interview, and it falls completely flat. The consequences are different, and it can impact the hiring decision.

Remember that all decisions and choices, and requisite actions or behavior changes, will give you a result. And those results have consequences. For example, actor and comedian Kevin Hart, in his audiobook *The Decision*, rightfully contends that one's emotional state will influence our actions and behaviors as well. Emotions may also impact the decisions and choices we make. I will build on Kevin's point and say that our emotional state will definitely impact the manner in which we move through our decisions, choices, actions, and behaviors. It's probably not a good idea to "decide" to get married right after you won the lottery.

I include "no result" as a result. The fact that absolutely nothing happened or changed *is* the result, in this case. Remember Sir Isaac Newton's third law of motion, "For every action, there is an equal and opposite reaction"? It's similar with decisions and choices. For every decision and choice that is followed by an action, there's a result. And it's worth saying again that *those results have consequences.* But, unlike Newton's law, results and consequences *may not* be equal or opposite to the decisions and choices you're making. You may think you're making an inconsequential decision or a simple choice, and the results and consequences are huge. A quick response to a text message while driving can be deadly. *You never know.*

MANNERS

What happens when the decisions and choices you make are about manners? Here's an example from my own family. My father got inspired to quit his job as deputy attorney general for the state of California to take a leadership position in the newly established Peace Corps. He decided this without consulting his wife—Momma. He came home, as I understand the story from Momma, and announced that "we" had this great opportunity and "we" were moving to Accra, Ghana. In Africa. On the other side of the world. This decision and other decisions and choices my father made foreshadowed the future of my parents' marriage—decisions that impacted my brother and me significantly.

Remember when I said that there is no value judgment on decisions? Dennis and I will never know if the decisions my father and mother made were "good" or "bad" for us. We'll never know if our lives would have been better or not had our parents made different decisions. We don't have a parallel universe to see how other decisions might have played out. The point is that the decisions significantly impacted our life's trajectory. I was not around to see the choices that my parents made, nor did I remember most of Dad's or Momma's actions and behaviors. The results were that we moved to Accra, Ghana. I remember that. I also remember that Momma left Dad in Ghana and brought us back to California, and soon thereafter my parents divorced. Those were factual results. In hindsight, the consequences of those decisions and choices my parents made were fine for Dennis and me. The consequence for Momma may have been a different matter. She became a single mother rearing two Black boys during a tumultuous time in our nation's history. And she never remarried.

A person's manners are revealed in their actions and behaviors. This is the place your decisions and choices show up in the eyes of others. Your manners, as you act or behave, may determine the quality of the results you get and the impact of the consequences. Two people who make the same decision and similar choices, but who act or behave with different manners and are perhaps influenced by emotion, as suggested earlier, may get different results and experience different consequences. In chapter 8, "Am I Being Interviewed?" we'll focus on the interviewing process. This experience, similar to courting, is the one area where you can grasp the importance of your actions and behaviors and focus your attention on them.

Remember that Saturday evening international gala in Toronto for which I had two thousand dollars' worth of brand-new clothes? Funny thing. While I was waiting at the front table where the NASA administrator and his entourage and I would sit, the woman in charge of the event came by and whispered in my ear that the administrator's plane was late. "Would you please give the NASA welcome address?" she asked. Did I have a copy of his speech? Of course not. I grabbed a pen and notebook and frantically began channeling the administrator in preparation for my first speech on my first international trip in front of representatives of more than twenty-five countries, including heads of space agencies, while wearing my brand-new two-thousand-dollar suit. This was one of those "you're out the door of the airplane and you either pull the parachute cord or you die" scenarios. I pulled. I got ready. And just when I was about to go to the stage, the administrator walked in. I glanced at him and his party. My jaw dropped.

The NASA administrator. The man who works for the president of the United States. A retired two-star general. Marine. Ramrod locked. NASA administrator Charles Bolden walked in wearing blue jeans, a turtleneck shirt, loafers, and a sport coat. I glanced at the other members of his party. They too were dressed a notch or two below business casual. "What da . . . ?"

The administrator was ice cool. He sat down at the table, politely greeted us, and proceeded to the podium. "I would like to first apologize for being out of uniform. Due to the extreme lateness of our flight, we skipped going to the hotel to change in order to come directly here and be on time." With that, he gave his speech without missing a beat. I was in awe of his performance and his cool. He didn't dwell on the reason for his attire, and he took responsibility for it with humor.

I concluded two things that evening. First, I absolutely did the right thing by making sure I was dressed appropriately. Second, if you have a flub-up due to things beyond your control, acknowledge it succinctly and move on.

* * *

How can you use your knowledge of the decisions and choices you make to polish your manners? Once you appreciate that every decision and choice you make may have a result and a consequence—and will have if you acted on your decisions and choices—you can then consider the end you have in mind first, as Stephen Covey suggests. What do you want to accomplish? How do you want to be perceived by your friends and colleagues as you take actions to accomplish your mission? Do you want to be known as someone who is trustworthy? Then what decisions, choices, actions, and behaviors can you make to engender trust with people? The NASA administrator had a choice: go to the hotel to change in order to look good, or be on time. I had a choice: show up in casual clothes and tennis shoes, or spend two thousand dollars to look good.

Manners are a consequence of *conscious* decisions, *wise* choices, and *appropriate* actions. It could be as straightforward as handwriting a thank-you note from the heart, using your best penmanship. I assumed this was prevalent. On several occasions, I have literally received appreciation notes, both verbally and in writing, for the thank-you notes I have sent. Imagine that—a thank-you note for a thank-you note.

Manners can mean deciding to bring a homemade dish to a friend's house when you're invited to dinner. Since you know the friend is vegetarian and eats gluten-free, the dish you choose honors that. You also bring the recipe. You made this dish; you didn't conveniently pick it up from a grocery store.

In my last job, I passed by a colleague's cubicle one day. I stuck my head in the door to say hi. She was eating lunch. I noticed she had collard greens. I *love* collard greens. My granny made them the old-fashioned southern way. My colleague's greens looked and smelled like Granny's. I made a scene right there in her office about the greens, joking that anytime she wanted to bring me some, I would not argue.

A few days later, I had a package on my desk. I opened it to discover a dish of greens. The dish was carefully covered in cellophane, and it was accompanied by a nice note to enjoy. Those greens lasted less than a New York minute. I returned her empty dish the next day, clean and with a handwritten thank-you note. The only thing Momma might have frowned upon was that I didn't share the greens. Since I was living by myself at the time, there was *no one* with whom to share. I thought about it, though. For a second. Okay, maybe not that long.

These actions may seem trite, old-fashioned, or unnecessary. I believe differently. I believe that decisions, choices, and behaviors like these reflect good manners and an intentional way to show up authentically and properly in the world. People appreciate being appreciated and respected. People appreciate it when you acknowledge them for their gift, whether it's a gift of time or a tangible thing. As you develop a practice of good manners, you're cultivating a narrative about yourself, and importantly, this continues when you aren't in the room. This is key. You are fashioning a mannerly reputation in people's minds. To the degree that people respect you because of your manners, they will tend to think well of you in general.

Getting the "low hanging fruit" from the manners tree builds your ability to handle the bigger manners matters. If you are a sedentary person who is overweight and complaining about a range of aches and pains, you cannot expect to run a triathlon in a week. If you start out slowly and steadily in a supported training program, there is a chance you can do that triathlon—in a year. Perfecting the basics of manners strengthens your ability to handle the higher consequential matters. You may conclude that certain encounters with people are not worth your concern manners-wise because you know you got this. Or do you?

A LIGHTHEARTED "PRACTICE" DECISION

Try this simple practice decision. The next time you put on fresh underwear (yes, this is about underwear!), instead of starting with your right leg first, start with your left leg, or vice-versa if you're left-handed or left-legged. I'm assuming that you always start with the same side. My hypothesis is that when you change something you've done repeatedly, then you'll realize you've been oblivious to your previous habits. And it is a habit. Now you must consciously think about what you're doing when you change behaviors. I know I did.

The first time I did this exercise, I nearly fell over because my balance was off. I invariably stepped on my underwear rather than dunking my big foot through the leg hole. To effectively do this assignment, you first must *remember* to do it, then you have to plot out your specific actions, and *next* you'll have to think about where your body's center of gravity is. *After* that, you'll have to execute the action. This is a lot of thinking for the simple act of putting on your underwear, isn't it?

The purpose of this exercise is to experience and feel what it means to be mindful about a decision and its possible results and consequences. Mindfulness and awareness, especially during the actions you take or behaviors you exhibit, are two powerful states that I strongly encourage you to cultivate. The more aware and mindful you are as you make a decision, the better your choices will be. The more aware and mindful you are as you make your choices, the better your actions and behaviors will be. This is how you mitigate the effects of your emotions. If you're mindful that you're angry, you have the opportunity to consider if your decision is you talking or the anger talking.

ASKING FOR HELP WITH THE BIG ONES

One of the most courageous requests you can make is this: "I need this result, and I don't know how to achieve it. I need help."

If there is a result you absolutely must have, and it's consequential, then back into it by carefully examining all the decisions, choices, and actions you have to make and take. And the more important and consequential the result, the more important it may be to seek help. There are many paths to the throne, and the journey on any of them should not be lonely. Ask for help when you need it.

Some decisions are so consequential that they demand support. Choosing where to live and which house to buy; choosing a mate; choosing where to take your vacation; choosing which university to attend; choosing a major; and choosing which job to take are examples of consequential decisions. For best results, I recommend that these decisions and choices be made with support from others. Getting support regarding your actions and behaviors is about developing your manners skills.

A good analogy is parachuting. No sane person would do this without training and support. Unless you're tied to a jump partner as you exit the plane, you're on your own, and your actions and behaviors may well determine whether you have a good result or not. The time to develop your manners is *before* you jump out of the plane, metaphorically.

The simplest and most useful question a mentor asked me regarding a pending consequential decision was, "Why?" If I didn't have a clear answer as to "why," then I probably needed to think about the decision more. Sometimes you have a gut feeling about something, and you cannot articulate a "why." That's fine, though I don't advise solely relying on a gut feeling.

It can become a crutch. You may get seduced into always trusting your gut without being open to other inputs or data.

A related question is, "For what?" I learned this from the late Rona Ramon, the widow of Israel's first astronaut, Ilan Ramon, who died in February 2003, when the space shuttle Columbia disintegrated upon reentry. Mrs. Ramon was interested in the why or purpose, but her question of "for what?" implied that the purpose had to be for something good or beneficial. A consequential decision thus includes both a sense of purpose (why) and the good it will do (for what).

HONING YOUR DECISION-MAKING AND CHOICE-MAKING SKILLS

Decisions start in your mind. Sometimes you aren't aware that you made a decision. You just act. You don't recall thinking first. In most cases, our decision-making process is not overt, thoughtful, or deliberate. We don't sit down and make a list of decisions we need to make and evaluate and prioritize each for execution. We just kind of "decide and do," without giving it a lot of thought. This doesn't mean that what we've decided is not up to par.

Ask yourself, "What three decisions am I going to make today?" Your decision list may include exercising, being in class on time or early, and making a healthy dinner. Notice that these are different than the choices you will make. You'll choose which exercises you'll do; you'll choose a strategy for ensuring that you'll be in class on time, including the time you'll leave, plus some margin in case of unforeseen interference; and you will choose what to make for dinner.

Before you rip your hair out and scream, "No way am I going to do this for every single decision I make!" please know that the invitation is to *consider being more mindful* of this formula with the *significant* milestones, events, opportunities, and especially those pink suits. I can assure you that I did *not* do this when I chose the college I went to or chose my major. I wish I had. Although I got lucky and attended a college I enjoyed, in hindsight I would have employed a different strategy in choosing where to spend probably four of the most important years of my life.

YOUR DECISIONS AND CHOICES IMPACT OTHERS

Every day you make hundreds of decisions and choices. You probably don't give them much thought because they're not big decisions with huge consequences—when to get dressed, when to take a shower, whether or not to eat breakfast. Compare these decisions with *I think I'll buy a new car, or get a graduate degree, or move to Zimbabwe.* These are more significant and consequential. I recommend examining the types of decisions you make and being deliberate and mindful about the ones that may have a big impact on your life. And, good manners include considering the impact and consequences of your decisions on the people in your life. Obvious examples include such decisions as driving under the influence (of alcohol, drugs, or cell phones), smoking around others, dumping oil down the drain, or cheating in school.

A NOTE ABOUT TRADE-OFFS AND POTENTIAL SACRIFICES

Let's assume you are determined to improve your decision-making skills. It's important to note that you'll also need to consider the possible trade-offs and even sacrifices that come with making one of those "super" life-altering decisions. We're not talking about sweating the small stuff here, but say, for example, you decide that you want to create a plan to pay for your children's college education. Let's say $50K per year times 4 years times 2 kids = $400K. You "choose" to sock away *no matter what* 10 percent of your net income to a college savings account. This is a consequential decision when you consider the sacrifices you may have to make over the years: no new cars; no expensive vacations; no eating out, no five-dollar lattes. "Manners" will play a role in your actions and behaviors, as a decision of this magnitude means enrolling your family and friends in your plan, which means learning how to politely decline invitations to dine out, go to sports extravaganzas, attend Broadway shows, and many of the other wildly fun but unaffordable things that will bubble up. The trick when contemplating a significant decision is to be brutally honest with yourself. Are you really willing to make the necessary trade-offs and potential sacrifices that such a consequential decision may require?

* * *

My big takeaway and strong recommendation about honing your decision-making skills is that you spend quality time being aware of those major decisions, and plan backward from your desired outcome to your present actions. In other words, *get to the airport early!* I believe you'll feel more powerful, be more committed, and be willing to do almost anything to accomplish your goals because *you'll know exactly why and for what good* you are deciding "X" and can easily explain it to someone.

In the next chapter, we'll explore the notion of being authentically present, perhaps the core ingredient of good manners. If one's outward behavior is akin to a software program, then authentic presence is the firmware, or your operating system. It's the core of your being that will inform all manner of how you show up in the world.

CHAPTER 7

AUTHENTIC PRESENCE

During a talk I gave in Berlin, speaking about NASA Education, I recounted the story of the effect one of our education programs had on a student who used to get in trouble as a gang member. I spoke about how this young man became involved with NASA's robotics program and the way his experience transformed him. I felt a sudden rush of pride and purpose for being associated with an organization—NASA—that could spark such a transformation. That profound influence impacted not just the student (one person) but also his family, maybe his proud parents or siblings. And maybe even society, as there was now one less violent gang member.

I got caught up in this story as I told it, as though I was both storyteller and audience. There was a moment when a convergence of emotions—which I could observe, as if I were having an out-of-body experience—overwhelmed me. I was so proud of being involved with an agency that inspires and moves people such as this young man—NASA transformed his life—that I felt humbled to have the privilege of working for NASA and being an agent for inspiration. I experienced a young man, who was once part of a social circle that harmed and even killed people, as transformed into a force for good. I wondered to myself, *Is there a person who is literally alive today because this young man has a different purpose now?*

My voice lowered, not as a speaking tactic, but naturally, in response to the emotion. I gazed softly out into the audience and made direct eye contact with several people, holding our connection long enough to communicate without words. During that pause, the kind of pause people do to control emotions, my emotions spilled over. As I surrendered to the moment, the audience erupted in applause. At that moment, we were resonating fully—a part of each other. I was equally sincere, vulnerable, and strong. I was *authentically present,* and so were they. Nothing else mattered to me at that moment. Authenticity emanating from one person helps those nearby to free their own authentic nature. For an excellent treatment on the whole notion of "presence," I highly recommend Amy Cuddy's book *Presence: Bringing Your Boldest Self to Your Biggest Challenges.* Cuddy is best known for her TED Talks on body language and how it influences what people think about you.

* * *

Some years before my talk in Berlin, I interviewed a candidate for an internship at NASA. She arrived on time and was pleasant, composed, and confident. She proudly gave me her résumé. After welcoming her and thanking her for coming, I took a few minutes to scan her résumé. It was decorated with Advanced Placement (AP) and honors classes plus a 4.0 GPA. She was a musician and was involved in numerous extracurricular activities. I was into her résumé for about twenty seconds when she started talking about herself and volunteering her accomplishments. At this point, I hadn't asked her any questions beyond "How are you?"

When I finished skimming, I looked up at her and said, "This is quite impressive. You must be proud of your accomplishments." I then asked her what she thought were the top three key takeaways from her AP US history class.

"Also," I asked, "what was the relevance, if any, of the key things you learned in that class to the current political climate?"

Pause. Long, awkward pause.

She forced a smile while staring at me with that deer-in-the-headlights look. I could tell her internal computer was working overtime, desperately trying to figure out what she should say. *What was the right answer?* To be clear, her answer had no bearing on the internship for which she was applying— but she probably thought it did, or I wouldn't have asked it.

She mumbled something but never did enumerate three things she had learned in her class. She didn't name one thing. I don't mean to be too critical here. I caught her off guard. One understandably might conclude that it was unfair to ask her a question about something irrelevant to the work she'd be doing at NASA. But I was not looking for that; I assumed that she'd thoroughly prepared and rehearsed the answers to the typical interview questions. I was looking for her authentic self. I wanted to hear from the real person, not the "I-know-all-the-right-answers" person. She could have responded with "That's an interesting question, Mr. James. For one thing, we didn't learn about the history of the US space program. Given its importance to the science and technology prowess of the US in the twentieth century, it occurs to me that would have been a good topic to cover. I *did* learn . . . *blah, blah, blah,* but I haven't considered its relevance or implications to what is happening today other than . . . *blah, blah, blah.* Thank you for encouraging me to think about this topic." Or she could have conjured up something she knew about and creatively made it relevant to the question. This is called a pivot. And she could have made this request: "I'd love to hear your recommendations for a particular book/link/source/article on the subject."

I wasn't interested in the content of her answer. I was interested in *how she thought through an unexpected question,* or how she "thought on her feet." I wanted to know if this person was naturally curious. Most NASA scientists and engineers *are.* They are simply curious about a myriad of topics. *Why is something so? What does this mean? How can we make this work? I wonder what Dr. So-and-So thinks?* I've seen prominent astrophysicists show deep interest in poetry and music as well as in black holes and galactic collisions. They form study teams and share their papers. They aren't afraid *not* to know something. I was looking for a different kind of AP—*authentic presence.*

For students, the common meaning of the acronym AP is "Advanced Placement." In this chapter, AP stands for *authentic presence* and refers to the style and tone of good manners, particularly when you're applying for admission to a college or university or applying for a job, for that matter. Advanced Placement is an important part of the conversation about college admissions, so we'll explore that in addition to authentic presence and manners. We'll question the meaning of cheating (to get into school), the meaning of "best" (the best school for you), and the role of manners for early-career professionals.

In the 1950s, school districts introduced college credit in high school. I attended a small private college-prep high school in Sacramento in the 1970s. We didn't have "honors classes" or "Advanced Placement" classes. We just had classes about subjects. We got grades, and we took the SAT and maybe the

ACT and obtained teacher letters of recommendations before applying to college.

Today, most high schools, public or private, including the one I attended, offer "honors" this, "AP" that. These classes have blossomed over the years. My understanding is that students, educators, and their parents are driving the proliferation of these specialized courses that sound tougher, more demanding, or more advanced than regular classes and are believed to provide a competitive advantage for college applicants.

The growth and interest in AP classes may help students get a leg up heading to college. But my work experience and training have taught me that people with a high degree of "presence"—that is, *authenticity*—tend to be admired and respected, regardless of what school they attended. I view the character trait of authentic presence as essential to developing sound manners skills that, combined with the appropriate education, will, as Momma said, "take you anywhere." I have concluded that if students focus on the other AP—authentic presence—they'll get a leg up in *all* aspects of their lives: college, career, and relationships.

Students and parents have also gotten the memo that many colleges look favorably on student applications that show extracurricular activities such as music, community service, and other nonacademic endeavors. The belief is that it's insufficient to get good grades and a high SAT score. Getting straight As is the new B. Hence the AP and honors classes to distinguish between levels of achievement. An A in honors chemistry is viewed as more valuable than just getting an A in regular chemistry. Many high school students take college-level courses, either to impress the college admissions officer or to seek ways to avoid taking Chemistry 101 in college. Their purpose may also be to save money or make room for additional classes later—perhaps to get a minor degree.

Any of us who had our heads in the sand about the fiercely competitive nature of being admitted to the "best" colleges and universities had an unexpected awakening when, in March 2019, the FBI indicted and arrested several people who were involved in an elaborate scheme to defraud the college admissions process. People were so driven to get their children into a "great" school, they cheated by illegally gaming the system. I confess this didn't shock me, knowing what I know about the intense pressure on students to do extraordinarily well to get into the "best" colleges. This scandal is an extreme example of this pressure. Ask yourself the next time you go in for surgery or fly on a plane or seek a lawyer, "I wonder if the (doctor, pilot, or lawyer) cheated to get into that prestigious school he or she proudly touts?" Cheating has consequences. We just don't know when those consequences will present themselves or how serious they will be.

Why are parents and students so driven—to the point of cheating—to get into certain schools? A great college education at a prestigious university, and of course getting good college grades, means getting a good, well-paying job, right? Attending a prestigious university is a badge of honor for many parents and students. A student's college choice may be about legacy—perhaps their parents went to that school. Getting into the "best" college is viewed as a student's ticket to success. I understand this.

As part of my executive training at NASA, I had the opportunity to participate in special classes and seminars and to go back to school. I didn't have to, but I elected to attend Harvard University's Senior Executive Fellows program. "Harvard" just sounded cool. Wow! *I went to Harvard.* Well, sort of. I didn't have to compete with a hundred thousand other prospective students. Because I was already in NASA's Senior Executive Candidate Development Program, getting into Harvard was *pro forma.*

The Harvard program at the John F. Kennedy School of Government was five weeks long. You didn't get a degree; Harvard handed you a certificate—but my ego sure enjoyed it. I bought and proudly wore my Harvard shirts and hat, and I think I even donated money to the school. Harvard, Yale, Stanford, Ivies, and military academies *mean* something, whether or not they're the right choice for a student. We want the "best" schools, the "best" doctors, and the "best" teachers. Yet we usually don't know what "the best" really means. By whose judgment and by what standards? Are these standards universally accepted? Do we know that the fit is right? My guess is that we have a belief about the labels we slap on institutions and people, and that belief, even though often unexamined, drives our thinking, decisions, and choices. I mean, it's *Harvard*, after all.

To be sure, for many high school students, getting into a preeminent university is a stretch, not because they aren't smart enough, but because the costs are prohibitive. I have a friend who is sending his child to the college of her choice, and my jaw dropped when I learned the annual cost. The United States is experiencing an epidemic of student debt. I assume many students and parents believe that going into debt to get into university is worth it, as opposed to, say, going to a less expensive local community college. Many universities offer need-based scholarships, especially to promising students, but even so, unless the scholarship includes stipends for food, living, transportation, and other nontuition expenses, a quality university education may be elusive even for so-called middle-class families.

Who can blame students for feeling as if they must overperform in order to stand out better to an admissions officer? With the fierce, almost cutthroat competition, how do you grab the attention of someone who's reviewing five hundred applications? What will make that admissions officer sit back, glance up with a welcoming smile, and say to herself, "You are exactly what Harvard needs."

I have spoken to several admissions officers who shared with me that in their weeding-out process, they start by eliminating all applicants whose GPA or SAT score is below a certain level. Once they've done that, they examine the full application. Of course, colleges across the country have different strategies, and there's even a movement by some colleges to avoid conventional methods for determining who should get in, including eliminating the SAT requirement.[5] This may be standard practice by the time you read this.

Savvy students and their parents have hunted down the decoder rings that they believe will help them get into the "best" universities. Their logic is this:

First, you must have top grades and a high SAT score in high school. Straight As are good, but your transcript should be spiced up with AP and honors classes.

Second, you need great teacher recommendations. I learned that admissions officers are savvy at reading between the lines of teacher recommendations. What if a teacher wrote "Jessica is a good student. She tries hard and gets along with her peers"? This sounds good, but it's likely code for "Jessica isn't the cream of the crop." Ink the "reject" stamp.

Third, you must demonstrate acumen in one or more disciplines and/or sports. Playing a musical instrument and knowing how to speak another language or two, along with being the captain of the volleyball team, are bonuses. Scoring an original symphony, working part-time as a translator for foreign dignitaries, and being an all-state athlete are better.

---

5. Valerie Strauss. "A record number of colleges drop SAT/ACT admissions requirement amid growing disenchantment with standardized tests." https://www.washingtonpost.com/education/2019/10/18/record-number-colleges-drop-satact-admissions-requirement-amid-growing-disenchantment-with-standardized-tests/.

Did you start a business or nonprofit in high school? The Ivies are looking better.

Fourth, you must have done something unusual, as if the previous accomplishments weren't enough. Perhaps your Eagle Scout project involves building a library for your local senior center, or perhaps you started a nonprofit to help underserved children in a less affluent neighborhood. Perhaps you were the one who got Webster to change the definition of racism.

Fifth, universities are interested in your struggles and sacrifices. Maybe your parents didn't have a college education, and you're the first to attend college. Did you work through high school to help your family make ends meet?

Sixth, you need to have the ability to write well. Many university applications require one or more essays. When I was in high school, there was no "common application" where the same essay was used for different universities. An original, well-thought-out essay is expected, not one that skims the topics in general terms. Remember authenticity. Writing well—and proofing your work—is critical. You must have zero misspellings, and you must avoid grammatical errors. I learned from admissions officers that applicants get careless here. They copy and paste their essay for a different university's application and forget to change the name of the previous school. This is an easy rejection. I hope by the time this book is published, all my typos are fixed, misspellings corrected, and poor grammar exiled. Otherwise, Momma will ask for a Heaven hall pass to descend back to Earth with her green pen in hand. I really appreciate my editors and proofreaders!

* * *

Students and parents have figured out these six key requirements and have begun to game the admissions (get-into-the-best-university) process, especially if the student falls a little short in one of these six areas. I've heard stories of parents fighting to get their child into the "right" preschool or kinder-garten—one that stresses academics. The kicker? *Their child hasn't been born yet!* The list of ways to circumvent the require-ments is long, but the one thing families aren't yet doing (to my knowledge) is "creating" a deliberately exaggerated "poor" or extra-challenging environment for their child so that their child's exceptional academic and social résumé looks even bet-ter. If you sense my cynicism, you're right. I'll explain.

Professional college admissions coaches (which you may have heard about during that March 2019 scandal) are every-where. Seminars on taking the SATs are a given. Preschools, elementary schools, and high schools with the best reputations drive expectant and young families in their choice of where to live. This is the game that parents feel they must play to ensure their child has a leg up, can compete, and can get into the best universities in order to get a good job.

It is imperative now that I share in full disclosure that I, as a parent of two, thought about many of these things as our kids were growing up. We sent our kids to private schools from kin-dergarten on, starting with Montessori. We changed schools when we thought it made sense. Our goal was to find the right academic environment for our children's personalities. We will never know if we chose correctly (but we're satisfied with our decisions). We were privileged to have those choices.

What we did not do was insist that they take honors or AP classes in high school. If they wanted to do so, fine. We hoped that if they had a choice, they would do so because they were *inspired* to do so, but not as a check mark to get into so-called great colleges.

Certainly, I wanted our kids to attend college and get a good education. I applaud parents and students who think and plan strategically about education. Parents and students *should* think about this. I've spoken to hundreds of students throughout my career. While my goal is to be as helpful as I can, I often conclude that what some students *say* they want isn't really what they deeply desire. They may not be fully aware of what they want, although indicators emerge that reveal some of their deeper interests. I assume there is, within each student, what I would call an *authentic want* or desire, and this is what I'm interested in exploring with them. My experience as an administrator of education and as a parent is that if the student's higher education strategy is aligned with something purposeful—a "calling," if you will—then the college experience is more meaningful and productive. I caution against a strategy that says, "If I do all these things, then I (or my child) will get into Harvard, or great university X, and that will equal my (or my child's) success." The results and consequences you desire may *not* follow from the decisions and choices you make.

This faulty thinking can easily be applied to one's career. In the earlier part of my career, I was motivated by what I needed to do to get a good performance rating (and, to be honest, I was also motivated by my paycheck). Even though I worked for NASA and was exposed to amazing people, technology, science, and really cool missions, I still wanted to know what I had to do to get an A+.

When I began to discover my calling at NASA and found my voice, my motivation shifted. For sure, I still wanted to do well in my performance review, but I wasn't inspired to *perform* for the review. *I was driven by my purpose of working for NASA.* It really helped that everywhere I went to give a talk, whether it was a school, a Rotary club, or a big convention, people loved NASA. NASA just seemed to bring out the kid in everyone, especially me.

LET'S TALK ABOUT CHEATING

HARSH, BLATANT CHEATING

Most of us understand blatant cheating. The type that's clear-cut, black and white, nothing subtle about it. Cheating on a test or on the job is the ultimate risk-free path to (assumed) success. I won't list all the ways it could be carried out—you've already heard about them or observed someone who blatantly cheated. A cheater gives up nothing in exchange for the assurance of money, the next promotion, or getting into the best university or the right club. Well, let's rethink that: a blatant cheater gives up integrity and character, but I assume a cheater doesn't care about that. Cheaters take.

HONEST CHEATING

Is there such a thing as honest cheating? Or subtle cheating? Is it cheating if everyone does it and it's accepted by most people? Is it cheating if most people understand why you did it and look the other way? Is there a cheating curve, a continuum that allows us to "get by" with being dishonest if it's acceptable and everybody does it? Slippery slope, right? We need an entire book to really get into this subject, but for now, let's talk about some of the circumstances relevant to students and parents—those that someday may be up close and personal for you. Here's a simple one that you've probably heard before: you've got a summer job, and once in a while you take home pens, paper clips, maybe a stapler—odds and ends that you could use, that you know aren't expensive, but there they are for the taking. Besides, *everyone does it.* It's not like you're stealing money from the company safe—or stealing a computer! How much harm can this do? Is there a victim?

Well, my take on it is *yes*! The first victim is *you*, the harmless, "honest" thief. The second victim may be the company you work for—even if you don't like them and think they're unfair. And the third victim is me—the person who has to pay more for every office supply I need because, according to Yannick Griep, an assistant professor of industrial and organizational psychology at the University of Calgary and author of "This Is Why Everyone Steals Office Supplies from Work—Including You," petty theft may be responsible "for 35 percent of an organization's annual inventory shrinkage."[6]

Okay, it's pretty clear how this kind of "ordinary" theft (cheating) hurts you, others, and society at large (not to mention, it's absolutely the worse kind of manners), but let's go a step further into a subtler area: Can you cheat or steal for a greater good? How about blocking off a street without a permit so that you can protest climate change? Hmm . . . a bit grayer? Is this "good trouble" to be in? Well, definitely yes, if you're passionate about climate change. But what if you aren't? Or what if it was your car that was blocked from taking a shortcut to the emergency room with your critically ill child?

And now, an even more subtle example: Is there any dishonesty in students who, encouraged by their parents, take classes because they've been programmed to see them as their ticket to success and not because they're particularly interested in the classes? Is it harsh to call this honest cheating? Might these students wake up one day at fifty years old, realizing they had never studied the very things they really loved? Is there such a thing as "soul cheating" in which you "cheat" others by keeping your true passions hidden, and you cheat yourself by not honing and offering your passion and gifts? And what if that well-paying job you took, and now hate, was the exact calling for someone else who couldn't get that job because you

6. http://theconversation.com/this-is-why-everyone-steals-office-supplies
-from-work-including-you-96448.

"took" it? If we place a high-level spiritual or "Momma spin" on a wider meaning of taking what doesn't belong to us, and participate in the really bad manners of cheating, even if it's condoned, are we both physically and energetically contributing to harming ourselves, others, and even our planet?

I'm suggesting that if a student takes an AP class to check a box called "do one of the following things and you'll get into the best schools" and doesn't actually care about the class, then I believe their motivation is misguided.

Here's a test: Let's say I presented research that concludes that students who take AP and honors classes have no better chance of getting into an Ivy League school than those students who don't do these things. (Note: I know of no such research on this topic.) Would a student still take the AP and honors classes? Maybe. Maybe not. The student realizes that those classes provide no advantage. Would this knowledge inspire a student to explore what really *does* speak to them?

Would it be more authentic if students took courses for the love and interest in the subject and not for the labels of the course and what they believe that label will get them? Don't get me wrong—I'm certain many students love their AP courses. They discover they're good at math, love the challenge, and decide to take as many math classes as they can. That's wonderful. This is the healthiest (for the student) reason for taking these advanced classes.

Consider one's work environment. Would it be more authentic to work at a company or agency for the love of the mission? What about the project or team? Would it be more authentic to show up because of the love of the work instead of just the paycheck? Who are we cheating when we work for the paycheck and not because we love and relate to the work? What about that calling? That job that would put us in integrity with our deep desires—and still pay us?

AP and honors classes don't "make" students smarter because they are so labeled. My parents didn't have AP or honors classes in college in the 1950s. They were pretty smart people. I've never seen Einstein's college transcripts, but I bet he never took AP physics—he hadn't invented it yet.

* * *

As you know by now, I'm an enthusiastic advocate for authentic presence because of the long- and short-term benefits it offers—essentially, liberation and joy. I believe that if a student takes a class because they genuinely love the subject, they'll be more authentically present for the class and get more out of it than a student who takes it to check a box. I believe the learning will be natural and more likely to stick. This student won't be tempted to cheat. No need. They'll love and master the material. They may struggle, but they'll have, in the common parlance, "grit" to stick to it, along with what Carol S. Dweck, author of *Mindset: The New Psychology of Success*, terms a "growth mindset." Yes, you can have both a genuine interest in the class and an intention that taking it will help you get into the college of your choice. It doesn't have to be either-or.

How do we know if we're authentically present? Or making decisions from our place of true calling? There are some indicators for students (and their parents) and professionals that can help us determine if we're operating from a genuine desire to be present or because we feel we "have to" perform in some way in order to get ahead. Not all of these may be exactly right for you, and you can add your own measurements to the list, but I think you'll get the gist of where I'm going.

- Are you usually a few minutes early to class?
- Are you prepared with questions, concerns, and issues regarding the topic of the day and

interested in discovering what's in store? Eager to talk about a topic and excited to know more from the teacher?

- Have you completed your assignments and sometimes read ahead?
- Do you take advantage of office hours or any other means of teacher/student communication available to you?
- Are you comfortable asking for help when you're stuck, from a fellow student or your teacher or a different teacher? Are you interested in how your peers approach a problem or subject? *Can you* share your own thought process and be comfortable asking for a critique?
- Does Momma's Rule #2 resonate with you?
  "What others think of you is none of your business."
- Are you here (wherever you are—school, career, in a relationship) because you desire to be?
- Are you taking honors physics, or any new class, because you're excited to master something new?
- Do you love to stretch outside your comfort zone and sometimes volunteer to be the project lead for a challenging event at school or on the job?
- Do you tend to stay away from "easy" because easy doesn't help you grow?
- Do you learn a new language just because it excites you to know that you can communicate with someone in their native language and feel more connected to them?
- Do you welcome pink suits, and are you at peace with ambiguity and confusion?
- Are you studying this book because you really want to and not because your teacher, mom, or

friend gave it to you, saying, "Here, you'd better read this if you're going to be successful"?

Let's take a second and mention two things that may disguise themselves as authentic presence but really are (very) bad manners.

Always blurting out exactly what's on your mind as a charade or pretense for authenticity or truthfulness. ("You asked me what I thought of your presentation, and I told you truthfully that it sucked. Why are you defensive?")

Speaking without thinking or without filters can be just as harmful. This isn't authentic presence; it could be using the guise of authenticity as a weapon that your ego wields.

Authentic presence is about being focused, aware, and mindful in the moment. It's also about nurturing and cultivating your connection with others for *mutual* benefit. It's about telling the truth with a balance of sincerity, vulnerability, discernment, and strength. Remember my talk in Berlin? I was telling a story that moved me so deeply that I was overcome in the moment by the power of the way in which one life had been changed. My true emotions arose and left me speechless. The audience felt my personal connection to the young man's story and joined me in honoring the moment. Curiosity with love. Had I not been authentic, or if I had taken credit for the young man's transformation, it would have been just another story. Don't get me wrong; I wish I could say that every story I tell comes from my most authentic self. I try. Momma inspired me to be real as much as possible. So I strive for this. I am very much a work in progress.

If you're convinced by now that it's important to be authentically present, then I'm certainly with you and applaud your conclusion. Authentic presence is the essence of good manners. Manners are how you show up in the world. Good manners are inspired by giving, goodness, and graciousness. Good manners are about giving to others more than you ask of them. Good manners are about resonating with others in a loving manner. Good manners are a gift to others and to yourself. Good manners are about the very best qualities of our humanity.

CHAPTER 8

AM I BEING INTERVIEWED?

Consider this scenario. You're a college senior majoring in electrical engineering, and you're home for the holidays. You want to go to graduate school. You focus on securing a good internship at a reputable company to strengthen your résumé, make more contacts, and earn a little money. After all, maybe your parent(s) spotted you for your undergrad degree, but they let you know you're on your own for graduate school.

During the holidays, your parents tell you that the Johnsons—you went to high school with their son, who liked you more than you liked him—invited your family to come and celebrate Hanukkah with them. You don't want to go. Your dreidel days are long over, but the lure of latkes is just too much, so you agree.

You arrive at the Johnsons'. There are other people there, mostly older folks you don't know. You're thinking, *I could be home playing my video games. I deserve it. Last semester was a bear.* Besides, senioritis has kicked in big-time, and you're not interested in small talk with old people, and for sure you're not interested in Joe (the Johnsons' son). Because you're an enlightened college student, you have opinions about the politics of the day. And since you've been in your comfortable collegiate bubble, you've forgotten there are people who may perceive the world differently than you. Then some man of about sixty saunters over and, after a few pleasantries, asks, "So, what are your plans after graduation?" He says his name is Fred.

Something about the question, the person, and the context annoys you. You aren't interested in chatting with Fred. You give a curt answer. Perhaps something canned, such as "Well, I'm not sure; I hope to get a job next summer and go on to graduate school." Your eyes are scanning the room for someone cooler to talk to, maybe someone your age. You aren't aware that you've turned your body, including your feet, away from Fred, and you are ignorant of the implications of your body language or that anyone might notice or care. You're respectful in your responses but not authentically interested. No vibe emanates from your pores that says, "I appreciate you and this conversation, and I want to know more about you." Ha! Just the opposite. You're thinking, *I've got to get away from Fred.* You are not present.

You just blew your interview. And you didn't even know you were being interviewed! You see, "Fred" is the CEO of a major tech company, and he's always looking for good talent. He's a close friend of Mrs. Johnson, whom he greatly respects— any friend of Mrs. Johnson is probably "good people." But you gave Fred zero reason to believe that. You probably blew your chance to secure a great internship at a reputable company. Fred may or may not have been a creep, but you never gave him a chance, so now you've lost yours.

Had you showed the most basic manners and stayed just a few moments longer, making a genuine connection, you might have gotten around to telling Fred about your interest in electrical engineering. Fred might have mentioned that he's the CEO of CoolTech, Inc. You probably would have perked up at this new information and asked Fred about internships. Fred's company must compete fiercely for engineering talent, so he might have looked past your initial aloofness, and something else he couldn't quite put his finger on, and suggested that you send your résumé to HR for an internship consideration. Your grades are good, and your professors give you high marks for your engineering acumen. Should be a slam dunk, right?

Good luck with that. You see, now you're sending your résumé to join hundreds of others. It's up to someone in HR to discover you and figure out that you're a great engineer and a great person with potential. All from your résumé. This is not the strongest strategy.

There are few milestones that are more consequential than a job interview. The outcome can significantly change your life. The job interview that brought me to California from Maryland resulted in major life events—I met my wife, and we have two incredible children. That would not have happened had I failed to convince the people in California that I was the right person for the job. I don't know what would have happened had there been a different result. I may have met "Mrs. Wrong" and ended up in a nasty, expensive divorce. Maybe I would have cursed myself for moving. Fortunately for me, my move worked out well.

The outcome of a job interview is more consequential than mindlessly crossing the street, unless you get run over by someone who is texting and not paying attention. I sincerely hope you never make a decision that exposes you to a similar tragedy. You never know. Any decision you make, followed by your choices and actions, can lead to disaster, fortune, or the infinite in-between. I'm not talking about long odds, chances that may or may not lead to a desirable or undesirable consequence. I'm talking about something that you know will impact your future. Examples include what your GPA is, what SAT score you get, which university you get into, which company you work for, whether or not you get your start-up funded, whom you choose to marry, and whether or not you choose to have children.

"TELL ME ABOUT YOURSELF"

Have you heard people suggest that the interview is over before it starts? How is that possible? It's possible, and it happens. As our college friend may have learned had she engaged with Fred authentically, *the way you show up matters.* Having impeccable manners, as in the manner in which you present yourself to the world, makes a difference. (As I mentioned in the previous chapter, Amy Cuddy's *Presence* is an excellent source for a scholarly treatment of this concept.)

I invite you now to broaden the concept of a job interview. In a narrow, traditional sense, a job interview means there is a position for which you apply. You might physically go to a place, sit across a table from one or more people, and answer questions, or you might be video conferencing remotely. Either way, you may be asked, "So why do you want this job?" Or "Tell me about yourself." And the classic, "So what are your strengths and weaknesses?"

Expand the possibilities of what the broader concept of a job interview could mean. Of course, a job may mean a position you seek (perhaps you answered an ad) that pays a wage or a salary. But it can be a different kind of job. It can be the job as a potential mate, the job as a friend, or the job as a business partner for a start-up. Some of these examples are not jobs in the classic sense, but they are *opportunities that may present themselves, depending on how you show up.*

As you traverse the world, you show up in a certain way. People notice or react to your words, your body language, your mood, your clothes, your grooming, your entire persona. Their reaction may range from no reaction to having a transformative experience. Some people have had a life-changing experience in the presence of a spiritual leader, a prominent political leader, a schoolteacher, or a therapist. You've heard people say, "That person changed my life." The interview is not just the formal half hour you have face-to-face with someone. Bottom line: you are *always* interviewing for a job. Always.

Now let's take another look at our college friend. How could this connection have potentially played out? Well, for starters, had she used her manners and communicated authentically, Fred might have been so impressed with her as a person that he might have asked this potential job candidate to send her résumé directly to him. He'd send it to HR. Now, put yourself in HR's shoes. You get an email from the CEO of your company that says, "Met a young woman last night who's pretty impressive. She's an electrical engineering major. Here's her résumé. Take a look, and perhaps we can find a suitable internship for her this summer. Let me know what you think at the end of the week." This is what's known as a "house deal." Meaning: the internship is yours.

There have been many times in my professional career that I have met people who so impressed me with their gift of rapport—their manners—that I thought to myself, "I would hire that person in a heartbeat." Why? Because I could teach them the technical skills they would need to perform the work. It's difficult to teach the so-called soft skills required to be successful. I'm not a fan of the term "soft skills." The term itself implies that soft skills are less important than "hard skills," as if "hard" is better or more useful. I learned hard skills and made it, so la-di-da, I must be better. There's a sophisticated term for this thinking, and it rhymes with "base hit."

What, exactly, are soft skills? Let's start with manners, meaning personal skills, rapport with others, and the ability to communicate well, get along with people, and listen well. You can extrapolate from here. Good manners take time to master, and failing to do so puts you at a significant disadvantage to those who have mastered them. Giving priority to a hard skill, such as technical skills, isn't a helpful distinction. I can assure you that people such as Bill Gates, Warren Buffett, and Oprah Winfrey have a *range* of skills—technical and nontechnical, hard and soft, if you must—that helped them become the people they are. And what exactly does "technical" mean? The word is related to "technique" and roughly means the manner in which you carry out or perform a task. It often refers to artistic or scientific work. Note that technique isn't about an ability to solve differential equations, or program a quantum computer, or calculate delta-v. It is a way, a style, a method. The goal is to learn "ways" that work.

Please do not get hung up on whether you have hard or soft skills, technical skills or strong communication skills. Once you graduate from MIT with a neuroscience degree, the one thing that may distinguish you from your competition for that "perfect job" is your manners. I have met many aspiring students who want to work in aerospace. They're convinced that by getting the right degree, learning how to program, and going to the right school, they'll get a leg up. Please do not misunderstand what I'm advocating here. If you want to be a neuroscientist and go to MIT, I'm your biggest cheerleader. What I will advise you, though, is to pursue those goals while also learning good manners. Remember what Momma said: *Manners will take you where brains and money won't.*

GABRIEL'S STORY

This is a story about Gabriel, a young man I wanted to take under my wing, hire, mentor, and watch in amazement as his successful career at NASA unfolded. The only problem? Gabriel was eleven. What did he do that impressed me so much? Gabriel embodied the essence of this book.

Gabriel "had me" in the first thirty seconds of meeting him. I was attending an air show at Fox Airfield near Lancaster, California, in my official capacity as associate administrator for education. NASA's Dryden Flight Research Center (now named Armstrong) is nearby and had a presence at the airfield with booths, demonstrations, and educational exhibits. Our NASA Education office at Dryden arranged for several local middle and high schools to set up small booths where students could show off their science or engineering projects. NASA engages students at this age to inspire them to pursue interests in disciplines that NASA requires to carry out its mission and deliver what the nation needs to be economically strong and maintain leadership in aerospace. A NASA investment in students is an investment in NASA's and the United States' future.

I've attended many events like this, and after a while, patterns emerge, especially with students. Most know their project and can explain reasonably well what it is. Some aren't as articulate as others, and some assume their audience knows a lot more about the subject than they do. I've listened to middle school students talk about various topics, and I've nodded my head as if I understood them, but I didn't. These are not students doing simple volcano science fair experiments. They're exceedingly smart. So, what got to me about Gabriel?

As I walked down the aisles, listening to the students pitch their projects to me, I noticed something different in the booth I was approaching. The two boys were smiling in my direction, already making eye contact and seemingly eager for my visit.

As soon as I reached their booth, Gabriel and his partner stood up, flashed a smile, and extended their hands to me, saying, "Thank you for coming, Mr. James." Gabriel spoke right up.

"I'm Gabriel Rodrigues, and this is my partner, Robert, and we'd be delighted to share with you . . ." I don't recall much of what he said after that. I was enthralled. About five minutes after they began talking, I stopped him to ask, "How old are you, Gabriel?" Because of Gabriel's and Robert's last names, I assumed these young boys might be of Mexican heritage. Since one of NASA's goals is to focus our efforts on underrepresented minorities, I am particularly interested in promising students of color.

"Eleven, sir," he replied.

He then proceeded, in tag-team fashion with Robert, to explain their project. They had a challenge, they had a hypothesis, and they talked about their experiments, the data they collected, and all the standard scientific methodology that many students understand well.

Gabriel did most of the talking. He was smart, and his firm grasp on his subject matter equaled his firm handshake at the outset. He was a skilled speaker. There was something about his authentic connection with me that stood out from all the other students that day. *Gabriel was authentically present.* When I first approached their booth, they had stood up without hesitation—with purpose, eagerness, and respectfulness. Gabriel faced me directly and confidently, eyes softly locked on mine, with enough deference to communicate that he respected me and the position I held. He called out my name because he took the time to look at my name tag. No other student did that. Gabriel didn't wait for me to extend my hand first. He put his hand out with a whiff of vulnerability and openness— an unconditionality that said, *I am here, and I want to shake your hand if you will take it.* I did so eagerly. Gabriel answered my questions without hesitation. He stopped periodically to ask if I had any questions and ideas on how they could make their project better. Wow. This young man was prepared and present!

I was struck by his presence and the articulation that flowed from him naturally. His communication did not feel scripted. I thought of the movie The Matrix. Tank must have inserted the "how to use impeccable manners when talking to adults" program into Gabriel. As we neared the end of our time, I asked Gabriel if his parents were there. He said yes and pointed to them. I thanked him for his time, excused myself, and went up to his mom and dad, who'd been standing in the background, watching their son with obvious pride. I introduced myself and said, "Whatever you did in rearing your son, you deserve a gold medal. I have rarely seen such a mature, fine young man like Gabriel, with such impeccable manners. I would hire him tomorrow if I could. I can't believe he' s just eleven." I continued to shower the parents with praise on their parenting skills. As a parent myself, I know how tough it is to compete with the many influences on a young person's life. And yet here was this kid who had just impressed the hell out of me.

The key was the authentic way in which Gabriel had handled himself *and me*. I didn't feel he was "acting." This is an important point. I've interviewed hundreds of people for various positions, promotions, or just informational purposes. Often, I sense that I'm the audience watching an act—the act being the "interview act." I do appreciate when the interviewee knows the conventional interviewing practices—they've dressed the part, arrived ten to fifteen minutes early, had a fresh résumé ready, and answered the obvious questions with what sounded like well-rehearsed answers. But this kind of preparedness, though important, leaves me wondering what they're really like when acting time is over and the credits roll.

People have a way of sensing an act, though they cannot always pinpoint the precise data they receive that makes them draw that conclusion. It's similar to the famous answer given by former US Supreme Court Justice Potter Stewart in 1964 when he was talking about how to define pornography: "I shall not today attempt further to define the kinds of material I understand to be embraced within that shorthand description ["hard-core pornography"], and perhaps I could never succeed in intelligibly doing so. But *I know it when I see it*, and the motion picture involved in this case is not that."[7] (Emphasis mine.)

Having said this, I will forgive someone for putting on a good interview act if I conclude they're trying hard to get it right *and* be real. What is difficult to know is whether they truly believe the stories they're telling or if they believe they will get the job by telling the "right" stories. Do their stories come from their head or from their heart? Sometimes the words don't seem to match the body language. At NASA, we had a saying about this disconnect: the "video doesn't match the audio." This brings me to a critical point about not just interviewing but communicating with someone in general—nonverbal communications.

You may already know that research provides strong evidence that nonverbal communication is powerful, oftentimes more powerful than verbal communications. Cuddy addresses this in her book *Presence*. I have studied body language and also recommend Joe Navarro's *What Every Body Is Saying*, if you want to know more on this topic. It's fascinating. People tell you a lot by how they hold and move their bodies. You're probably more aware of this than you know. Recall if you have ever been in a conversation with someone, and somehow you just sensed that they weren't that interested in what you had

---

7. Jacobellis v. Ohio, 378 U.S. 184 (1964).

to say, or they seemed to be looking past you or through you instead of at you. When this happens, their words may say, "I am with you," and "I am communicating with you," but their body says, "I am somewhere else."

Let's look at what constitutes a worthwhile interview, the one that comes closest to putting both you and your interviewer in a place where authentic exchange might take place.

PREPARE FOR YOUR INTERVIEW

Okay, I can't emphasize enough the value of preparing for your interview. This is one of those times that winging it simply won't do. Here are a few ways you can get yourself ready:

- Think about what you're going to say and how you will say it; identify at least three powerful points you must convey to your interviewer.
- Think about your body: How will it help you to communicate your messages?
- Film a mock interview of yourself so you can see yourself in action. Are there any distracting habits you have that you can address before the actual interview?

It's vital to be prepared for the possibility that the interview may not go well. When you become aware that things aren't going well, you must take a deep breath and pay attention to your talking cadence, your tone of voice, and your body language. Notice when you're uncomfortable in any discussion, including your interview. Do you fidget more, get more physically energetic, or do the opposite—freeze, or get that deer-in-the-headlights look? Your body will tell the truth, regardless of what you say. Don't allow your body to betray your true feelings: *I am so toast; I just want to get the hell out of here.*

You may be anxious, or the interviewer intimidates you or challenges you with a question that really throws you off. Your tendency will be to cover up your feelings and pray that the person will not notice that you're scared to death. You must master managing your emotions and feelings to avoid betraying what is true. The best way to do this is to practice. Pay attention to your body the next time you are in a heated discussion about politics or some other hot-button topic that gets you going. How you are in those situations is what you must work on.

Are you a bit puzzled? Earlier I spoke of the importance of being authentic and exhibiting impeccable manners. Now I'm talking about masking your true feelings. What gives? This is a fair question and a critical distinction to understand. *Master this and you will master the interview.*

Consider a theater actor. I've met a few; in fact, my daughter is an actor. I've learned that some actors get nervous before a performance. Some are so terrified that they throw up before going on stage. What is also true is that when you, the audience, see them, you'd never know they felt this way, nor does their body betray their true emotions, at least the ones that immediately precede their performance. Their emotions are present at that moment. They cannot change that. What they can change is their feelings *about* their emotions. This is a distinction artfully discussed in Brendon Burchard's bestselling book *High Performance Habits.*

The actor's emotion may be anxiety. But their feelings are of power and determination. They experience anxiety and may say to themselves, *I'm grateful for this anxiety, for it will give me the power to give the best performance possible. If I don't have anxiety or am not nervous, then something is wrong.* Anxious actors learn to use their anxiety. Their anxiety *affirms their humanity and keeps them focused.*

Actors may be anxious because they really care about what they are about to do. Like fight or flight, actors use their nervous or anxious energy proactively to laser focus their energies. This includes not just what they will say, but much more importantly, *how* they will speak it and how their bodies will say it. Good actors don't allow their anxiety to dictate how they will perform; they allow it to fuel their performance.

The feeling you choose, as Burchard says, is a matter of your intention. If you're going to be interviewed and you're nervous, then you must articulate your intention, *out loud,* before you even get in the room. You must prepare. You must plan for what you intend to accomplish in the interview. Visualize the interview. See the room. Picture the interviewer(s). Imagine the furniture. Smell the environment. Allow your mind to fully experience what is about to happen. Devise strategies if the interview doesn't go according to your plan. Here's an example:

I interviewed for a high-ranking position at NASA. I was nervous and afraid of screwing up. I was anxious. I prepared long and hard. One of the things that concerned me was, *What if I get a question I haven't prepared for or considered?* I know myself well enough to know that when I "wing" an answer, I talk too much. I call it verbal shotgunning. It's when you spew out a million shot pellets of words and hope that a few hit their target. This isn't a winning strategy for an interview or for most discussions, for that matter. Perhaps you keep talking to avoid the "awkward silence" and believe that if you keep talking, you'll accidentally stumble upon the right combination of winning words that will nail the answer. Next time you're tempted to do this, just think "slot machine." If you keep putting enough money in one, maybe you will get the three 7s. Sure.

I researched this question and concluded that the best strategy for the stump question is to thank the interviewer for the question, then *stop talking*, get out your notepad, and start writing your thoughts about your answer. The silence may be loud, but resist the temptation to ramble. Just start writing. When this happened to me, I said, "Great question. Thanks. I'd like to take a minute and collect my thoughts." I then closed my mouth and worked through my answer on paper. I scratched out some lines; I added more. When I had the right content, I wrote down the three points I wanted to make. I then memorized the points. This lasted about thirty to forty-five seconds. I put my pen down and proceeded to respond. After my last point, I stopped talking.

Note: You may want to ask for time to consider your response. This acknowledges and respects the interviewer's time. If the interviewer seems rushed, looks at their watch, or makes a comment about time, then you know you don't have a lot of time to ponder. You must "read" the interviewer, especially their body language. Usually it's okay to simply state, "I'd like to take a minute to collect my thoughts."

Why did I feel this was the best strategy for handling the question that had caught me off guard? Consider my alternatives. First, I could have given him the verbal shotgun. That would have told him, *This guy doesn't know what he's talking about. He's making up stuff and hopes I won't notice. He's playing me for a fool.* Second, I could have admitted that I didn't know the answer and just said, "You've got me there." I don't know. Depending on the question, this is usually the wrong response. The interviewer may not care if you know the right answer. They're probably trying to see how you handle a difficult question, scenario, or situation. They want to know how you *think*. Why? Because your job will require that from you. You won't always have the right answer. The better candidate knows *how to manage* the situation in which they are unfamiliar and uncomfortable. The operative word here is "how." Don't forget that your body may give you away, tipping off the interviewer to the idea that you don't know what you're talking about, while you chatter on. Savvy interviewers will notice this discrepancy.

You may get a question for which you really have no clue of the answer. If it's a question that has a right answer, like a math problem, and you just don't know, then *tell the truth*. If you sort of know or think you know, you may preface your response with "I am not sure I have this right, but I believe the answer is X." Depending on the question and context, you may have an opportunity to qualify your answer. Another option would be to acknowledge that you don't know the answer, but express that you will find out and report back. Then it's imperative that you do just that, and earlier than you promised. This strengthens your credibility.

Being nervous, if you are, is authentic. Use your nervousness as your "invisible friend" to help you power through the moment. Nervousness or anxiousness may be about your fear of failing, of looking bad and blowing the interview, or of not getting the job and feeling worthless and ashamed.

My own nervousness in interviews is directly proportional to my desire for the position I seek. Nervousness and anxiety are at my side before and during an interview. They will keep me company and remind me to be mindful, aware, clear, and focused. These partners are like ambient internal noises to which I must really pay attention when I'm talking to someone or doing something important. If I admit I'm scared, I can use my nervousness and anxiety to help me. If I pretend that all will be cool because I've studied the right answers, then my partners might become my instant enemies. If my partners aren't watching out for me, I might get sloppy and make mistakes. They can be unforgiving. If I screw up, they will be right there to remind me just what a screwup I am. This is a critical point: my partners never change who they are. I just change my relationship with them, and when I'm finished, I thank them.

THE BODY SPEAKS

Consider the person who approaches the interview with a prepared "act." The act is "I am the great interviewee and I know all the best strategies. I'll check all the right boxes, so they'll be impressed, and I'll get the job." The experience may be different. Something may change once you get into the interview. Maybe you land one of those savvy interviewers who doesn't ask predictable questions, and you unexpectedly find yourself confused and now nervous. If you haven't brought along your "partners," your body or voice may expose your truth as you mouth the lines you practiced. The video does not match the audio. And if you're really nervous and haven't made a deal with your partners, your body may noticeably fidget or just freeze. You may talk too much, believing that your words will save you. Or you may clam up and stare at your interviewer, praying they will save you. You may want to get out before the harder questions come, so your body literally might start pointing to the door or away from your interviewer. You may project overconfidence or even arrogance, so you lean back in the chair, cross your legs, or even put your hands behind your head. You project fear, so you fold your arms to protect your heart or basically send a message that your heart is closed for business.

I have observed interviewees clutch their neck or put their hand over their heart. I'm not sure what it means, and perhaps it means nothing. In Cuddy's *Presence*, she discusses the hand-over-the-neck gesture as a tell for the feelings of powerlessness. However, body language expert Joe Navarro warns us that body language is not always correlated to a particular message.

Sometimes there are alternative explanations. He suggests that it's easy to draw the wrong conclusions. Folded arms may just mean the person is cold, or—and I have done this a lot—tired; I use my folded arms to get a little stretch. To be clear, our body does send messages. They may not be the messages we intend to send, or the receiver may interpret a message incorrectly. Nonverbal communication is powerful. If you know that nonverbal communication matters and communicating in an interview is critical, then understand this dynamic, and don't take chances on inadvertent messaging. Your interviewer may misinterpret your body language. If an interviewee's body language screams "nervous" to me, at the very least, I get distracted. At the most, I assume there is an issue.

Back to our young friend, Gabriel. When he greeted me, I got these messages: *I'm happy to meet you. I respect you* (he took the time to learn my name). *My heart is open. I trust you.* (He faced me directly and "showed" his heart to mine without protecting it.) *I want to connect with you* (he extended his hand first). And when he spoke about his project, he didn't drone on and on, as if he'd memorized a Shakespearean soliloquy and couldn't wait to impress me with a bunch of big words he'd recently looked up. No. His speaking was measured and focused, and he periodically stopped to ask if I had any questions, including asking me what I thought about his project.

If you will forgive the NASA cliché, young Gabriel had what we call "the right stuff." The good news is that the right stuff can be learned. I don't believe we are born with the right stuff, though our odds of learning it improve depending on our parenting, schooling, friends, socioeconomic status, and general environment. Like most skills, if you're determined and focused, you can develop your right stuff enough to make a difference in your career.

The bad news is that the playing field is *not level*. Some people are at a bigger disadvantage than others. Some people may have talented parents or friends who have mastered the right-stuff recipe and consistently do well in interviews and in their careers. Some may have had the resources to train themselves in the skills needed and do so with fierce determination and conviction. Others may have been born into an environment where just making it to school and back alive is a challenge; or, if they have a parent around, that parent is so preoccupied with putting food on the table that long-term investments like interviewing skills don't register on the hierarchy of needs.[8]

It's true, unfortunately, that life isn't always fair, and it's definitely not equal. Everyone does not begin at the same place at the starting line of life's journey. Some people have way more challenges and obstacles than others. Some cannot even get to the track, while others are blessed with so many opportunities and wonderfully supportive people, and an abundance of resources, that it's newsworthy when they don't succeed or when they take a turn for the worse.

As with many journeys in our life, we must start where we are. The hard part is determining where we are, and I don't mean our zip codes. Regarding interviewing, start with *your* knowledge, skills, and abilities. How knowledgeable are you, not just about the interview process, but about yourself? Do you really know yourself *in an interview*? If you have never interviewed for anything, then you probably don't know much about that.

And if you have interviewed, then did you follow up with an assessment of your performance? And if you did, how deep did you go? Did you reflect on your attitude going into the interview? Were you nervous, anxious, confident, determined, prepared? Did you assess your verbal communication? Did you talk more than listen, ramble a bit, use too many "uhhs" and "mmms"? Did you talk too fast? Did you feel inarticulate or

---

8. See "hierarchy of needs," a theory made popular by American psychologist Abraham Maslow in the mid-1940s.

forget to answer a question? Did you review your nonverbal communications? Did your hands or legs fidget; were your arms folded; did you clutch the area between your neck and chest? How was your eye contact? Was it fleeting or minimal, or did you perform the dare stare? Were your feet and body aimed toward the exit? How much did you learn about the person who interviewed you?

There are many books and articles on interviewing techniques. I recommend studying as many as possible. It's important to *practice* and *practice* and *practice* again. Reading a book, including this one, will not magically make you better at interviewing if you don't practice what you're learning. And practicing by yourself is insufficient. You must practice with great awareness, as if you're having an out-of-body experience and watching yourself. Arrange for mock interviews, and video them. Watch the videos and critique your performance. Show friends a video of your interview, have them watch it without sound, and ask for their impression. After an interview, mock or real, demand candid feedback. If your friend says, "You did well," ask for specific examples of what you did well. Probe. Question. Test.

If you arrange a videotaped mock interview, you may see things you have never noticed or considered. Have you ever looked at a photo or video of yourself and reacted with horror? Remember, you've seen the exact same "self" in the mirror hundreds of times and never reacted that way. There is something about seeing yourself through the eyes of others, or a camera, that reveal our blind spots. This happened to me in a profound way.

In my second year of graduate school, I began to think about life after school. One of my advisors suggested I consider applying for the Presidential Management Internship program. This was a US government program designed to bring master's level students, mostly in public administration, into the government at a GS-9 level. As I mentioned earlier, "GS" is the government's designation for the civil service, and it stands for General Schedule. The General Schedule goes from GS-1 to GS-15. Higher than that is the Senior Executive Service (SES). There are variations and other schedules, but GS is the main one.

To me, the Presidential Management Internship program, or PMI as it was commonly known, seemed a good way to start out. The government, specifically the Office of Personnel Management, accepted only about 125 to 175 PMIs a year, so it was selective. In my case, at American University where I attended graduate school, in order to be allowed to apply to the PMI program, I had to first apply to the university. Then the university had to nominate me. Only then could I apply to the federal government's Office of Personnel Management.

I made the American University cut, and they provided in-depth support to prepare us for the government's application process. This included preparing us for the interview. The government's interview process would be a panel of senior federal officials. I imagined sitting in front of a table of gray-haired people who were glaring down at me, barking out question after question. The scariest thing in the world is a bogeyman you have never met.

We were put through a series of mock interviews, some of which were videotaped. The video was used to critique our performance, similar to the way sports teams review tapes of their games. I thought I performed well in the interview. I was confident, I knew most of the answers, and the ones I wasn't sure of, I thought I handled reasonably well. Then I watched the video.

Remember how you felt when you first saw yourself on video and how that made you feel? I watched my video, and without my coaches needing to say anything, I knew I had sucked. I was riveted on my performance, including the biggest faux pas I committed—during about 75 percent of the interview, I *never* looked up from my notebook. *Never.* I might as well have been interviewing the notebook. I had no clue I'd done this.

I noticed that I mumbled and linked my thoughts with uhhs, ummm, and yeahs, like trashy verbal grout. I would drone on, long after I'd answered the question or made my point. With hindsight, I realize what I was doing—filling silence with my verbal pollution. I also fidgeted more than I thought. Maybe it was nervous energy that I ineffectively tried to cover with a confident act. Not sure. As nauseating as this experience was—watching this video and enduring the deserved tough-love coaching from the support staff—it may have been the single most important gift I have received about interviewing. It took a video of my performance, and my own focused awareness and assessment, along with the honest coaching of others, to see where I was in the interviewing skills continuum. I was nowhere near where I needed to be to master the process of interviewing. I had to perform deep introspection with a healthy dose of external observation and criticism to discover where I was in order to know what I needed to improve. And if you don't know where you are, it's difficult to get to the top of your skill level because you'll wander or, worse, you will be lost. Examine carefully and lovingly where you are. Practice, practice, practice, but *mindfully.* Make time to reflect, assess, and adjust as needed. Trust yourself and trust the process.

About checklists. While they have their place, you may not want to write down a checklist of interview reminders because you'll be so busy trying to remember your list that you may botch the interview. Just take some time after an interview, whether actual or mock, and reflect on what you noticed about your behavior and actions. Make a note of what the interviewer was like. I suggest writing down your action assessment notes immediately afterward. Be as specific and detailed as possible.

There are classes and support organizations and, of course, many books on the subject to explore this in depth.

Remember: *You are always interviewing.* Master the interviewing process, and you will construct many paths to opportunity. If the term "interview" doesn't resonate with you, then perhaps the terms interaction, communication, dialogue, or engagement better characterize your experience. There is a purpose here, whether it's getting a job, influencing someone, learning something, or getting to know someone. A mannerly approach to your purpose, and an authentic, respectful, and caring approach in situations where you give of yourself with presence, will yield positive results and desirable consequences.

If you think about the whole domain of human engagement as part interview, then the skills you develop are more than just about getting a job or moving forward in school or in your career. There's a possible "catch" that sometimes makes developing your skills much more than just about interviewing. And that would be a plot twist—something unpleasant that jumps into your path. It's the scene in the movie that suddenly increases your heart rate. You didn't see it coming. Being human means that this is going to happen to us sometimes. Without a doubt, manners will make the difference in an interview, especially the interview you didn't know you were having.

CHAPTER 9

INJUSTICE AND MANNERS

About a year and a half into my tenure as associate administrator for education at NASA, I received an unusual text from my wife. Unusual in that it was uncharacteristically short. It read, "What's this?" followed by an embedded hyperlink to a website. Within an hour of viewing the website, I found myself briskly headed to the "ninth floor" or the "A-Suite" at NASA Headquarters in a fog of turbulent emotions. Everyone at NASA knows the A-Suite is where the administrator, deputy administrator, and other top brass at NASA reside. For those who go to the A-Suite for the first time, the trek can be a bit intimidating. Everything about the space says greatness, elegance, power, importance. And there I was, in my dream job, finally an OIC (official in charge), running up to tell NASA administrator Charles F. Bolden—former Marine general, naval academy graduate, four-time space shuttle flyer, NASA's first Senate-confirmed Black administrator, and the man who worked for President Obama—about the website link my wife had sent me and praying to God that I was the *first* to tell him and assure him that what was said about me was utter and complete hogwash. My second prayer was that he would believe me. This was a defining moment in my professional career.

* * *

Sometimes we follow the rules and practice good manners. Events beyond our control catch us off guard, impacting us significantly, and often not in the ways we want. We suffer an injustice. I'm not referring to a legal injustice, but a violation or offense against our character, such as gossip, libel, slander, or some form of potential damage to our good name and reputation. We feel helpless and struggle to own this unsettling moment we never asked for. No one likes feeling powerless and out of control. How do we get back on track after a distressing incident that has the potential to derail our personal and professional lives? In this chapter, we will see that almost all of Momma's Cardinal Rules of Life are needed to move forward from an injustice of this magnitude. Let's start with Momma's Rule #2:

> "What others think of you is none of your
> business."

This may seem contradictory after I've just mentioned that what people say or think about you can disrupt and harm you both professionally and personally. Why might it matter what other people think of you? Just because what others think of you is none of your business doesn't mean that what they think about you, or write about you, can't impact your life. Sometimes we don't even know that we've been impacted by what someone else thinks of us, let alone why they think it. Caveat: I would be lying if I said that regardless of what people think of me, I'm never bothered by it. In fact, 99 percent of the time, what is swirling in my mind is what I *think* someone else thinks of me, not necessarily what they *are* thinking (remember the "three me's"). Most people will not tell you the complete truth about what they think about you anyway—for many reasons, and some very legitimate. Would you easily tell your friend any of these things: that they talk too much, sound arrogant, constantly talk about their problems, always judge people, dominate the conversation, only care about themself, or always need affirmation and approval from others? Probably not, unless you've been specifically asked, and even then, you'd likely tread lightly. There are more personal examples that almost never see the light of day: the person smells, looks scary, "looks" or talks like a racist, or always comes across as negative. Yet stories about you, private or public, can impact and even harm you. And this is the position I found myself in as I made my way down that long hall on the ninth floor to the NASA administrator's office.

So, what was the link my wife sent me that resulted in my unscheduled visit to the A-Suite? The link was to a website called "Cheater Report." I did pause before clicking on the link, remembering my security precautions, but I was confident the message was really from my wife. It didn't appear that anyone had hijacked her account. What I saw and read sent shock waves of disbelief through my whole body. If anyone had walked into my office in that moment, they would have observed me with my mouth gaping open in a frozen state of shock. My head was spinning as I stared at the "About" page and read: "All posts in the site are the opinion of their authors, we do not represent that any information is true, use your own discretion (sic)."

This meant that someone could anonymously post something about you, true or not. The site didn't verify a post's accuracy and seemed designed to "out" people who acted nefariously or did inappropriate things. Men and women cheating on their spouses. People who were real jerks or worse at work. Yes, people were anonymously posting some pretty awful things. And I was one of the subjects.

The link led to a section about me. There I saw one of my NASA professional headshots and an article apparently written by a woman who was making claims of my sexual interests in her. I was dumfounded reading references to my family, including the mention of my wife by name. Some of the facts in the article were accurate.

Some context is important here. At that time, the news cycles had been dominated by accusations against actor and comedian Bill Cosby. Several women had come forward to accuse the celebrity of many criminal acts of a sexual nature, although Cosby vehemently denied the accusations. His wife, Camille, vociferously defended her husband. I do not know what is true. I know only what I read online and what I saw on TV. The media narrative about Cosby implied guilt.[9] Honestly, I had a hard time believing that all the alleged victims, many of whom did not know each other, could make up a consistent story about Cosby's indiscretions. At great risk to them personally, they came forward. The Cosby episode was the tip of the iceberg of revelations of powerful and notable men harassing, denigrating, and raping women and men. Women from all over the country, fueled by the #MeToo[10] movement, exposed a national sickness that is still shaking the country, including

---

9. Bill Cosby was convicted of crimes and sentenced to prison.
10. #MeToo was a movement against sexual harassment that began in an effort to raise awareness of the magnitude of the problem by asking victims to tweet about their experiences.

allegations of misogyny and inappropriate sexual behavior by the forty-fifth president of the United States.

So there I was, reading allegations about myself in an environment where people seemed ready to listen to the women who were making similar claims. As Senate Majority Leader Mitch McConnell would say about an accused pedophile, Alabama State Senate candidate Roy Moore, "I believe the women." I was going crazy. Someone had the gall to take easy-to-find information about me and stitch together a fake story about indiscretions. I was a public figure, and much about me could be found online, through LinkedIn, Facebook, and NASA.gov.

I called my wife, not knowing what she believed or thought. I was curious how she'd discovered the site. If someone had forwarded it to her, then who and why? Someone out there was trying to damage my character. I searched my memory, frantically to remember if there was a woman I may have offended in some way that would cause her to write this. My conspiracy theories grew sensational. Perhaps I was the unwitting victim of a two-bit hacker having fun at my expense. Or maybe there was someone inside NASA who had it in for me, and this was their way to discredit me and my reputation. Who would do this? Why? *What on earth did I do to warrant this?*

I found it nauseating that I actually had to say to my wife of twenty-five years, "Honey, this is pure fiction. None of what I'm being accused of is true. I don't know who did this or why." I reminded her that in our relationship, when I slipped up, I was the first one to tell her about it. If I messed up, I fessed up. I reminded her that if I had ever acted in as sinister a manner as this "report" suggested, that to do so would be inconsistent with my character, my history, and everything I stand for. And if Momma ever found out . . . well, all I can say is the grits would be quite hot.

This may have been the lowest moment in my life—talking on the phone, wondering if my wife believed me. Would she believe me but always wonder? Would she always harbor a sliver of doubt? Once we got through this piece (she said she believed me), I turned to the question of how she'd gotten the link. The depth of my despair over this report would be the beginning of an even deeper despair once I realized the many arms and legs of this kind of public accusation and humiliation.

After hanging up, I sat at my desk, shell-shocked. Then I was overcome by a sudden awareness of the "holy crap" variety. If this Cheater Report thing was online and someone had found it and sent it to my wife, then it could be a matter of minutes, if not seconds, before it might "hit the news." I'm not a physics expert, but I know electrons move fast. Though I was a senior official at NASA, I was not at a level where, if the Washington Post got hold of this, they would run a story. But there were plenty of other news outlets and websites that follow NASA matters that might find this story too juicy to ignore.

One particular website was run by a former NASA employee who prided himself on revealing hidden insights about NASA. He wasn't above trafficking in gossip or reporting on matters not found in the regular press or reported by NASA Communications. Unlike news outlets that try to follow journalism standards, this site didn't necessarily check facts or get alternate points of view. Many NASA people turned to this site to learn what might be happening behind the scenes—whether accurate or not—in the agency. I confess: I often did, too.

When you reach a certain level in an organization, as a leader and a public figure, appearances or "optics" can become a liability. This means that you don't have to do anything technically or legally wrong, but there is a saying that if what you did "doesn't pass the Washington Post test," then you could be in hot water. What does this mean? It means that if something about you warrants a story in the most important news organization in Washington, DC, and it's not a "good" story or one to be proud of, then, justified or not, *accurate or not,* you can become a liability. This can cost you your job, your reputation, or both.

So just imagine if someone happened to see this report about me and decided to send it to the Washington Post. What if the Post decided it was a story worth running? The Post, unlike the other NASA-oriented nongovernment website I mentioned, is required to do journalistic due diligence. They would call NASA and ask for a comment. Our NASA PR machine, now apprised of the report, would work with me and others to craft a "statement or response"—or, in this case, probably a "nonresponse," such as "NASA does not comment on personnel matters." So now, let's say that the Post has at least tried to get a response from NASA and me and decided to move forward with the article, publishing it with a lead that might read something like "Senior NASA official accused of sexual misconduct. NASA declined to comment, citing personnel-sensitive matters."

You can see that it doesn't matter at this point if I'm guilty or innocent, or that the NASA-focused nongovernment website doesn't adhere to strict journalistic protocols. I am probably toast. One "oh, by the way" comment in a phone call from someone in the White House to the administrator is all it would take. They might say something diplomatic like "Charlie, the president hopes you'll look into this and ensure that our senior executives are behaving properly." Now in reality, no one in the White House would have talked to the president. And the US federal civil service system has some protections against willful political interference with a civil servant's job. But the message is clear. And to demonstrate resolve over zero tolerance for misbehavior, I may have been "reassigned." We called it going to "NASA jail"—exiled to a remote facility most Americans have never heard of.

All of this swam through my mind as I anxiously waited to see the administrator. Major General Charles F. Bolden is not what you would call an imposing physical figure. He came of age when fighter jet cockpits weren't exactly "economy plus." For sure we have had tall astronauts, but General Bolden wasn't one of them. I mention this only because on three separate occasions, people, including a NASA employee, confused me for Charlie. One of the confused people was a Black man in the DC metro. He was so excited to see the Black NASA administrator! I wanted to play along just for a minute to experience what that was like, but I came to my senses. I found this amusing, since Charlie is eleven years older than me, eleven inches shorter, and in far better shape than I ever was. We did share the same skin tone, so perhaps that is what threw people off. Imagine that. As a Black man, it meant something to me to work for the first Black NASA administrator, who in turn worked for the first Black president. This was an honor.

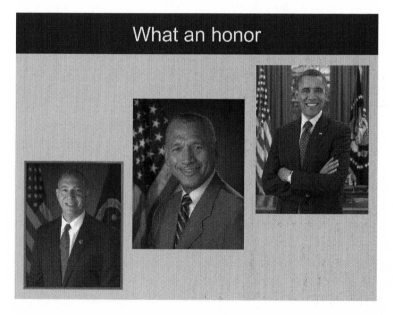

What an honor

I was determined not to mess up or do anything to cause my boss, my agency, or my president embarrassment. As my NASA colleague Karen B. use to preach, "Do *not* shame the family."

Some in the Black community have a saying called "representin'." Appropriately or not, it means that as a Black person, especially a Black man, you are Black *first*, and as such, if you screw up, you indict "the community—the Black community or, more particularly, the Black male community"—usually in the judgment of those *not* in the community. As a kid, I remember my mom, after watching the news, lamenting that a perpetrator of a crime was Black. Though she cared about the person (who obviously hadn't followed her list of rules), she was more concerned with the way that others might judge *all* Black people because of this person's crime. Especially Black men. As a mother of two young Black men, she feared that due to the actions of other Black men, we could be unfairly judged or even worse. So here I was, not only laying potential scandal on the doorstep of a man I highly admired and didn't want to disappoint, but also a Black man who might feel I had "shamed the family."

After what seemed an eternity, his secretary, Kathy, a wonderfully warm and delightful woman, said Charlie was ready to see me. As was customary, the administrator was working on something, but he eagerly welcomed me and motioned for me to have a seat at his round table. The TV was on—it was always on when I went into his office—and it was tuned to CNN.

Charlie, as we all called him, is one of the most kind, caring, and considerate human beings you could ever meet. He loved the NASA family and loved people. He wasn't afraid to show emotion or shed a tear, one that always seem to trickle straight from his heart. He's a proud family man, a loving husband, father, and grandfather. He's a devoted Christian who believes that all of us should pay attention to our physical as well as spiritual well-being. Family and well-being superseded everything for Charlie when it came to the NASA family. In the work environment, though, safety was our number-one core value, followed by integrity, teamwork, and excellence.

Charlie was always more than gracious to me. He knew I sacrificed to move to Washington to take this job, even though for me it was my dream job. I never viewed it as a sacrifice, other than being away from my wife and kids for long periods of time. I had the utmost respect for him. Here's a Black man who grew up in the Jim Crow South and, against all odds, achieved things few rarely do. There are over seven billion people on the planet. Just over five hundred have been in space, and Charlie is one of them, having flown four times! You would have to win the lottery twice in a row while simultaneously being struck by lightning to equal these odds. I don't use the word "hero" easily because throwing it around devalues the true meaning of the word. In my mind, Charlie was a hero, and an American hero, and he was and is my hero to this day. And here I was having to tell him about the Cheater Report. I'd rather have had a root canal without anesthesia, or a proctology exam in church, than talk to him about the Cheater Report.

I had printed out a couple of copies of the Cheater website and had it open on my laptop. I began by saying how sorry I was to be sharing something that I had just discovered. I showed him the website and summarized what it said. Then I looked him straight in the eye and, in a measured but firm tone, said, "Charlie, this report is not true. I have no idea who this is, or why this person would say these things. I believe it would be easy for anyone to learn the few details about me in this report that happen to be true and use them to fabricate this story. I am sincerely sorry this is happening, and I do not want to bring shame or embarrassment to you, the agency, or President Obama."

Somewhere during my account, Deputy Administrator Dr. Dava Newman walked into the room. It was common for Dr. Newman to join in meetings I had with the administrator. She'd been nominated by President Obama to be the NASA deputy administrator in January 2015. Prior to coming to NASA, she'd been a professor of astronautics and aeronautics at the Massachusetts Institute of Technology (MIT). She was well known and highly respected in the aerospace community and was known for her pioneering work on new, highly advanced astronaut space suits. Dava is a wonderful and inspiring person, and incredibly smart. Like Charlie, she cares deeply about people and isn't reluctant to allow her emotions to show. For some reason, people like this, who are so comfortable in their skin that they allow others to take a peek underneath, greatly endear themselves to me.

As soon as Dava came into the room, she greeted me warmly, quickly apologized for being a bit late, and asked if what I had on the table was related to something about NASA Education. Charlie saved me by saying that, no, this was something serious about Donald. He outlined the report's content.

So there I was, sitting with NASA's top two officials. They'd been appointed by President Obama and represented the pinnacle of America's technological prowess. I should have been talking about our ongoing strategy for inspiring the next generation of explorers and future Mars astronauts. Instead, I was talking to them about a bogus report of alleged sexual indiscretions on a website with no accountability. This was the lowest point of my thirty-five-year NASA career.

Charlie and Dava did their best to console me, and I did my best to manage my composure. I was hurt, I was embarrassed, but mostly I was angry. Very, *very* angry. I clung to the belief that the people who knew me would know better. Unfortunately, the narrative in American society, particularly when it comes to men being inappropriate with women, was

"Well, if there's smoke, there must be fire." To be honest, I'm often in that camp. I don't believe that the myriad of women who bravely come out and expose men for their indiscretions would make up a story for some possible gain or retribution if their stories were not true.

What hurt me more was not just the actual report. I knew it was fiction. I thought that between my reputation and a no-accountability site akin to the tabloids, reasonable people, especially my family and friends, would laugh this off. What really got to me was wondering *who* might do such a thing. I wanted to know this person's identity. I wanted to get to the bottom of this attack on my character. Charlie instructed me to meet with our security to see if there was a way of finding out. Unfortunately, their answer was "No, not even the National Security Agency could find out." I explained to the two security officials my incredulousness over the way my wife had received this information. But they actually laughed, saying that not only were they not surprised that no one had contacted me directly, but added, "Why should they?" Anyone who would stoop so low as to create such a harmful story certainly wouldn't want to give me a heads-up about their dishonest deeds. Security assured me that "this kind of thing happens all the time." *Really*? I thought.

I felt zero understanding or empathy from the security officials. They couldn't see this situation from my point of view; the assertions on this site threatened both my marriage and my career! There was nothing funny about it. I left the meeting convinced that maybe I was the crazy one.

* * *

Before discussing why this story is important from both a career and a manners standpoint, I want to say that, yes, I can still get angry over this incident, though I no longer have negative feelings against the people who passed this link to my wife. As it turned out, I knew all of them well. My wife told me she got it from person three who got it from person two who got it from person one. I was disheartened that none of the three had the courtesy of warning me directly and immediately. Mercifully, this incident did *not* drive a wedge in my marriage. My wife rightfully can and probably *should* check out any nefarious report about her husband. After all, if she didn't care, she wouldn't have bothered. She'd demonstrated her love for me and her dedication to our marriage by coming to me right away. It still bothers me, though, that someone who knew me well put me in a position to have to defend myself against something blatantly not true, and put my wife in a position to have to wonder, even for one millisecond, that my fidelity to her might be in question.

WHAT WOULD MOMMA SAY?

At some point in your career or personal life, you may find yourself in a cesspool of confusion that you didn't create. This cesspool can cost you dearly—your job, your friendships, your marriage, or your reputation. What distinguishes people is how they handle the situation in which they find themselves. During that painful situation, desperately seeking a way to soothe my wounds, I turned to the tried-and-true wisdom of most of Momma's Rules:

#1: Make peace with your past, so it won't screw up the present.

#2: What others think of you is none of your business.

#3: Time heals almost everything; give it time.

#5: Stop thinking too much. It's all right not to know the answers. They will come to you when you least expect it.

#6: No one is in charge of your happiness except you.

#1: MAKE PEACE WITH YOUR PAST, SO IT WON'T SCREW UP THE PRESENT.

Do you want your present, your *now*, to be clear, free, fulfilled, peaceful, and joyful? Then you *must* make peace with your past.

What happened had happened. Every second that I spend thinking about this matter keeps it rolling around in my head. This event is history. My choice is to make peace with my past or allow that past to screw up my present. This is *hard*. *Very* hard. I know. I still get angry, and I occasionally imagine what I might do to the person who posted that report. But Momma knew better. Making peace with your past doesn't mean that you acquiesce to a wrongdoing or validate a negative narrative. You aren't admitting defeat or surrendering. You're letting go of your past's chokehold on you so it no longer controls you. One way to do this is to *thank* the situation that caused you pain. As Brendon Burchard would say, see this as a gift you've been given. Enjoy it.

#2: WHAT OTHERS THINK OF YOU IS
NONE OF YOUR BUSINESS.

My concern with what my wife, my children, my friends, my colleagues, Charlie, Dava—or anyone, for that matter—thought about me yielded me no solace. Momma said that what others think of me is actually none of my business. For sure, I don't enjoy having my character questioned, and I hate the thought of being judged based on inaccurate information. But what can I *do* about it? I cannot make people change their opinion or their thoughts, even if I know them. I can continue to cultivate my behavior in a way that represents what I believe is good and right. I'm not looking to win a prize on my deathbed for the fewest number of people who judged me negatively or inaccurately.

#3: TIME HEALS ALMOST EVERYTHING; GIVE IT TIME.

Rule #3 is one that, upon reflection, has been consistently true for me. Over time, the wounds I have do heal and the pain lessens. And I've learned there are things I can do to help speed the healing. The most important thing is to change my attitude about the purpose of the wound. The wound is there to teach me something. It's a gift that will help me grow and be stronger.

#5: STOP THINKING TOO MUCH. IT'S ALL RIGHT
NOT TO KNOW THE ANSWERS. THEY WILL
COME TO YOU WHEN YOU LEAST EXPECT IT.

I'm human. I may find it hard to appreciate this gift or comprehend why I received it at the time. But I need to hang on and trust that I'll get it. This is a plea to quiet the mind. Be still and listen. This is hard to do when you are essentially struck by lightning and as a result are agitated. The answers don't always come right away; they may even take a lifetime. The point is this: it's hard, if not impossible, to see and appreciate the gift that comes from something horrible while your mind's "committee" is working overtime rebelling, judging, defending, whining, and complaining at a million miles a second. It's okay not to have "the answer." I was with a Holocaust survivor who rhetorically asked, "Why did I survive? I don't know. I don't have an answer." That was his conclusion. Sometimes there is no answer, and you must learn to be at peace with that.

#6: NO ONE IS IN CHARGE OF YOUR HAPPINESS EXCEPT YOU.

Rule #6 cannot be overstated. No one is in charge of your happiness except you. At first, this seems obvious—one of those sayings that everyone has heard. If you're bothered by something, or feeling unhappy, disgusted, or angry, do you assign responsibility to someone or something other than yourself for your feelings? Maybe you don't do this, so I'll speak for myself because I do. The lie to oneself is generally found somewhere after "because," as in "I'm angry about the Cheater Report because _____." Well, this isn't exactly accurate. What is? Something happened. I got angry. I, and only I, created causality.

The "thing" in "something" did not *cause* my anger, like a germ causes a cold. I could have been giddy. Seems a stretch, but really, I could have been happy or appreciative to have had this experience. Yes, it's difficult to separate the action and the reaction here. If my reaction, such as anger, moves into my heart like a bad tenant, then I have to wonder, who was in charge of signing the lease?

Early in my career, when I worked in public affairs, a NASA colleague told me he would never again do an interview with the news media.

"Why?" I inquired.

"Because I once did an interview, and in spite of my being precise and deliberate in my answers, the reporter got the story wrong and made me look bad."

"Wow," I responded. "When did this happen?"

"Thirty years ago," he replied, without a hint of irony. Thirty years! That was long enough to fully pay off a mortgage. Wonder how much that grudge cost him?

Things will happen that you don't like. They may not be your fault. You may not get that promotion because of biases and misinformation about you. You may not get the job because you're not a "good fit." You may never know if it is your skin color, your gender, your religion, your weight, your hair color, your age, what you wore, what you said or how you said it, how the interviewer's mood was that day, or whether it was raining or sunny. Most people will not tell you the truth if it's something "politically incorrect." If they did, it would probably be illegal, unethical, against company rules, or just foolish.

There are two things I believe about the Cheater Report experience. First, I believe that the manners I learned from my mother, including her cardinal rules, gave me the foundation to handle this experience in the best way possible, especially given how painful it was. Second, I believe that the people who really know me knew that what was said about me did not match their experience of me. My manners preceded the Cheater Report! In my close circles, it was a nonissue. And if it was an issue for some people, then that is for them to live with. I'll say it again:

Momma's Rule #2:

"What others think of you is none of your business."

Sometimes life simply is not fair. There is injustice in the world. Embrace it! "Embrace it" is *not* synonymous with "accept it and agree with it, or leave it alone." Embracing it means not resisting its existence. There is a wise saying, "What you resist persists."

There's nothing like putting things into a larger perspective in order to release their hold on us. Sadly, painfully, and regrettably, Americans, and citizens all around the world, are reeling from the mass murders of students, teachers, peaceful protestors, and even vacationers at the hands of gunmen, who often use semiautomatic rifles that literally tear people apart. Children have been separated from their parents and placed in internment-like camps and facilities; police have shot or killed unarmed Black men and women, sometimes in the back; extreme weather from climate change has wreaked havoc on lives and property; homelessness and opioid abuse has increased significantly; fires have raged through entire towns; COVID-19 has killed many and changed the world . . . Sorrowful, sometimes shameful and tragic events happen every day somewhere in the world. Some things *really are* more important than a phony article.

My message is this: please don't dwell on an injustice. You may or may not have experienced something similar to the one I experienced. I believe that *injustice is a fact of our culture,* and injustices are not meted out equally. Salacious libel isn't in the same league, by several orders of magnitude, as the violent, tragic loss of children, or any human being.

An injustice is what happens to *you*. You didn't ask for it, and you cannot possibly think that you deserve it or had any hand in creating it. You experience a loss of control. The impacts of injustice are real. The consequences are unfair. The purpose of this book is to empower you to do your best not to give someone a reason to do you harm, to misjudge you, to close a road to you, or to prevent you from fulfilling your dreams. But should an injustice befall you, think about Momma's Rules and how you can be lifted up instead of taken down by someone else's attack. You may need these skills just to survive.

We are more powerful than we know. With our power, we can move past injustices and perhaps go on to channel our emotions toward rectifying an injustice, as so many great people have done. What is essential to moving forward out of a "mess" is to have a team of people who will support us. Who's on your team?

CHAPTER 10

WHO'S ON YOUR TEAM?

In April 1992, Daniel S. Goldin took the helm as NASA's ninth administrator. He'd been appointed by President George Bush, kept on by Bush's successor, Bill Clinton, for both terms, and retained again by George W. Bush until November 2001. Even though NASA is one of the most bipartisan agencies, a new president often means a new NASA administrator because the NASA administrator is a presidentially appointed, Senate-confirmed position.

People who worked at NASA during the "Goldin years" are familiar with his personality, character, and temperament, which was quite different from his predecessor, former astronaut Vice Admiral Richard Truly. It would be impossible to distill Mr. Goldin's career and what he contributed to America's space program to one paragraph. To be fair, to describe Dan Goldin and his tenure as NASA administrator would require an entire book. Dan Goldin was a smart man, New York born and educated. Direct and brusque in nature, he didn't do much to counterbalance the stereotype of the streetwise and highly educated New York City breed. He probably could win most intellectual bar fights. Ask any NASA person who worked during Mr. Goldin's tenure what three things stand out about him, and they will likely name these:

- He was known as the promoter of the concept of "faster, better, cheaper." Instead of taking ten years to build a big, billion-dollar Battlestar Galactica spacecraft, build spacecraft faster, cheaper, and better. Do more with less. Quick. Take risks. Let's return to NASA's roots.
- He was famous for making the decision to change NASA's logo back to the original one established in 1958, the blue circle with the red "vector" swoosh and stars.
- We'd learned about the concept of a RIF, or reduction in force, and feared our jobs could be in jeopardy.

The Clinton administration made "reinventing government" a domestic policy priority. For most federal workers, reinventing government meant fewer federal employees. There are two main strategies for reducing the federal workforce: attrition, when someone resigns, transfers, or retires and their position is not filled; and involuntary separation, meaning the government determines that your position is no longer needed. Involuntary separations are known as reductions in force (RIF).

In the early 1990s, the internet was growing, including a proliferation of websites. A former NASA scientist established an unofficial NASA-oriented website, RIF-Watch, which later became NASA Watch, to help the NASA workforce, understandably nervous about job cuts, get an inside jump on information about reductions. People could post anonymously. The site became a repository for uncorroborated stories and a haven for the NASA underground communication system. We found out about personnel changes before they were officially announced. There was no other way to learn about these changes because the agency maintained a policy of not sharing personnel matters until they became official.

Because Dan Goldin's acerbic personality was well known, fear among the workforce swelled. He'd even played the "race card" when he referred to NASA leadership as "male, pale, and stale." Ironically, Goldin, a Caucasian, could get away with saying that. Though many of us knew that NASA had a leadership diversity problem, some believed that Goldin's way of articulating it was unprofessional, unnecessary, and divisive. In my view, it was insensitive, and he should have been called out.

This is what I knew about Dan Goldin on the day he visited NASA Ames Research Center. I was a member of a diversity group at Ames called the Multicultural Leadership Council. Since Goldin's famous "male, pale, stale" trope, Ames leadership, predominantly Caucasian, thought it might be a good idea to showcase Ames's commitment to diversity by asking the council to meet with Mr. Goldin. I'll never forget that day. There were about twenty-five of us seated around conference tables, in a room usually used as a special dining room adjacent to our cafeteria. We waited somewhat nervously for the administrator, his staff, and Ames leadership to show up.

The director of Ames at the time was a soft-spoken, Stanford-educated career engineer named Dale Compton. Smart, quick, nice, and unflappable. Think Mr. Rogers as an engineer. It was Dr. Compton's job to escort Mr. Goldin to the various locations at Ames, including the meeting with the Multicultural Leadership Council.

We had been advised that when it was our turn to speak, we were to introduce ourselves and describe our jobs succinctly. One of the underground memos we received from a NASA center that Mr. Goldin had visited previously advised us not to engage, push back, or argue with him.

"He's smarter than you and probably knows more about your discipline, your project, or your work than you do. Don't challenge him, and for goodness' sake, get rid of any worms." "Worms" meant the new NASA logotype, created in 1975, the one with red, curvy letters. When Mr. Goldin decreed that NASA would return to the original "meatball" logo, the blue sphere with red vector and stars, he was obsessed about not wanting to see the worm logo anywhere. We heard that he'd stopped a briefing and publicly berated a senior NASA leader who'd dared to have a worm logo in his PowerPoint presentation.

Dr. Compton began by welcoming the administrator and summarizing the council's mission. Administrator Goldin made a few remarks. Nothing noteworthy. Compton then asked each of us to introduce ourselves. I recall being the ninth person to go. My colleagues were quiet, observant, and nervous. They were brief in their remarks, just as coached. As each person spoke, Administrator Goldin listened with steely-eyed focus. He may have asked a few follow-up questions, but given what was about to happen, my memory of anything up until that point is, at best, fleeting.

"My name is Donald James, and I work in the Public Affairs Office. My role is—"

I never finished my sentence. Somehow, the term "public affairs" was the match that lit Mr. Goldin's short fuse. He exploded. What followed was the longest ten minutes of my career. I imagine law students subjected to the harshest Socratic interrogations would have cowered under Goldin's tirade.

"Public affairs?" Goldin bellowed, leaning back. *"Public affairs?* Public affairs is *terrible!* Nobody outside of this place knows what you do. *Nobody.* Public affairs is *crap!* Why is that?" Goldin demanded.

At this point, I thought he wanted me to answer, but as soon as I inhaled, God willing, to exhale the right answer, he reignited.

"How are you reaching nontraditional audiences?"

Again, no reply expected. By now I saw that this was a one-way diatribe. Note: If you ever find yourself on the receiving end of a verbal barrage from an irate superior, do not attempt to jump into their lane. You will be driving the wrong way and become roadkill. Just take it and know your redline. By "redline," I mean you don't have to tolerate personal attacks or any "ism" comments that are clearly out of bounds for you, such as sexist, racist, anti-Semitic, or homophobic comments. You should clearly and respectfully articulate your boundaries and remove yourself from the toxic moment should someone cross your redline. Continue your "fight" after you've calmed down by taking appropriate administrative or even legal action (if it's a work situation). Good manners don't mean *not* fighting. Good manners are about how you fight.

Goldin excoriated NASA's public affairs operations. I was the reactant for his product, and that product was righteous indignation. Mr. Goldin's tirade centered on the NASA Public Affairs Office's lack of outreach to nontraditional audiences. He wanted to know, for example, if we translated our news releases into Spanish. No. He wanted to know if I knew the demographics of the greater San Francisco Bay Area and if we cultivated relations with these communities. No. And on he went. My knees shook. No one came to my defense. Compton and his deputy, Vic Peterson, stared in stoic silence.

I don't remember much after his tirade. I was numb, embarrassed, and confused. No one spoke to me the rest of the day.

I walked around as if I had leprosy. Early the next morning, I made the trek to the "head shed"—Building 200—where Ames leadership worked. As a young and junior NASA employee, I rarely needed to go to the head shed. But now, I went with my tail between my legs, feeling as if I'd let the whole center down. It was early. The building was quiet and empty. I made my way to the second floor because I knew Dr. Compton was in. He always came in early. I knocked on his door and asked to speak to him.

He welcomed me in. Before he could say anything, I said, "Dr. Compton, I'm sorry about what happened yesterday. I didn't mean to cause any embarrassment to you or the rest of the group." I asked Dr. Compton what I had done or said to cause the administrator to explode like that. I wanted to know how to make it right.

Compton put me at ease right away with his Mr. Rogers–like personality. He put his arm around my shoulder like a grandpa might do and said, "Oh, Donald, you got this all wrong. That had nothing to do with you at all. He just has several hot-button issues, and you reminded him of one. You did everything right. That was never meant to be a dialogue. He wanted to make a point in front of everyone, and you happened to be the lucky one holding the bag. Don't worry about it. That's just how he is. Welcome to your NASA initiation."

Compton went on to talk about Mr. Goldin's rather interesting personality and to convince me that tolerating his "tirade" came with the job. Compton's key support to me? *Do not take what Mr. Goldin said personally.* Goldin didn't have issues with Donald James. He had issues with NASA Public Affairs. I happened to be the unfortunate schmuck who reminded him of this. Compton said gently, "We're good, Donald." I desperately needed to hear that.

Four years later, Ames planned an open house. My boss asked me and a colleague to cochair the organizing committee and take on the day-to-day responsibility for managing the event. We led a team of thirty to forty people who planned and produced the first NASA Ames open house. Goldin was to attend. Recalling his caustic communication to me during that fateful Multicultural Leadership Council meeting in 1992, I was determined to reach out to a broad spectrum of people across the greater San Francisco Bay Area. We were concerned about establishing the right target for the number of visitors. If we fell short and our visitors were not diverse, Goldin would ridicule us, or worse. We didn't want to set too low a number, but we didn't want to go too high and risk not meeting the target. After some internal debate, we settled on fifty thousand potential attendees. This felt like a stretch but doable. We went all out to meet our target. I personally did radio interviews on Chinese and Spanish radio stations, using translators. We attended many regional art and wine festivals with a display and handouts about our open house.

I arranged to have one of NASA's SR-71 hypersonic former spy planes, based at our Dryden Flight Research Facility in Southern California, to fly up for a touch-and-go. According to my research, an SR-71 had never flown at any air show in the San Francisco area.[11] Ever. *Wow,* I thought. *This will get the crowds out.* Though, of course, we could never really know if all our work to bring people in would actually result in hitting our target of fifty thousand.

As it turned out, our marketing worked beyond anything we imagined. In one day, Ames Research Center welcomed over a quarter of a million visitors. The diversity of the attendees was noticeable. We blew away all records for a NASA open

---

11. The SR-71 was on the tarmac at Edwards Air Force Base, ready to go, when there was a mechanical problem, so the former spy plane never made it. Thank God it didn't. At the appointed time of the touch-and-go, the historic Hangar 1 at Moffett Field, near the runways, was jammed with people. The sound of the powerful SR-71 engines in full afterburners may have caused a stampede of people rushing out the exit to see the plane.

house. My cochair and I received one of the highest monetary awards ever bestowed on a NASA employee. Our entire team received Outstanding Achievement plaques signed by Administrator Goldin. When I think about my thirty-five-year career at NASA, that open house ranks as one the top five achievements of which I am most proud.

As I see it, here's the moral/epilogue/wisdom of this story—my personal focus and effort to reach a wide, diverse audience can be traced back to *that dreadful day when the administrator went ballistic.* Think about that the next time you get your rear end handed to you. It may be the best gift you've ever received. In fact, as a result of that experience, any time I experienced a difficult encounter with a superior, after licking my wounds, I would say, "Well, there must be a pony in here somewhere."

You never know how support will show up. I didn't seek out Dr. Compton as a member of "Team Donald." To be honest, I wouldn't have had the nerve. But I reached out to him for comfort in my effort to show that I accepted responsibility for my blunder. His response to me demonstrated that, though he was three levels above me organizationally, it was possible to enlist him de facto on Team Donald. Even without an invitation from me, he played a significant role on my team.

WHO'S ON YOUR TEAM? FIVE SUGGESTIONS

I believe most people can benefit from a team. I've concluded through some trial and error who the best types of people are for my team. All your team members play an important yet different role. All may not be equally essential to your journey and success, as you define it. What's important is that you deliberately and carefully identify and recruit your personal team. Depending on where you are in life and what your situation and interests are, you may not have team members from all the sources I will describe. You'll also see that these five groups can be fluid, not rigidly divided, as they may seem.

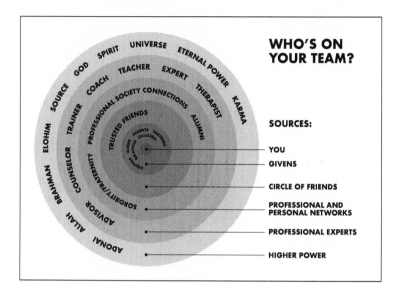

- Givens: Your Innermost Circle
- Circle of Friends
- Professional and Social Networks
- Professional Experts
- Higher Power

YOUR GIVENS: YOUR INNERMOST CIRCLE

The people closest to you are potential team members. Start with the people closest to you right now. With whom do you spend the most time? Parents? Siblings? Partners? Children? People like this I'll call the givens, or your inner circle. These are the people you're around all the time. And for the most part, you didn't choose them, partners excepted. (By partner I mean boyfriend, girlfriend, spouse, or a committed love relationship.) Perhaps when you first connected with your partner, you realized, *Wow. Now here's a smart, insightful person; I think I'll add this person to my team.* Your relationship is now both as partners and team members.

The givens for many will be family. If you don't have a traditional family, creating your own may be much better than trying to force a family tie that just isn't there. I could go out on a limb and say that everyone's family is dysfunctional to a degree, so expand the definition to mean those you really want to be around, who already have your back, *as though* they're family. These are the people who are a part of, and have impacted, your life in some significant way.

A good exercise is to think about how your givens have impacted your life. My givens improve my life immensely and make me a better person. Each member of my immediate family has had a significant and impactful influence on my life. They're on my team because I know they love me and want me to do well. They're excited about my journey, and they support me. They forgive me for my transgressions and faults. Both my parents were principal members of Team Donald. I learned from them, directly and indirectly. I am also blessed to have a wonderful wife and two wonderful children on my team, though not always as cheerleaders. Sometimes they're comedic hecklers, quick to point out that the new shirt I bought is just a tad young-looking for me. My brother Dennis, who's my collaborator for this book, and my cousin and mentor, Matti Dobbs, are natural givens for Team Donald.

As I reflect on my givens, I become aware of the sometimes not-so-obvious lessons that I've gleaned from them. Ask yourself, "What can I learn from my mother/father, brother/sister, wife/children, close relatives?" With family, this can feel basic, yet with careful observation, it can be highly significant. For example, one of the things I learned from Dennis came from observing him as an "end goal" person. He doesn't let the challenge of process stop him from working toward a high-priority objective. I'm more of a process person. If I don't enjoy the process, I tend to quit. I learned from Dennis that perseverance on priorities often rewards you with good results. This is why he's a pilot and I'm not. It's why he's a pretty good golfer and I'm not. From him, I learned to begin seeing the role of process much more than I ever would have on my own. His way of being in the world, though different than mine, worked well when I tried it. Borrowing from his approach improved my life and taught me to care less about the challenges and sacrifices inherent in the process and to focus more on my end goal. Elevating perseverance, perhaps like the journey of Homer's Odysseus, puts the challenges of one's journey in perspective.

I don't recall my father ever saying anything critical about my behavior, with one exception. During a trip to Athens, Greece, we shopped for a new piece of luggage. Apparently, I had a lot to say to the Greek woman helping us. After we made our purchase and left the store, my father made a point of telling me that I talked too much. His exact words were, "You have a big mouth." I didn't appreciate the discipline, but with hindsight, I appreciate his gift. My father shined a light on an aspect of my personality about which I wasn't aware. His comment came from love and support. From that moment on, I was aware of my propensity to talk more than I should. I still talk a lot and can be loud, but I'm aware of this tendency and, as such, I can manage it in order to exhibit better manners. This is the way I understand the wisdom we can gain from the givens with whom we surround ourselves.

YOUR CIRCLE OF FRIENDS

Beyond our inner circle is our circle of friends and acquaintances. These are people with whom we have a strong bond.

We may or may not live with them. We may have fallen into each other's lives via school, places of worship, work, the military, social clubs, or sports, but due to a strong affinity, we became friends. If asked, we could identify the reasons these folks shifted from new acquaintances to friends. These people care about us and may, through direct feedback or keen observation, teach us something about ourselves and help us approach our journey more effectively. We often need external eyes to see something that is right in front of us. Remember the story of my mock interview? When I looked at the video of that interview, I was astonished. With the help of experts, I was able to dissect the way I presented myself and make positive adjustments. There's a good chance that among your circle of friends, there are those who know you so well that they can see you as you might see yourself in a video or photograph. They are your mirror. They know your great qualities, and they know your bad habits and bad manners. Your best friend may have good instincts about why you aren't getting asked out on dates, why you were unsuccessful in landing that summer job or promotion, or even why some people may not like you. These are the folks who possess one of the greatest gifts our team members can offer—loving honesty.

If you want to enlist your friends as team members, be prepared to hear them give you their truth. A wise friend knows that many of our "issues" are beyond their ability to address. Their loving support may be something as simple as "I think you should see a professional on this one." We aren't usually looking for our friends to *solve* our problems. We just want to be heard and have our feelings and experiences understood. We may have checked all the boxes—education, relationships, work, you name it—yet we continue to find ourselves in a bad relationship, without that perfect job, or in poor health despite the new diet. Now we feel like a victim. Time to go to your team for an external review. Loving support from a friend, who may tell you what you don't like to hear, can be effective in moving you past your stuck point.

PROFESSIONAL AND SOCIAL NETWORKS

In addition to your circle of friends as potential team members, there's another pool from which you can draw. Consider your professional networks. There may be overlap between this group and your circle of friends (or even your givens). As I see it, a "network" is a group of people linked by a common purpose. Fraternities and sororities are examples of social networks. Organizations such as the American Institute for Astronautics and Aeronautics, or the American Institute of Chemical Engineers, or the Air Line Pilots Association, or university alumni organizations, are examples of professional networks.

Your professional networks have at least one thing in common—you. The difference between professional networks and your circle of friends is that you might not go to the movies or share a vacation with people in this group. Your professional network is composed of people you've met across disciplines and interests and with whom you have decided to stay connected.

Regardless of where you are in life—a high school or college student, a midcareer professional—haven't you marveled at people you know who seem to know everybody? My good friend Jack lives in a small east coast city, and I swear he knows everyone in that city and everyone knows him. This didn't happen by accident. Jack is one of the friendliest and most caring people I know. He's one of my closest friends. He always greets people in the street and asks them how they're doing. I think he walks his dog only as an excuse to talk to people. I've never heard Jack ask anybody for anything. He's a giver, not a taker.

He endears himself to others in a gracious and authentic manner. He's known around town affectionately as the "mayor."

Some may argue that it's just in Jack's nature to be, well, *Jack*; it comes easy to him, as if he were born that way. I believe anyone can cultivate their "Jack," especially in professional networks. It starts with being genuinely interested in somebody else—*just because*, and not so you can get something from them.

People love to help people. Look at the countless stories of total strangers who run into burning houses to save someone they don't know. Every news story or article I've read quotes the hero as insisting they are no hero. Captain Sullenberger, who guided his severely damaged airplane, US Airways Flight 1549, with great skill into the Hudson River after taking off from LaGuardia Airport in New York, was doing his job, and he saved 155 lives. He did what he was trained to do and used his intuition, rooted in years of experience. He is quoted in news articles saying that he was no hero and crediting his crew for the safety of the passengers.

PROFESSIONAL EXPERTS

Another source for your team are those I call professional experts. These are the experts in a given field. They could even be famous, and you probably don't know them personally. Examples include a therapist, a personal trainer, a music instructor, an English tutor, a personal performance coach, a religious leader, or a financial planner. In many cases, you usually buy the services of this kind of expert.

For example, you may need a health care expert on your team. My health care team includes a general physician, a cardiologist, an acupuncturist, a dentist, a chiropractor, and a yoga master. This is a mix of experts, close friends, and, of course, my best friend and biggest supporter, my wife. They're all committed to my health and well-being, and I am grateful for that. You may say that yes, you too have good doctors to support you. That's great. But I'm suggesting you shift your perspective. How does it feel to say "I have a doctor appointment" versus "I have an appointment with an expert member of my health team"? If they're on your *team*, they have a responsibility to you, and you have a responsibility and are accountable to them. The shift can be palpable.

YOUR HIGHER POWER

There's one more category of team member, and this category is deeply personal. You can define and relate to it in the way that works best for you. Or you can choose not to include it. There are many names and labels for this intangible team member—Higher Power, Spirit, Divine, Teacher, Allah, Buddha, Nature, Source, Master, Universe, God, and more. Each of us has our own name and way of relating to this "unseen" team member.

The concept of a divine source confuses some and brings crystal clarity to others. And some don't care. I'm not here to tell you what works for you. I'm simply inviting you, to the extent that some aspect of spirituality is important to you, to include this as part of your team. If your relationship with a higher power is important and is a source of peace, strength, and guidance, then include this support on your team. For me personally, I strive to connect with the immense energy and power of the universe, from the molecules inside my body to the trillions of matter and "not matter" that are light-years away.

HOW YOUR TEAM CAN WORK FOR YOU

Support from family, friends, professional and social networks, professional experts, and your higher power can play significant roles in your growth. Let's look at an example of how your team might help you with a specific issue.

Issue: You feel stuck in your career and would like to move up or on but don't know how. Who on your team will help with this?

Givens: You share your story with a family member on your team and ask for their support. What can this look like? Being honest and authentic about where you are with the issue of being stuck in your career will allow them to support you better. Being straight with them frees you from having to pretend. You aren't seeking their solutions to your problems. They have your back, and that strengthens your resolve. The goal is to let them into your story and see the dynamics that play out in your head. If they do nothing more than really "get" your story, then you have engaged this team member well.

Circle of Friends: There may be someone on your circle of friends team with whom you're reluctant to share your story. You may fear you won't get the feedback in the way you'd like. This team member will give you what you *need* to hear, not necessarily what you *want* to hear. You remind them that you are friends now and you will be friends afterward, no matter what kind of insight they offer. If your friend doesn't have thoughtful (or relevant) feedback for you immediately, follow up with, "Say more. What are you seeing that I may not be seeing?" You're looking to get to the part where it could hurt, because the hurt may reveal where the truth is. The paradox is that once you get there—at bottom—you are in a place of incredible possibility. The old narratives, beliefs, and structures around which your present condition lives are now called into question or dismantled, freeing you to explore new possibilities, new options.

The truth may simply be that you are not qualified for that promotion you want. The truth may be that you are in the wrong career. The truth may be that you are an arrogant "taker" that nobody wants on their team. Who knows? Your team member's job is to move past what you can see and show you what they see. Perhaps you were passed over, or were discriminated against, or someone higher up picked his buddy or just doesn't like you. Maybe . . . You. Are. Not. Ready. Seeing this liberates you and now reveals a range of possibilities so that you can prepare for the next opportunity.

Professional and Social Networks: These sources can help you see what it might take to break through that wall. This is where you find your better tennis players. (We'll talk about better tennis players in chapter 11). Ask them to mentor you. Ask if you can shadow them. Interview them. Ask how they might handle certain situations and include examples from your own experience. Perhaps it's dawning on you that you're in the wrong profession. You realize you're working to earn a paycheck instead of manifesting your true calling—and, by the way, getting paid for it. A team member from this source may help you see ways that your passions and skills apply to other disciplines. It's entirely possible that your team member has changed jobs or careers and will relate well to your dilemma. Ask what sparked that change for them. Ask if they were fearful of change and if the risks they feared were realized. Ask them, specifically, what they did to make the leap. Chances are they will tell you, "I just knew I had to jump. So I did."

Professional Experts: There are better tennis players, and then there are the pros—trained, certified, or demonstrated experts. Professional experts are highly skilled. People usually pay for their services. Your team members from the professional expert category are *trained* to examine your situation and can offer their expert counsel or guidance for resolution. Like others on your team, your professional expert team members may see something in you that you cannot see, nor do you have the skills to ferret it out and address it. For example, you may go to a therapist to understand better why "they" aren't promoting you, and what the therapist discovers is that *you* have deep-rooted unresolved issues with a parent or have suppressed abuse experiences. He may guide you to see that these issues have long shaped your personality or manners and, as such, they should be addressed as a prerequisite to getting unstuck. If your manners are based on a dysfunctional or challenged history, you may need to address the history first. I am not a trained therapist, nor do I know therapeutic protocols. My message is that a professional expert may be able to address your issues from a place you never would have considered. This happened to me when I attended an intensive relationship seminar. I had no clue beforehand that I had deep-rooted emotions that would erupt like an uncontrollable volcano. This emotional release became the key to a joyful freedom I didn't know I'd been missing. Find your professional experts and trust their work with you; be open to what may emerge from the experience.

Your Higher Power: Okay, this one is immensely personal, and I can tell you how it works for me. It's commonly known as a prayer or meditation. Trust that the universe will provide what is right for you to receive. I really wanted freedom, so that is what I asked for. If you ask for something more tangible, you may not get it, and then you may hate your universe for failing to get you that promotion, or that right partner, or straight As, or into the "best college," or slimmed down to the weight you covet. Before I went into my interview for my last NASA job, I didn't pray to get the job; I prayed for the right outcome for me, for my interviewer, and for NASA. This is my approach. Remember, there are many paths . . .

CHAPTER 11

PULLING YOUR TEAM TOGETHER

Growing up, I was tall for my age and was often asked if I played basketball. I delighted in revealing that my main sport, and where I'd discovered my athletic passion, was tennis. I also played the three most popular American sports: baseball, football, and basketball. My hero was Arthur Ashe, one of the best tennis players in the world in his day. I'd had the good fortune of watching Ashe play in a tournament, and I wanted to be like him.

There was a racquet club down the street from our home in Sacramento. My dear, fatherlike friend and mentor, Bill Rutland, was also an avid tennis player who took me and some of my friends there to play. Over time I got pretty good and developed a powerful serve that often made for quick points. There were many people of all ages and abilities who played at the club, so I could usually get a game.

At some point, I started getting more serious and began taking lessons from the resident pro. He was a lefty with bushy red hair, a gregarious nature, and a sense of humor. He asked me how I thought I was progressing after several months of lessons. I told him I didn't think I was making much progress. There were a couple of guys I thought I should be able to beat but never could.

He asked me how many times I played each week and who I was playing against. After I told him the names of my usual opponents, he thought about it for a minute and then almost commanded, "Stop playing people worse than you! Only play against people better than you!" I protested with a lame story about how the better players didn't always want to play with me. And in my head, I also knew that I liked playing people of lesser ability because I enjoyed winning.

"Losing sucks," I confessed candidly.

"Exactly!" he agreed. "What you need is constant butt-whippings on the court. You need to insist on playing the scariest players around. You'll never improve your game if you play only weaker players. When you play the better players, just remember, they weren't born that way. They struggled, lost, learned, persevered, and practiced—a lot. That's how they got good, and that is what you have to do."

There have been times in my life when I've been the beneficiary of what educators call a "teachable moment." Teachable moments don't always feel uplifting, but more like an "aww, crap" feeling. Yeah. And you know instinctively and instantly that the person involved in your teaching moment is right, even if you don't want to admit it. The reason you may not welcome the teaching with open arms is that you would have to give up a narrative to which you have become attached. The *racket* you have been running is *busted* (pun intended).

Your original story was a story you developed to make yourself right about something. We humans can be addicted to being right. How many times have you been in an argument with someone, and after about ten or fifteen minutes, the person with whom you are arguing stops and says, "You know, I see your point and I think you're right. I think I had this all wrong. Thank you." Or, how many times has someone persuaded you that you were wrong and you yielded?

This admonition from my tennis teacher was a teachable moment. The lesson has had an enduring impact. His support was perfect for my tennis game and perfect, metaphorically, for other areas of my life, too. This is nothing new, and others have written about it. If you want to excel in school, among other strategies, hang out with the smartest kids in the class, and pester your teachers with demands for more work and learning opportunities. If you want to be a great poet, subject your work to the criticism of those who would paint poetic circles around you. If you want to lose weight, get healthy, or more physical, find people who are beyond your physical abilities, and hang with them. If you want to get promoted and grow in an organization, ask to do the hard projects, and spend time with the managers and leaders you want to emulate. If you want to be a better tennis player, play against better tennis players.

My tennis coach wasn't just a teacher of tennis; he was "on my team." He really wanted to help me, even if he had to use a little semitough love. Who's on *your* team? Unless you're a recluse and never see people or are stranded on a deserted island, there are already people in your life who are on your side. I firmly believe we all need a support team. The people who already support you can be the start of that "official" team you'll want to build from the ground up. But this can be tricky, because not everyone we love (or who may love us) belongs on our official team. Some people are fascinating, lovable, and great fun, though of questionable influence. How many parents lament someone in their child's circle of friends? How many young people grow up in environments where their "team" consists of bullies, dropouts, street thugs, or thieves? Ask yourself these questions as you establish your support circle:

+ Who's already on my team?
+ Is this person good for me?
+ Who's missing from my team?
+ Where are the better "tennis players"?

The term *team* generally conjures visions of sports teams and is popular in organizations, too, especially when it comes to projects. A team comes together to achieve a common goal. People on teams have specific roles and responsibilities and often different skill sets. In American football, the quarterback has a different skill set and plays a different role from the punter. At NASA, the systems engineer has a different skill set and plays a different role from the project's financial manager.

In considering your personal team, you're proactively choosing people with different skill sets who agree to support you in achieving your goals. One difference between your personal team and sports and organizational teams is that the people on your personal team have a relationship with *you* and not necessarily each other.

Be proactive in identifying the people in your life who can be on "Team You." There's a good possibility that once you determine who those better tennis players are, you may realize you need a larger or broader selection on your team. You'll have to recruit, including people you don't know. You may be pleasantly surprised that with a little perseverance, charm, and even ego massaging, many capable people you seek out will gladly support you. Why? They remember working with a coach or mentor or someone else better than they were and how it helped them reach their goals. People appreciate when their guidance and expertise is sought. Successful people are often inspired to help others. If you ask them why they enjoy helping others, you will usually hear that they received help in their formative years, and now it's time to give back. This is my story exactly.

HOW TO ASK PEOPLE TO BE A PART OF YOUR TEAM

There's a way of asking people to support you that is almost impossible for them to decline. It's hard to explain, and there is no script I can give you to study. Ironically, scripting a support request usually comes off as a script that you're stiffly acting out, and people may see it as disingenuous. It's like bumping into Warren Buffett, the American multibillionaire investor and philanthropist, at the airport and asking him, with a broad grin, for the keys to getting rich. If he bothers to answer you, he may give you a curt, "Buy low, sell high," and move on. He probably lost a million dollars just talking to you instead of doing what he does to be wealthy.

The people who ask me for support or help or even advice *in a certain way* will almost always get a thoughtful response. If I sense someone is interested in my support without condition and not looking for me to affirm a decision they've already made or a path they have already chosen, then I'm even more motivated to join their team. I may sense a vulnerability in the request and recognize they're entrusting me with that vulnerability. They have lowered the shields over their hearts. This brings up a tremendous sense of responsibility to ensure that I treat their story or journey with the utmost respect and care. I was the first person to "catch" my children as they were being born. I handled my vulnerable babies as if their lives were 100 percent in my hands. Because they were. *This* is the kind of care I mean. When someone gives you the privilege of their vulnerability, it's worthy of newborn baby treatment.

If you are open to receiving support, if you are vulnerable and expose your heart, you become the "baby" that is the gift to the new parent. This doesn't mean that every time you ask for help, you'll bare your soul. It means remaining open to someone's service to you without condition, without a preconceived notion of the kind of help you'll get. It means that you trust that someone gets something you may not, or has had experiences you haven't, and they are therefore positioned to shed light on your darkness or suggest a different path forward.

GIVENS: ASKING YOUR INNER CIRCLE

As you survey your givens, you may identify two or three who could be liabilities. However, I'm not suggesting you estrange yourself from them. For example, you may conclude that your sister and father, who love you dearly, would be unhelpful team members. They may not be able to offer a helpful response to a particular purpose, endeavor, interest, or dream of yours, and though you love them, they just may not be the right people to support you in your pursuit of greatness.

Remember, you don't have to recruit from your immediate family—your givens—if you have a dysfunctional family. Ironically, a dysfunctional family may help teach you how to navigate dysfunctional work teams. But it takes determined effort and probably professional help to translate what you've learned from your family to your professional experience.

ASKING YOUR CIRCLE OF FRIENDS

Caution: *not all of your friends are qualified to be on your team.* I have friends I love, but they don't belong on my support team. I just like to hang out with them and have fun. I would not necessarily call them at three in the morning and ask them to listen to me while I vomit my problems and expect them to offer the support I need. How do you know whom to choose? This is difficult and somewhat subjective, but there are a few clues:

- Who among your friends tends to talk less than you do?
- Who seems to have few judgments and opinions about the things you tell them?
- Who tends to listen to you with eyes of kindness and compassion that seem to actually *see into your soul*?
- Who is comfortable with silence during a discussion?
- Who seems keenly aware of you and your moods?
- Who asks questions for clarification that suggest they really want to "get" you?

INVITING YOUR PROFESSIONAL NETWORK

Professional networks are solid sources for people who can support you. Most people like to feel needed. Some like to be heroes, even if they reject the label. Asking someone in your professional network to be on your team affirms their sense of worth. You are telling them that they have something of value that you need. Remember, deep down, most people want to make a positive difference for others.

In order to find people for the professional networking part of your team, make a list of people you've met recently who are not in your circle of friends. Those who make the list should meet these criteria:

1. You've met them face-to-face, even if it was just a brief introduction.
2. You have something in common. This could be a discipline, a career interest, or an organization.
3. You may see them as a role model, someone skilled in an area that interests you.
4. You know instinctively that you'd like to connect with them again, even if you're unsure why.

For my professional network, I include this additional standard: I feel that I *should* meet with them again. I say this because I've met people professionally that I did not like at first. They may have rubbed me the wrong way. Perhaps I judged them as arrogant. But there was something about them that spoke to me, and what I "heard" was my inner voice saying, *I'm not sure why, but this person is somebody I should get to know.*

Start with the obvious ones for your network, the people who bubble up right away. You've remembered them for some reason. Add them to your list. Make notes about each person. Where you met them, what you recall discussing, what you may have found interesting about them . . . anything at all you can remember, including any funny tidbits. When I can, I make a note about who introduced us and where. If I get a business card, I'll write the date and place of the meeting and why I should reconnect with this person. I make a note if I agreed to send them something or do something for them. As Momma would say, *keeping agreements and promises is a hallmark of good manners.* These notes come in handy later when I contact the person and can remind them about where we met.

When I became the associate administrator for education, I discovered people who wanted to be in my professional or even social network. I sensed they wanted something, even if it was just access to NASA leadership. They weren't calling me to give me anything or ask how I was doing. I didn't necessarily mind. I knew this came with the NASA territory. It's like walking into a car dealership and, magically, a salesperson appears from nowhere, hand extended, asking me my name and how I'm doing. I'm sure they care about me, but let's be honest, car salesmen want to sell me a car. They *want* something. They want to make me happy, but they also want to close a sale and earn their commission.

If you approach professional team scouting with an attitude of "How can I get something from this person?" then yes, you may be a taker. But what if adding someone to your professional network is *an act of giving*? You're giving someone the joy of supporting you. You may even be willing to try on their pink suit—an act of trust.

DETERMINING YOUR PROFESSIONAL EXPERTS

Remember rethinking your perspective on your doctor? "I have an appointment with a member of my health team" versus "I have a doctor appointment." Start with those experts you're already seeing, and build from there. Are you trying to stay physically active and healthy while working a job that never stops? Maybe a nutritionist or a personal trainer should be part of your professional expert team. Perhaps you're being triggered by something from your childhood that is creeping into your relationships? Maybe a therapist becomes one of your professional experts.

Your "expert" team might shift as your life shifts—at one point, you may need a speech therapist or a writing coach, but they may not be as important in the next project. Only you can determine the kind of professional experts you need on your team.

SEEKING YOUR HIGHER POWER

As mentioned previously, this one is personal. When building my team, including one around a project, I include the "universe" and ask for the energy and humility to do what is right, *especially if I am unsure of what is right.* I have a recommendation—if you ask your higher power for support, ask for the best *outcome.* Note: this may not be the specific outcome you'd like, but it's often one of those "hindsight" things where you look back one day and realize that it was the right outcome. I also ask for the wisdom to use my body and my manners to serve— me, my family, and those who ask for my support.

COMMUNICATING WHAT YOU WANT
AND NEED FROM TEAM MEMBERS

You must be clear with those you recruit for your team that you want feedback *as they honestly see it.* Anything and everything can be fair game, if *you* can handle it. You need your team member to be the video camera and the critic. You don't need a friend to tell you that your colleagues are the problem and that you just need to put your foot down and insist they do what you want them to do. In my NASA experience, I learned the hard way that this just doesn't work. I was a manager and a leader, not a pharaoh. Give your team member a sensitive example of an area they can observe and work on with you. In other words, *give them parameters* so they know exactly what is fair game—maybe you don't want to hear that your birthmark isn't that attractive, but you do want to know if you talk too much in an interview, or that you have bad breath. You want to know if you show up like a righteous, controlling person.

If you're lucky, you have one or two team members who will call it as they see it. You will need to give them permission to be honest with you. Furthermore, you won't want them to stop at the punch line, but you'll insist they explain what that "something" is that's off. A rude awakening of this sort, if you can take it, can move you light-years toward improving something you weren't aware of that may have been holding you back.

RISKS TO THE RELATIONSHIP

Your circle of friends may be reluctant to tell you something that might imperil the friendship. They may tell you that your outfit looks "cute" or "cool" but not tell you that your sagging pants make you look unprofessional to say the least. Your friend might ask, "Why would someone hire you?" Part of the holdback is that someone's "truth" about you is their biased judgment. Biased judgments usually say more about the judge than the judged, unless, of course, you recognize yourself in the criticism. Then you must decide if you're tough enough to welcome the support and appreciate it as a gift.

If you're the one telling like it is, the person you're speaking to may reject you, curse you, or walk out of your life. They may just "ghost" you. Or they may crumble, sobbing, realizing that a painful truth has just been exposed, and deep down they know it. The truth you pass along to your friend will change them, and it will change your relationship with them. The thought of this possible outcome is discomforting, so tread carefully with your relationship if you want it to survive this level of commitment. It's a big deal when your friend cares enough about you to offer their truth and know you'll consider it without becoming defensive.

I'M *WHAT?* ACCEPTING WHAT YOUR
TEAM MEMBERS OFFER

HEALTHY CRITICISM FROM A TRUSTED TEAM
MEMBER IS A DIFFERENT FORM OF LOVE

If my team member tells me, "Donald, the way you ran that meeting just sounded arrogant," initially, this would be hard for me to hear. Who wants to be told they're arrogant? I don't want to come across as arrogant, but I don't know what to do or stop doing to change. I am unfamiliar with, or not practiced in, the specific behaviors and communication styles of a nonarrogant person. I look up the opposite of arrogance and see that it is humility or modesty. I study the definition of both. I need to be coached on my way of showing up that shouts "Arrogant!"

What can my team members tell me that is helpful? Remember, I asked them to be on my team, and I gave them full permission to call me out. When this happens—meaning you're really caught off guard by the observation—you genuinely don't know how to change this perception. You must ask for specifics. What behaviors are you exhibiting, or what is it that you're saying (and how) that is being interpreted as arrogant? Ask. Probe. Reflect.

My friend may tell me that every time one of my colleagues speaks, I immediately say something. I start talking before my colleague finishes—gotta jump in before somebody else does. I *know* the answer. *I may lose my brilliant thought.* I put myself first. So, now I can ask my friend to offer suggestions to help me overcome these bad manners. They might suggest that I listen, wait a second, nod my head to indicate that I heard my colleague, and then perhaps paraphrase what the other person said, or use their point as a basis for my point. This is known as active listening. This is something concrete that I can practice.

When my team member suggests I take a different approach in my communication and provides specific examples of how to do that, I can practice making a change in my behavior. I invite my team member to let me know when I falter, and especially to give me the details. This is much more effective than just telling me I'm an arrogant jerk. I work on my team member's recommended behavioral changes. But it's important to remember that memorizing new lines and adopting new behaviors isn't the same as *transformation*. To transform, you must do sustained work over a long period. You must struggle, be coached, reflect on your progress, and learn. You don't recall exactly when the *act* of "not jerk" shifted to the authentic "not jerk." Your shift in behavior over time illustrates the essence of what's in your heart.

"TEAM YOU" POINTERS

First, remember that declaring to yourself or to others that someone is on your team gives you power. This invokes mutual responsibility for your intentions. There's a difference between saying "My algebra teacher is helping me with my college applications" and "Mr. Pignata is a critical member of my college application team."

Second, team members help you see alternate paths to the throne and perhaps invite you to try on a pink suit. If everyone on your team simply affirms what you tell them about what you want to do or how you want to be—the so-called "yes" person—then you probably won't have an effective team, nor will you grow, transform, or change.

Third, your team doesn't magically self-assemble. You must build your team. At first, write down their names and their roles—the givens, friends, networks, professional experts, and, if it's right for you, your higher power. These are the pools from which you select your team members. Make your own labels for your pools if you prefer. What matters is that you are deliberate about who's on your team and why.

Fourth, articulate your support needs to your team members, and give them permission to offer as many pink suits as you can tolerate. Remember, healthy criticism from a trusted team member is another form of love.

Fifth, your openness and willingness to receive support in any area of your life is the most important variable for a successful team. If you're unsure of the issue or you struggle to explain it to your team member, then share what you can and hear what they say until you can articulate your challenge yourself. Equally, if you struggle to understand the support offered, continue to seek clarity until you can articulate their message. When you and your team member are on the same page, only then can you decide to accept or reject the support. Caution: If you *do* reject the support, try to understand why. If it goes against your core values, that's one thing. If you're afraid to do what you're being supported with, that's another. Examine the fear closely. Is this the part where you always quit?

Sixth, you must cultivate your team. It's like planting seeds in a garden. The garden needs tending. Some plants require more love than others. Don't just sow, do nothing, and expect to reap later. Keep your teammates apprised of your efforts. Send them little gifts out of the blue. Invite one for dinner or an evening out purely for social purposes. Call them. Your teammates want to feel important in your life. Help them feel the value of their presence in your life.

Seventh, don't be surprised if some teammates occupy more than one circle. This is perfectly okay. The boundaries between circles are porous. My acupuncturist began as my health professional expert and evolved to a close friend. I have friends who overlap with my professional networks.

Eighth, unlike sports and other teams, your team doesn't have to be together at the same time to support you. Many members of my team don't know each other, though they know they're a part of my team. Additionally, you may get conflicting observations, counsel, advice, or support. This could be a sign that the paths to the throne are many and equally viable. If you meet with five different people at different times and they tell you the same thing, then you can be confident that the road revealed is the one you should take. Trust your instincts.

As I see it, the most important area of support you can ask for from your team comes back around to your manners. Not politeness, as in the "please and thank you" pleasantries, of course, but in the whole presentation of your manner:

- how you carry yourself
- how you are received by others
- how you understand the unspoken narrative about you
- how you speak, listen, react, or respond
- how you give or take criticism
- how you judge and evaluate, and by what standards
- what your body language may or may not say about you
- how you defend yourself
- how you argue or promote
- how you relax and enjoy life
- how you do things when no one is looking

Skillful, authentic "manners will take you where brains and money won't," as Momma said. Add a crackerjack team, and you have a chance to meet, equal, or surpass your most ambitious goals, or just be a better person.

CHAPTER 12

MONEY, BRAINS, AND SUCCESS

I admit that in elementary school, I was occasionally called out in class for "bad behavior." As you might guess, this didn't go over well with Momma. After one of these incidents, Mrs. Burns, my fourth-grade teacher, must have really filled Momma's ears with unpleasant warnings about my miscreant behavior. Perhaps Mrs. Burns feared that my behavior would guide me toward a dark path instead of a future as a NASA employee. In that long, slow walk to our car after their meeting, Momma measuredly turned her head to me and said, in a frighteningly soft, yet stern southern voice, "You're going to get a whipping when we get home."

Note: Momma later said her biggest regret in rearing my brother and me was using corporal punishment. She came to realize, like many others, and this was backed by research, that spanking or hitting your children is not the most effective way to change the root cause of whatever bad behavior warranted that physical punishment. The American Academy of Pediatrics strengthened its call to ban corporal punishment within an updated policy statement, "Effective Discipline to Raise Healthy Children."

Yikes! I'm sure I deserved it. That said, I never recalled my mother or my father saying they would mete out a similar punishment when I received a bad grade or tested poorly. My father once told me he was proud of a D that I'd received in a class "because it was an honest D." He'd rather I got an honest D than a dishonest A. He never once scolded me for poor grades. Momma would say, "Be as smart as you possibly can be. Just remember that brains alone will not get you to where you want to be."

Momma expounded on this sliver of golden wisdom in her expression *"Manners will take you where brains and money won't."* We've discussed success as an illusion and that chasing it is like chasing your shadow. Yet success as a concept in Western culture seems to be about money, power, titles, the number of "things" you have, or how many goals you've accomplished. We might think this is what Momma means—that manners will take you to this kind of success. But let's probe this notion further to find out if that is, in fact, what she meant.

FULFILLMENT AND MEANING

I'll start with saying that I believe what most people want is fulfillment and meaning. For an excellent treatment of meaning, see Emily Esfahani Smith's book, *The Power of Meaning.* What does a "successful" parent, sibling, or friend mean, anyway? If your child doesn't get into a "good" college, does that mean you weren't a successful parent? If your child got to be an adult without getting shot, does that mean you were a successful parent? For many parents, the latter just means they got lucky. Fulfillment and meaning are more multidimensional and nuanced than success. There are multiple factors that influence feelings of fulfillment and meaning. Some people are, by common criteria, quite successful. Yet, if you dive deeper, they don't feel completely happy. Something is missing. There is a hole inside that isn't getting filled. Fulfillment is an expanding universe of joy and delight fueled by curiosity, adventure, passion, relationships, giving, spiritual awakening, and love. Meaning emanates from belonging and a sense that you matter as a human being. You can have a lot of money and yet not experience fulfillment or meaning.

MONEY: THE MAGIC MONEY EXERCISE

Years ago, I took a training program in which the facilitator invited us to try an exercise about money. Please try this process on your own and see how you react. Get paper and a pen and follow along. If you have never done this, then welcome to your pink suit of the day.

The facilitator—I'll call him "Emil"—asked us to go on a thought journey. He introduced the exercise by telling us that due to his incredible magical powers, he could dispense *any amount of money* that we felt was necessary to take care of *all* our personal wants, desires, and needs—forever. He repeated this. *Any amount of money between zero and infinity.* No limit, no conditions, and no caveats.

"How much money will it take to handle your life?" He asked each of us to shout out how much money we'd like from him. This is a good place to stop and write down your own number. Go ahead. How much do you want or need to take care of *anything and everything* you can possibly imagine?

As people slowly began to shout out numbers, he was at the whiteboard, writing down the figures in one column: one million dollars, five million dollars, ten million dollars. Write down or say out loud your number if you haven't yet done so. This went on for a while, then Emil paused and said, "I'm not sure you understood me. I said, I have *amazing* magical powers, and I can dispense *any* amount of money you want. How much will take care of *everything* you need and want?"

People got more into it and started shouting larger numbers like one hundred million, two hundred million, even a billion or two. Emil was busy writing the numbers on the whiteboard in a column on the left. He paused again to challenge us not to hold back.

"Are you positive this is enough to handle all your wants and needs?"

Perhaps you may want to revisit your own number now. Is it high enough? How much do you *really* want?

At this point, many of us were into the exercise and thought, What the heck? This is the magic money exercise, and Emil has amazing powers, and he invited us to *really go for it*. Big numbers started rolling in now: twenty-five billion, one hundred billion. A trillion. I had the audacity to ask for sixty trillion dollars! This went on for a bit. Unfazed, Emil captured all the numbers with aplomb. He drew a vertical line on the whiteboard to separate the list of figures people shouted from another column in the middle.

Do you have your number? Have you identified a number that satisfies all your wants and needs? Write it out and take a close look. This is what it will take to handle, well, *everything*. Right? Last call.

In the blank column to the right of the figures column, Emil wrote at the very top: "Spend your money." He told us to spend all of the money we'd asked for. I repeat. You must spend *all* of the money. To illustrate, and to make this a group effort, he picked a random figure—five hundred billion—and asked us to spend this money. Please do this as well. Just take the number you came up with, and start spending it on actual things or experiences or whatever comes to mind. It's your money. Do with it as you see fit.

The key to this part of the exercise is that as you spend the money, you must identify a price or an amount of your expenditure. It can be a guess, but make it a good guess. For example, if you want to buy a mansion in the south of France, you may want to do an internet search for the market value of French mansions. Please go ahead and do this before reading on. Your castle in paradise awaits.

After a while, what emerged were the categories people spent their money on. First, most took care of their basic needs and wants. They paid off bills, and then they bought new cars, designer wardrobes, new houses, and fancy gadgets. Then people began giving some of the money to their family and closest friends. They would say, "I want to take care of my family." If they had children, they wanted them to be set for life. Close friends would get some of the wealth, too. Emil did the math. After all of this spending and giving, there was hardly a dent in the five hundred billion dollars. Assuming you invested most of the money until you spent it, you would earn even more money. A 2 percent return on five hundred billion is ten billion.

After family and friends, people tended to give money to their favorite charities, usually organizations that served the less fortunate. Some people wanted to build schools, libraries, theaters, or something for their community. Some people wanted to start a business or invest in businesses aligned with their values. Even though the cost of items purchased had to be realistic, it was difficult to spend five hundred billion dollars. Most people had to increase the amount they would give to their family and friends and charities in order to spend it all.

Cool exercise, right? Have you spent *all* of your money? Great. There's more.

Emil created a third column on the right. At this point, he asked us to think slowly and carefully about all the money we'd just spent. It was now all gone. He said he had a question for us to consider carefully.

"Please allow this question to settle in before you answer. Don't answer from your head; allow the answer to bubble up from your heart and soul. Please take a deep breath. Here's the question:

"What is it that you really got when you spent all this money?"

Silence.

Puzzled looks.

Confusion.

Rumblings from the deep.

Emil didn't mean for us to restate the things we'd bought, the adventures we'd experienced, or the money we'd donated. He meant something more profound. This is the part when you remember that on your deathbed, *none* of what you acquired will go with you. As I once heard Denzel Washington preach, "you'll never see a U-Haul behind a hearse." So the question remains, as you take the last breaths of your precious life:

"What is it that you really got when you spent or gave away all this money?"

Silence.

Less confusion.

Slowly, the words began to permeate the quiet room. This is what Emil wrote in column three:

> comfort
> contentment
> pride
> peace

personal power
freedom
love
spirituality
caring
respect
tranquility
happiness
fulfillment
meaning

What Emil said next, we didn't see coming.

"So, it's not money you ultimately want. What you ultimately and truthfully want is comfort, contentment, pride, peace, personal power, freedom, love, spirituality, caring, respect, tranquility, happiness, fulfillment, and meaning."

You could hear a pin drop. Some people wept. Emil continued.

"The truth is that money is meaningless *in and of itself.* You know that you don't have to wait to make five hundred billion dollars to get what you truthfully want? Yes, money enables saving, investing, purchasing, and giving. Usually you need money to get food, shelter, and clothing. In your heart, you know that a *causal connection* between money and what you really want is an illusion, right? You know there are miserable rich people. So, if this is what you really want," Emil mused, pointing to column three, "then why not focus your energies here? What is the possibility that each day, each moment, *right now* you can bring these experiences and feelings into your life?"

This exercise had a profound impact on me. I'd spent most of my sixty trillion dollars on solving homelessness and poverty around the world, even though I was already acutely aware that money alone would not solve these problems. Still,

I believed that doing nothing was not acceptable. Of course, I took care of my family and friends and built schools. I replaced *every* school building that was twenty years or older with a brand-new building tricked out with all the technology money could buy.

What really got to me was the obvious. That money—or maybe more accurately, "currency" as a thing—doesn't have inherent meaning. Money could be rocks. In fact, money used to be rocks. Money's value, and its subsequent meaning, comes from its agreed-upon worth in exchange for something we want and value. For example, you can have five hundred billion dollars, but the catch is that you have to live on Mars. You're the only one there, and you can never return to Earth. That five hundred billion won't do much for you on Mars, right? You might as well use it for wallpaper in your new Mars home.

We don't need to exchange money to get the meaningful stuff in column three, the things we truthfully want. There is a saying that "you can't buy happiness." For the most part, that is true. For some people, that which they do *in order to make money* makes them happy. The things they spend their money on might also make them happy, even if it is fleeting. Just knowing you have the freedom to spend your money or give it away when you want can make you feel free and content. I'm happy when I can give money to my children, but I am happier when I see them being responsible, taking care of themselves, and earning money on their own. I'm happy when I have the money to afford a nice "toy," but I'm happier when I can walk on the beach with my wife, enjoy the sunset, and celebrate our love.

What is it that you really want?

MORE ON MOMMA'S MANNERS

When Momma said, "Manners will take you where brains and money won't," she helped me see that having good manners was the best strategy for getting what I really wanted. Money won't buy me freedom, peace, love, caring, and fulfillment. As a reminder, manners, at this level, isn't about what fork to use; it's about the *entire way you show up to people, including yourself, and your environment.* Manners is about the *possibility* of what you really want in each moment, especially within your family, friends, and professional networks. Manners is also about your relationship with strangers—those who may do you harm, or those who are not like you in ways as varied as gender, race, religion, class, sexual orientation, or nationality. Manners is about your relationship with the physical planet—the air you breathe, the water you drink, the ground on which you walk, the birds, insects, animals, and all the plants and trees. This is your world, and you create your experience of this world.

BRAINS

I don't recall Momma spending a lot of time talking about what she meant by "brains." There were some clues, though. For example, I suppose like many mothers, my momma had her opinions about my choice of women—unlike my grandmother, who always hinted about what the "preferred" woman should look like:

"Ooh, Donald, just look at that pretty *brown-skinned* girl." Hint. Hint.

Momma didn't have a race, religion, or size standard. She *did* have what I would call a brains standard. She would say, "I don't care who you marry; just don't marry no dumb woman," intentionally brandishing bad grammar to make her point.

Momma was known to pass judgment on women she felt did not meet this standard. I never did ask her how her judgments squared with Momma's Rule #4: "Don't compare your life to others, and *don't judge* others. You have no idea what their journey is about." (Emphasis mine). Perhaps she believed that "brains" and "my child's mate" were an exception to her rules.

Momma also didn't spend time in the details of what she meant. She left it up to us to know. What does it mean to "have brains"? I don't think Momma meant the physical biological gray matter lodged between our ears. She meant "smart and intelligent." But what makes a person smart and intelligent? Is it their knowledge? Is it their ability to remember tons of facts? Is it their ability to consistently get good grades? Pass tests with flying colors? What about so-called street smarts? Aren't there different types of smart? Suffice it to say that "smart and intelligent," like "brains," are concepts that people have a sense about. Dig deeper, however, and you find that defining what comprises "having brains" is complicated and subject to interpretation. To measure and judge smartness and intelligence requires an agreement on what to measure.

I have met people who seem to use their intellectual gifts as weapons. Their knowledge prowess is expressed in such a way that it turns people off. I worked with someone at NASA who was like this—very smart and not shy about letting you know. It was hard to even have a discussion with her, because she was righteous, and she was armed with data to prove her point. She was dismissive if you couldn't outsmart her in a verbal exchange. I don't find people like this enjoyable company. They delight in flexing their smart muscle in front of you, like bodybuilders showing off their bodies' every ripple and striation. People like this tend to remind me of what I lack, and then I get frustrated trying not to compare myself to them.

You may be 100 percent right about whatever you're arguing about and feel no qualms about telling people what "the truth" is. I have two issues with this: First, if you deliver your knowledge bomb to crush your opponent into submission, you probably will not endear yourself to anyone, and you may end up being lonely or no longer invited to the party. Whether you are right or not misses the point. It's *why* you needed to be right and *how* you delivered your "rightness." A well-mannered person seeks to raise the proverbial sea of knowledge so that all the ships around it also rise. Second, if you are wrong, the consequences could be significant.

Unless you are trying to win a debate competition or litigate a court case, you may want to consider what your higher purpose is in your discussions, whether your interactions are at school or work. Go back to your epiphany in the spend-your-trillions magic money exercise. What is it that you really wanted? Was one of the answers that you always wanted to be right and win all arguments?

I offer this as a cautionary tale. The next time you say someone is "smart" or "not very smart," think more deeply and precisely about what you mean and why. Perhaps someone made a decision, or several, with which you did not agree, and the consequences were not so great, in your judgment. So you concluded that person wasn't smart. That same person may be a world-class chess player and get superb math grades. Now do you conclude that person is smart? Smartness and intellectual prowess can be situational. Just check yourself the next time you make the claim that someone is or isn't smart—especially when you make it about yourself.

The phrase "one who has brains" is often associated with these attributes: being quite knowledgeable; getting good grades; scoring well on tests; having strong memory skills; being skilled and capable in different fields or disciplines;

being analytical, articulate, and able to quickly grasp challenging concepts.

The danger is in thinking that if you, or someone you know, checks most if not all of these boxes, then *that is sufficient to achieve success.* I have met people who had all of these traits and were socially inept. If you define "brains" as someone with the qualities mentioned above, plus excellent social skills and great manners, then that may be a different story. Perhaps we will call these people well-rounded instead of simply smart.

Remember the cliché, "You're missing the forest for the trees"? If you are focused on the details of a tree—the branches, the aphids on the leaves, or the missing bark patches—you could miss the bigger picture, such as imminent deforestation or development creep. If you rose up high enough, you would see the forest—the big picture. "Success" is similar. Every time you judge yourself or someone else as successful, that is your cue to go a bit higher in the forest. Is it beautiful up there?

Momma never said don't worry about brains. Remember, she was rather judgmental about people who, in her opinion, didn't have any or were not that smart, *whatever* that meant.

To be clear, I am not arguing that one should not endeavor to be as smart as possible or forgo the pursuit of money. Go ahead. Be as smart as you can be, and make as much money as you can. Really. Please just remember what truly calls you once you are wicked smart or are the richest person in the world. Consider these questions along your smart and rich journey:

- Along your way, did you help and give to others?
- Are there people who are better off or more enlightened because of your journey?
- Is the planet healthier, safer, and cleaner?
- Is your family stronger? Safer? Healthier? More loving?
- Are you healthier?

- Is your community or country better off?
- Is the world more just?
- Was your journey more about you or something else?
- What made you happy and fulfilled?
- What did you sacrifice to be brilliant and rich? Was it worth it?
- Do people need to know how smart and rich you are?
- Were you a taker or a giver?

I don't know what your right answers are, nor all the relevant questions to even ask. Those are for you to contemplate. I do believe if you consider these and other questions, regardless of what stage in life you're in, you will inch closer to your purpose and what is truly meaningful *for you*. This is how you live in the magic money exercise's third column.

CHAPTER 13

GIVING ATTENTION

I spent the spring semester of my college junior year in Washington, DC, a magnet for students worldwide. I had been there before, but this was my first time free from the parental leash. Just being there was educational. Trips to museums and monuments, meeting other students, and nights on the town. I confess, I remember little of the academics, except for one thing that always stuck with me, nestled in the recesses of my memory, but occasionally bubbling up to remind me of its power.

University of Southern California professors based in Washington, DC, taught our classes on government, international affairs, and economics. Papers we wrote, classroom participation, a few quizzes, and final exams were the basis for our grades. At the beginning of the semester, one professor was reviewing with us his syllabus and grading standards. It was his grading standards that would be the basis for a powerful thinking tool. After he reviewed his class requirements, he said, "For your papers, if you cover the content and address the items I have asked you to address, and if your writing is impeccable—no misspellings, poor grammar, or sloppy word choices—if you do all of these things, you will get a B."

Most of us sat there in puzzled silence. Surely, he had misspoken. Professor Jones said nothing else. Then one brave soul slowly raised her hand and asked the question we all had: "Professor Jones, you're saying that if we write papers that meet all of your requirements and do so very well that we will get a B?"

"That is correct, Jennifer," he responded, without a hint of irony.

Jennifer probed, "If that is the case, then what do we have to do to get an A?"

Everybody was giving Professor Jones their full attention now. How could you do everything required, do it well, and get only a B? Professor Jones acknowledged the question, pondered his response, leaned back, and then said, "Well, I'm not sure what you have to do to get an A."

Right about this time, every unfairness and confusion alarm blared. Sensing our dismay, he continued, "It's not sufficient just to check all the boxes I have given you. You must go beyond what I ask of you. In fact, you must explore your paper's conclusion with deep thought by answering this question: 'So what?'"

So what? That's it? Well, what the hell does "so what?" mean?

What Professor Jones was telling us was that we had to think critically about our topic and work through our analysis with depth and discernment. We needed to discuss our argument's relevance to a broader principle or theme about which we might know little. Google, had it been invented then, would not have helped. This was not about the "right answer" or what the professor required in the paper. He was asking us to explore *"So what?"* Why would anything we write matter? Who cares? Why would your grandmother in Nebraska[12] care? Professor Jones did not define what "so what?" meant. He deliberately threw us into uncharted waters.

I had never had a writing assignment framed this way before. Yes, it was frustrating because there was no clear path to getting an A. There was no "if I just do A, B, and C, plus 1, 2, and 3, then I know I'll get an A." There was no script, map, or connect-the-dots that led to an A. The only support we had was our brain, the library, and our peers. Professor Jones had played a clever trick. I doubt he cared a lot about what we concluded in our "so what?" analysis. I think he hoped that those of us who were up to the challenge would realize that we must rely on our peers and our critical thinking skills. This worked for me.

We would be judged not on the correctness or incorrectness of our conclusions. We would be judged on the strength and logic of our arguments and how we blended disparate ideas and data. We would be judged on our ability to see what others may not. We had to determine if we were writing about something consequential or not. How did our topic relate to broader questions or issues? Years later, I understood that sharpening my "so what?" critical thinking skill helped me become a better leader. It's also a critical skill in cultivating good manners.

* * *

---

12. "Grandmother in Nebraska" was a favorite fictional person NASA public affairs people invented as a test of the clarity and simplicity of communication. "NASA speak" was often filled with technical words, acronyms, and phrases only known to Martians. The question was, "Well, can you explain it to your grandmother in Nebraska?"

Between the time I was in Washington as a student and my last job in 2017, Washington grew and changed—a lot. My awareness and understanding of what it means to offer someone my full attention—giving attention—evolved. I attribute this to my NASA training along with my cumulative life experiences. As a student, I didn't know I would visit Washington many more times, including four work assignments, several visits to see my dad after he retired (he's buried there now), and my final job as NASA's associate administrator for education.

"Giving" or offering attention, as contrasted with "paying" attention, infers something you want to do versus something you have to do. Paying attention hints at having to sacrifice something, such as spending money. Giving attention enriches both parties in a way that brings them to a place of deep mutual satisfaction. I've learned to recognize and appreciate how I feel when someone gives me their full attention. I notice, observe, and see things in human interactions about which I may have been previously oblivious. For example, I've learned to read cues when someone is ready to be finished with a meeting. I've learned to be better at sensing emotions in others. I've learned to observe the dynamics of group conversations during meetings and social occasions. I notice patterns and nuances that deepen my ability to understand. I sense who has power, who wants it, and who is just along for the ride.

Let's revisit and reflect on Professor Jones's grading standard and apply it to manners. Why do manners matter? Why should manners matter? *So what* that you or anyone pays attention to manners? You may ask, and rightfully so, "What about those people who have 'made it' without good manners?" Or, "I want to emulate people who are rich and have big houses; why don't I just do what they do?" And, "Aren't manners old-fashioned, anyway?"

Manners are not a static standard. The "so what?" question demands that we see what others may not see in the context of our time and culture. Manners are not like the laws of physics that have withstood the test of time. Manners differ between nations, cultures, religions, and any of the other ways we tend to label ourselves. Manners evolve. Some aspects of manners are what I consider foundational, meaning few would quarrel about their correctness and resilience. Because manners are not like physics or math, where there is usually a right or wrong answer, one must look deeply and think critically to determine the "so what?" behind their use.

So, what if you listen more than you talk? Why does it matter how I dress for an interview? I am who I am, and if they don't like it, tough. Besides, customs and standards change. I'm creative and a trailblazer. Soon everyone will be going into an interview saggin'. I'm just starting the trend. Does it really matter if you handwrite a thank-you note to someone? My text will reach them faster. Does anyone these days care if you wait until your host starts eating or if you start eating with the outermost fork?

Is it sexist if a man stands up when a woman approaches his table? I often examine such questions by exploring the counterfactual . . . what would happen if a man approached a table of men and women, and the women stood up? Gentlemen used to tip their hats to acknowledge the presence of a woman. And, I like to believe, to acknowledge her humanity. Do I tip my hat now? Well, I can't remember the last time I wore a hat, but the larger point behind these passé customs is what? Respect. One of the ways I try to show respect today—to *anyone*, man or woman—is to notice that person in a positive way. I look into their eyes and meet them with a genuine smile. Sounds a little corny, doesn't it? But can't you tell the difference between a disingenuous, obligatory greeting and one that genuinely acknowledges you? We all have this kind of radar, and we sense the difference. With my greeting, I'm saying that I acknowledge your humanity and, as such, you are worthy of blessings.

For me, this is more than paying attention to someone: it's *giving* or offering my attention, respectfully.

If you aren't used to giving attention to others, including people you pass on the street, then *practice*. A personal example: if I pass a Black man, plus or minus five to ten years of my age, I may offer what some euphemistically call the "brotha' nod." That means I will jerk my head upward while making eye contact and sport a quick Mona Lisa smile—body language for "how ya doin,' brother?" All of this takes place in about a second.

In my heart, I'm saying, *You are worthy of my respect and acknowledgment. I know that, as Black men, we share some common history and experiences, good and bad, that bind us, whether we like it or not.* I give him my full attention when I connect in this way—an entire conversation happens in what appears to be a simple nod. This connection remains long after we've passed each other. Yes, I do acknowledge men of other races, or much older or younger Black men, or women. Perhaps someday the brotha' nod will go the way of the tip of the hat.

The invitation is to communicate in your authentic manner. Think of it as *giving a piece of yourself to someone.* This person is worthy of our full and deep attention—they aren't a blur moving past us. We're affirming their existence. We're *seeing* them as they are, without judgment.

Note: If you're not interested in acknowledging that person with genuine regard, then consider not acknowledging them at all. No one is interested in your phony smile or fake greeting. I bet you aren't interested in receiving theirs, either. If your thought bubble is filled with judgment about someone, then just notice what's in the bubble.

How did something that appears so simple, like greeting a stranger on the street, become so complicated that we have to practice getting it right? Well, let's break it down. I used to wait to see if a person passing me would acknowledge me first.

Yeah, this is a little game we play with each other. Maybe you recognize it? If the other person greets me or smiles at me first, then I'll respond in kind. If they ignore me, I'll ignore them more—and better!

Now that I'm more aware, I practice giving an acknowledgment first. I initiate. Sometimes I get an acknowledgment back, sometimes not. It doesn't matter. That's not the point. *My blessing to them isn't based on whether they give me something first.* Specifically, in my practice, I'm mindful about the homeless, destitute, or those who appear to be cast aside. I believe they want to be seen and affirmed as human beings, not ignored, pitied, or judged. They are worthy of my acknowledgment and blessings as much as anyone else.

COMMUNICATING WITHOUT WORDS

People, families, communities, and social circles are always communicating, and often without words. But we may miss some of the communication if we aren't giving our full, undistracted attention. Our blind spots will betray us if we don't know how to observe or listen for the nonverbal clues around us—if we don't know how to "give" attention. Imagine Luke Skywalker fighting with the lightsaber while blindfolded. He had to use different senses in order to fight. Of course, we all know that he had "the force" with him. But we do, too. We must develop our "force" to *see* in ways we may not have previously.

Why is offering deep attention good manners? Giving close attention improves your ability to establish rapport with people—men, women, and gender-diverse people, and those from religions, races, or socioeconomic backgrounds that differ from yours.

RAPPORT

Rapport is one of the distinguishing characteristics of the most respected leaders. Great leaders can authentically connect with the janitor one minute and the chairman of the board the next, and then go home to their family roles of spouse, partner, or parent, not CEO. Yet rapport is a skill that's not easily taught, though I believe it can be learned. We speak of "establishing" rapport. How do we develop harmonious relationships so that we're open and concerned enough about others that our communication flows well?

One way to start learning and practicing is to identify someone who is unlike you and practice engaging them. How do you decide whom to choose? Quick! Who is the first person that comes to mind that you *least* want to talk to? That's your person! Your mission is to learn as much as possible about that person while giving them your full attention and showing genuine interest. You don't need to match their story with one of your own. If they talk about someone who died, this is not your cue to talk about someone you know who died. This is not about "your turn, then my turn." It's about simply being with that person and listening. How do we do this? As National Public Radio's *Fresh Air* host Terry Gross suggests, start with "Tell me about yourself." Then, listen to what is and is not being communicated through words and body language.

Caution: Use your peripheral vision to capture body language. Looking directly at someone's body risks the appearance that you're ogling.

When you try this, you really must stay focused and remember *this is not about you.* If the person wants to shift the focus away from themselves, skillfully pivot back to their story. Some people dislike talking about themselves for too long and maneuver back to you with something like "So, enough about me; what about you?" That's fine. Answer their questions with respect. Resist a long response. Your mission is to "get" who *they* are. Ask open-ended questions. For example, "Tell me more about how you got interested in acting." One of my favorite questions to ask couples is how they met, when they knew they were in love, and what the proposal was like. I ask what has surprised them in their relationship. I learn so much from their responses. I get the added pleasure of watching them look at each other as they reminisce about their original love attraction as it bubbles back up. I don't know anyone who's fallen in love solely from a written description of a person, no matter how detailed, effusive, or remarkable. (I admit I have fallen in love with a character in a book, thanks to the incredibly talented author.) You must be with someone for a while to "get" who they are. Great manners are about the ability to connect with someone in a way that *they get you and you get them*, and there is authenticity in the connection.

When I speak about "getting" people, I am reminded of an analogy I learned in a seminar that helped me grasp the concept of "getting." It is the "candy bar analogy," a fictional scenario. You're sitting on a park bench, and a stranger asks to join you. She seems okay, so you oblige. After a while, you notice she has a candy bar in her lap. You haven't eaten in a while. That candy bar looks *sooo* enticing. In a small gesture of friendliness, you ask her what kind of candy bar it is. She says it is a Galactic Cone Bar. You've heard of it, but you've never tried one. She peels off the wrapper, and you get a whiff of chocolate and nuts. You really want a bite. You steal quick glances and drool over the chocolate coating, with its gentle swirls. She bites into it, and you hear a low sigh as she projects satisfaction. It reminds you, the coffee addict, of the way it feels when you take that first hit of hot coffee on a cold winter morning.

You can't help yourself. It just comes out of you: "That looks like a great candy bar." You're doing a poor job of disguising your desire.

"It *is*," she says.

You're too much. You keep going. "I've never had one of those before. What's it like?" By now there's no hiding your true intent.

"Well, it has a chocolate outer layer that is sort of crunchy, but not too crunchy. There's an inner layer of something like marshmallow, but not really."

You understand the words but are blinded, like a little kid. Just as you're about to ask more questions, she pauses and asks, with her hand outstretched, "Care for a bite?"

You smile, blissfully embarrassed, and quickly accept her offer. You take the candy bar as you would take a swaddled infant child from a proud and protective mother. As you pull the wrapper back, exposing more of the bar, you open your mouth slowly, eagerly anticipating the rush of sweet sensation. Your teeth make contact with the outer layer of chocolate and slowly descend through the bar's inner layers; the salivary glands under your tongue burst like a geyser. Your tongue's receptors are alive with joyous recognition as your eyes gently close and your lungs fill with air. The intense chocolate flavor fills your mouth as you emit that universal sound of ecstatic pleasure . . . "Mmm." *Now* you "get" the candy bar.

DON'T OVERDO IT

Some people's efforts to establish rapport with me backfire. I appreciate their positive intent even though the delivery may have failed. On occasion, I've experienced people—mostly Caucasian—who, in their efforts to establish rapport with me, speak to me in what I would label a stereotypical "Black vernacular." Or they seem to want to establish their "I-am-good-with-Black-people" credentials by telling me about their best friend, "who happens to be Black." I admit, I have been guilty of doing the same thing, even with other Black people. I'm not coming from a place of no offense.

This is a tough one. When we want to establish rapport with others, we search for common ground. We want to connect through a shared experience. Since I'm Black—and that's what most people will see first—to find common ground with me, they may use my Blackness to connect. But it's not always about race. My NASA background has often been an opening to a connection. If I'm wearing something that says NASA on it, you would not believe how many people just had to volunteer that their Uncle Bob worked on the Apollo program. I like wearing my "NASA colors" because I love NASA and am proud to have worked there. I want people to ask me about NASA. This has provided many an icebreaker with complete strangers that often leads to fascinating conversations. (This also leads to a fair share of people who want to talk about space aliens and how we faked the moon landing. As Momma said, "They walk among us.")

For me, the rapport-building effort backfires when it feels inauthentic. I'm wondering if the person who spoke to me while trying to "sound a bit Black" speaks this way with his Caucasian friends? While well intentioned, it is inauthentic and patronizing. I prefer connecting not based on my race, or gender, or body shape and size, or politics, or even NASA, as desirous as that may be. I prefer to connect based on my heart, my karma, my history, my story, my truths, my ideas, my hobbies, or my dreams. I don't need someone to believe I'll like them if they speak in a way they assume will endear me to them. Nor do I feel more connected because they have many Black friends. *Je m'en fiche!*

I feel connected when people give me their attention. I feel connected when people are willing to be a bit vulnerable because this demonstrates their trust in me with something delicate. I feel connected when people are genuinely interested in my experiences and how I feel about them and what I have learned from them.

Having said this, I haven't always been successful in establishing rapport with people over the course of my career. I've failed more than I care to admit, especially when it comes to my female colleagues. I've deployed an occasional "honey," "sweetie," and "girl" epithet in casual conversations with females I know well. I still do sometimes, but I'm getting better at excising them from my communication. This language is inappropriate in a professional environment, and it doesn't belong in most other situations. If you're close to the person and you *each* use similar terms of endearment reciprocally, it may be okay, but beware. I've caught myself mid "honey," stopped, and apologized. I wouldn't address a male colleague, even in casual conversation, with a "hon" or a "sweetie" or, for sure, a "boy."

Note: I'd like to make an important distinction. If I am with only my Black male colleagues, and we consider each other friends, too, we may say "brother" in casual conversation. That said, it's rare that this is done in "mixed" (meaning not just Black) company. For me, unless I feel comfortable calling any male "brother" as a term of endearment, I refrain from doing so. I feel it communicates to my non-Black colleagues, "Donald doesn't see me as a 'brother' because I'm not Black." Not a winning formula for rapport building.

I've been the object of uncomfortable ogling. While in graduate school in Washington, DC, I was walking to my favorite bookstore, Kramerbooks, from the Metro station. As I was cutting across Dupont Circle, near the fountain, I heard "Oh, my! Hmm, hmm, hmm, check dat out." I eventually realized I was the object of the lascivious catcalls. I noticed that others noticed. I felt embarrassed. I confess that for a second, my ego was inflated. The fact that the oglers were men was unprecedented for me. I don't know if they were gay (I assumed they were) or if they thought I was gay. It didn't matter. I just felt weird. What I remember thinking was, *Wow, so this is what women must deal with.* This was, as it would be known in current vernacular, one of my more "woke" moments.

I'm aware of regional differences in the meaning of certain terms. I respect that. I've experienced more "honeys" and "sweeties" in the South than any other place I've lived or visited. But, in a professional environment, I don't believe it's okay for me to use these terms, even during watercooler banter with women or men, regardless of how well I know them or what part of the country they're from. For example, at NASA, I knew several married couples. Though I saw them together occasionally at work, I never heard one refer to the other as "honey," "sweetie," or "darling," yet I'm certain that in the privacy of their home, when they were in "couple mode," they might use these terms.

Check your language to see if you believe there's room for improvement. The key is checking your heart for where you're coming from and asking yourself how your language may make the other person feel. This is about building rapport and conveying respect, not about some universal assertion of what is right.

Context, circumstance, and history also play a role in what's respectful. If I'm the CEO of Company Z, and I go to the basement to say hi to the building's cleaning crew, it's bad manners to greet them with "¿Qué pasa, amigos?" (trying to be cool by using my awful high school Spanish), then head to the boardroom and say to one of my executives, "Good to see you, José. How's the family?" Obviously, there are exceptions. You just need to check in with yourself to see if you're being authentic and respectful, or whether you're appropriating something for your own benefit, without direct or implied consent, because you want to connect and be viewed favorably. If your desire is connection and rapport, remember, there are many paths to that throne. Let your knowledge, instincts, and heart be your best guide as you give your attention fully and graciously.

GIVING FULL ATTENTION TO *YOU*: WHAT YOU REALLY WANT

Let's say you practice good manners and your career stalls, your home life craters, or you feel isolated and frustrated at school. Or you experience a personal injustice, and Momma's Rules aren't helping. What then? There may be hundreds of reasons you aren't getting what you want or are having experiences you don't enjoy. Your life feels stuck in column two. Maybe God has it out for you, or maybe you're just plain unlucky. You can spend a lot of time dissecting your problems, and you may even conclude that all this manners stuff is for the birds.

But before you write off manners, I suggest you take a critical and honest look into how you're showing up in the world and what stories you are telling about yourself, especially the stories you keep to yourself. I strongly suggest *not* examining the stories or the secrets alone. You may find growth impossible or challenging unless you have loving, committed, and authentic support. Get some coaching. Go to your team, and throw yourself before their critical, loving inspection. This may be painful and scary. Your heart tells you that your team might offer you some difficult truths. Welcome these gifts. It's like the doctor who must tell you that you have incurable cancer. Do you want it straight, or do you really want her to dance around the topic, trying to make you feel better? In the long run, you won't feel better (or get well) if all you get is the dance.

Second, are you honoring your authentic self? Hamlet says, "To thine own self be true." The broader quote is "This above all: to thine own self be true. And it must follow, as the night the day. Thou canst not then be false to any man." If you know without a doubt, and are supported by external validation, that the way you're showing up in the world honors the authentic you, then there's no reason to change your manner.

Third, you may need to change other things, like the stories you have been telling yourself (and others) about yourself. If you are not "false to any man (or woman)," you may be telling a true story, like the alcoholic who admits she is an alcoholic and finally says so. Isn't this what you want? You no longer must expend energy showing the movie version of you as if it is really you. I believe this is freedom.

Remember what you gained from spending your billions—what you *really* wanted? Not the "things," but the feeling you had when you bought, gave away, and/or saved all your billions? Review your list in the magic money exercise's third column. As the saying goes, "Money can't buy you love." Of course, don't be naive. If you had billions, a whole lot of "love" will come looking for you. You may find people who want to be with you because you're rich. If you're lucky, it may just work out. Let me know if that happens to you, okay? And, oh, one more thing, and just for fun. After you are blissfully in love, tell your partner that you decided to give away your billions. It's just too hard to be rich, and besides, money isn't what you really wanted, anyway. Show your partner your third column and tell them, "This is what I'm working on." Just imagine that conversation.

Giving full attention isn't only about what you offer to others. It's about what you offer yourself. Look inside and find out more about who dwells within that home you call yourself. If you're living every day knowing that what you really want is available to you right now, that you don't need one hundred billion or five hundred billion dollars, you may discover that those lingering issues and problems are only there because you invited them to your party to serve some purpose. I am reminded of Momma's Rule #6:

"No one is in charge of your happiness except you."

Consider this: what you identify and label as an issue or concern is your decision. You're the one who decides to call a situation a problem. This label resides in your own mind. *You're powerful enough to change your mind,* or at least change the terminology and the labels you've chosen. To be clear, this is different from a feeling you may have. I am not sure I can control my feelings. I feel bad, down, joyful, angry, blessed. The decision is whether your feelings present a problem *that controls you,* or, like the anxious actor, you use it to power yourself forward.

My thoughtless labeling of thunderstorms, heavy rain, snow, fog, and high winds as "bad" weather is a fabrication in my mind. Why are these weather conditions "bad"? During years of drought, people pray to have rain, but then when it comes, suddenly the weather is "bad"? It's just rain. Rain doesn't, in and of itself, have good or bad qualities. It's part of the earth's weather system. I'm the one attaching significance to rain. Why? It may get my clothes wet. So what? It may cause traffic accidents, which will cause me to be late for work. So what? High winds may knock down a tree, causing damage to my house and maybe even injuring or, God forbid, killing someone. But these are possible side-effects of rain in a world overflowing with human beings and their lifestyles. People do bad things, and some people do very bad things, but weather is just weather. I no longer slap a label on rain as bad or even good, for that matter. Rain is definitely useful and necessary for life. I appreciate the rain. I actually feel a sense of freedom when I walk out in the rain now. Just the other day, I went out to help my wife load her car for work. The rain was coming down hard. I was barefoot and without a raincoat or umbrella. Everything got wet. And I felt *alive!* Previously, I would have been angry that the rain drenched me or irritated with my wife for expecting me to help her in the rain. Wow! Look at me—creating drama in my own life because of a natural phenomenon. What really happened is that I had a feeling that I turned into a problem, which I let control me. People and the earth need water! Why attach my projections onto something that is necessary for life? I changed the narrative, and in the process, brought myself back to a place of innocence, in which I can feel almost like a child running free in the blissful rain.

One more thought about using weather as a metaphor to practice shifting your perspective. As a young Presidential Management Intern during my first years at NASA's Goddard Space Flight Center, I had the opportunity to do team-building activities. One was an outdoor ropes course. The morning after we arrived, when we were to meet our course trainers, it was pouring rain and quite cold. Most of us whined and complained and conspired to leave. We felt uncomfortable, and that was a problem. I am a card-carrying cold-weather wimp, as you've figured out by now. I. Do. Not. Like. Cold. Through careful questioning and dialogue with the trainers, who did not have a stake in whether we stayed—they would be paid regardless—we realized that we really *wanted* to do the course. Somehow, the trainers skillfully moved us to our "third columns" to understand why we were there and what we really wanted. We eventually shifted our relationship with the rain and the cold and just embraced our discomfort. It was a transformative experience.

Looking back, I chuckle at how incredibly concerned I was with my comfort and how much I cared about what the rain might do. What terrible thing did I think would happen? I have no idea now. Many years later, I did a fire-walking exercise. I was scared at first, but I remembered my experience with the ropes course and decided to use my fear to help me walk. I dedicated the walk to my children and their Black and Jewish ancestors, who sacrificed so much for them. With that in my heart, I powered through the walk, twice. After walking on burning hot coals, I remember feeling like I could do anything. Heck, I walked on fire!

So, if I can rethink my "bad weather" issue, perhaps I can rethink similarly negative labels as well. There's a current saying about particular problems we experience. By "we" I mean middle-class Americans who, on balance, are living pretty good lives. In describing an issue or problem, someone will respond with "Sounds like first-world problems to me." The suggestion is that if you think *that* is a problem, share your story with people who walk miles for clean water, if they can find it at all. Talk to people who suffer from disease and malnutrition. Share your complaints with people who know that of their eight children, two or three may not live to learn to read. Tick off your challenges with the thousands of refugees who fled their homelands only to find harsh conditions in a country that didn't want them. See how they feel about your rain-drenched hair and goose-bumps. I'm confident that many of these people would gladly trade places with me and wrestle with my "problems."

I'm not arguing that what you experience and label as a problem or an issue is an illusion. Your experiences are real to you. What you feel is real, and the way your feelings and attitudes impact you is real. What can you do? I suggest Momma's Rule #7:

> "Smile. You don't own all the problems in the world."

And you don't have to own all of *your* problems, either. You don't have to invite them to the party. You can tell that "committee" in your head that they no longer have the authority to have themselves over. You may have to remind your committee that you've walked in the rain and you've walked on fire. Don't bother me!

There is a line I like in the Coen Brothers remake of the movie *True Grit*. The lead character, Rooster Cogburn, a crusty one-eyed marshal played by Jeff Bridges, gets into a gunfight that doesn't go well. When it's over, Cogburn says, in a matter-of-fact tone, "Well, that didn't pan out." There is something liberating when you face an unwanted result and can simply react, "Well, that didn't pan out." I wished I'd had that ability when Laura Smith declined my invitation to the seventh-grade dance, laughing at me while her friend listened in on the phone. I was humiliated. My life was just *horrible* at that moment. But what really happened? My invitation was declined, and I made up a story that this was horrible, and therefore I experienced humiliation. I could have just thanked her for considering my invitation, hung up, and shrugged, saying, "Well, that didn't pan out."

When something negative or unexpected happens, I often wonder how I created it. This is a way of keeping the power of the total experience to myself instead of giving it away to someone or something else. I often play with how I choose to interpret experiences. I can look back on one that, at the time, I labeled "bad" and change the way I understand and speak about it. I can ask, what was the gift I received? It doesn't matter if my conclusion is make-believe. "Bad" is make-believe, too. So why not entertain a different interpretation? Try a pink suit on, perhaps? Bad day? What did I do to create a bad day? I prefer to live in the question, What is the bigger lesson here?

CAN MANNERS CHANGE THE WORLD?

Now that we understand we are free to change our perspectives, what do we do about heinous crimes against us? Can we blithely tell parents of a slain child to shift their perspective and see the gift in their violent, cruel loss? Of course not. Catastrophic incidents against human beings—the Holocaust, slavery, abuse, war, or devastating illness, like COVID-19—are horrific. They can kill the light inside us, take away our will to live, and leave us emotionally broken, unable to function. And many who suffer unimaginable cruelty are often forgotten.

Sometimes, there is a light in the darkness—the Anne Franks or Edith Eva Egars[13] of the world. Those who have suffered unimaginable crimes against humanity but are able to lift us up and give us hope because they are somehow able to find a higher purpose, a gift within the tragedy. Their personal development growth does not discount their horrific experience but offers a way to live in a world that includes that experience.

What do I do when I cannot change history or social illness? Good manners guide us to care about each other and about the planet. And yet, as I write this sentence, hundreds, maybe thousands, will lose their lives to violence. Girls and women will be abused, raped, harassed, and disrespected. Gay, lesbian, and gender-nonbinary people will be killed, taunted, ostracized. People will die because they are Muslim, Christian, Hindu, Jew, or a religion someone does not believe should represent man's interpretation of God. Why? What are the root causes of this? Are we relegated to living with this, like "death and taxes"? Or perhaps, as Martin Luther King said about human progress, it "does not roll in on the wheels of inevitability. Human progress is neither automatic nor inevitable . . . Every step toward the goal of justice requires sacrifice,

---

13. Edith Eva Eger, Holocaust survivor, psychologist, and author of *The Choice: Embrace the Impossible*, Penguin, Random House, 2018.

suffering, and struggle; the tireless exertions and passionate concern of dedicated individuals."[14]

I believe the popular song by Jill Jackson-Miller and Sy Miller, "Let There Be Peace on Earth," gives me a starting place. Peace really does begin with me. I can do my part to help create a better future. I can refuse to participate in promulgating cruelty, destruction, or tolerance of hate in all its incendiary forms. Throughout history, courageous people, in the face of impossible odds and defying significant challenges, have taken a stand for justice and a better world. They have given their attention to matters greater than themselves. Here are some who come to mind for me:

- United States President Abraham Lincoln, who promoted the cause of a *United* States and the end of slavery
- Indian nonviolent activist Mahatma Gandhi, who motivated and mobilized the masses in India regardless of language, religion, caste, creed, and sex, to come together and fight for the cause of freedom
- Susan B. Anthony, the American nineteenth-century women's rights activist who fought for a woman's right to vote and for the end of slavery
- Mother Teresa, the Nobel Peace Prize winner and saint, who loved and fought for the most destitute on the planet
- Harriet Tubman, who risked her life to save many lives during American slavery, through the "Underground Railroad"

---

14. Martin Luther King Jr., "The Future of Integration" (speech, New York University, February 10, 1961).

- the soldiers of World War II, considered the vanguards of the "greatest generation," who endured unspeakable challenges to save the free world
- South African leader Nelson Mandela, who, after enduring nearly thirty years of incarceration at the hands of the apartheid regime, emerged not a bitter or spiteful man, but a man of compassion with a vision for an inclusive, more democratic South Africa
- Dolores Huerta ("sí, se puede" / "yes, we can"), the tenacious and skillful leader of the United Farmworkers Association, who, together with Cesar Chavez, organized and fought for farm workers' safety and rights and for the rights and dignity of women and people of color

For every name on this list, there are thousands of unknown soldiers of goodwill who will do good deeds today by *giving their attention to and for others.* Each of us can do our part, too. If you're not sure where to start, begin with a simple and genuine smile at someone you don't know; give them your attention, and in your heart, bless them. Remember that the person serving you at a restaurant is your server, not your servant. If you mess up, fess up. Introduce yourself to a neighbor you don't know. Look for an organization whose mission you can get behind, and volunteer if you can. Or drink fewer lattes, and offer that saved cash as a donation. Best of all, give someone the gift of your personal time and your heart.

Give attention to yourself. Forgive yourself for misdeeds. Forgive others who have wronged you. Give more than ask. Listen more than talk. Meditate more than pontificate. What is it that you really got when you spent all your money? What makes your heart sing? Make it so. Today. Right now.

CHAPTER 14

MANNERS IN PRACTICE

After I retired from NASA, I traveled to Germany to attend the world's largest international aerospace conference, where almost all the aerospace entities came to show their capabilities to each other. Next to the NASA exhibit was the United Arab Emirates (UAE) exhibit. A few years earlier, the NASA Education Office had arranged for UAE students to intern at NASA's Ames Research Center, and I knew Dubai would be hosting the conference in the future. I was eager to connect with them about their current education efforts in hopes that I could be of support.

I approached their exhibit counter, where two women, each wearing the head scarf traditionally worn by Muslim women, were waiting to talk to conference attendees. I introduced myself, mentioned my UAE student experience, and did my very best to pronounce their names correctly (good manners and rapport building), an effort that was received with friendly head nodding and grins. When we finished talking, I thanked them both for their time, and without thinking, I thrust my hand out to shake theirs. One of the women obliged. When I went to shake the second woman's hand, she pulled her hand up to her heart, leaving my extended arm and hand in the air. *I'd made a mistake.* I was embarrassed because I knew better. I mirrored her gesture, smiled, nodded to communicate that I understood, and turned away, feeling stupid.

You would be forgiven for wondering why I would care so much. After all, we were in a Western country at an international conference with most attendees from non-Muslim countries. Why should I have to mimic their cultural norms? Why shouldn't they respect mine, in this country, including my gesture of gratitude, expressed by my handshake? This isn't an unreasonable question.

Well, you guessed it—Momma taught me to care, and I pride myself on being at least minimally aware and respectful of a culture where observant Muslim women, in general, don't touch a man to whom they are not married or who is not a relative. It's irrelevant whether I endorse that norm or practice. Respecting cultural norms is a sign of respect similar to Momma's insistence on pronouncing her students' names as their parents did. It's why I wear a yarmulke when I go into a synagogue. As a non-Jew, a yarmulke has no special meaning to me, but I respect its purpose and honor the sacred space in which it is worn. This is good manners.

STEPPING UP OUR MANNERS SKILLS

So, how do we know if we're advancing our manners skills? There's not always a solid wall between good and bad manners; sometimes there's a gray, murky area that shrinks, expands, and changes, depending on the situation. A football coach, a

NASA flight director, a doctor, or a student intern can each display wonderful manners, yet their manner of person-to-person engagement may differ. Good manners do not all look the same—good manners may share characteristics that are hard to quantify, challenging to teach, and impossible to get right 100 percent of the time. The key is training yourself to be aware of your own *presence* within a situation, as well as the presence of those around you who are engaged in the same experience.

Presence is your "firmware," which manifests itself externally through your words and actions. If you can develop your sense of presence, you'll learn to focus your awareness on that which precedes your behavior: your thoughts and beliefs, and the ways in which your experiences are encoded. Think about the rain example. Do you experience a thunderstorm as "bad weather"? Then that's how you have encoded your experience of rain. I experience people a certain way and will encode that with a label, like "moody" or "arrogant" or "authentic."

My ensuing behavior, then, is based on how I've encoded that experience. When I'm aware that I'm responding to a label that might not be an accurate or full representation of that person, I know that I have a choice. I can be open to something more authentically true if I just bother to look carefully. I have had this experience with several people in my life. Usually, I have realized rather quickly that my initial labels were wrong. It's the labels I held on to for a long time before a more accurate picture revealed itself that I find both embarrassing and transformative. I am embarrassed that I showered that twentysomething handsome kid at the reception desk with a couple of labels (privileged summer intern who probably knows the doctor, so that's how he got the job), only to be transformed when I realized that he *was* the doctor. Oops.

Examining how you may be wired to react to a person is key to good manners. This wiring has been programmed into our being over many years, by multiple people and experiences, and especially by our families. Not to mention cultural and environmental influences. That woman in the car in Los Angeles who locked her door when I crossed in front of her labeled me not based on knowing *me*. Perhaps she rethought her labels when I stopped in front of her and pretended to be a mean, growly monster, leaving us both in jolly laughter. Our individual wiring becomes who we are, so much so that we usually don't see our patterns. This is why it helps to have our support teams standing by to help us see ourselves more clearly.

What are your knee-jerk or unconscious reactions? When have you instinctively locked your car door, metaphorically speaking? The stories we tell about others (or the labels we convey upon people) influence how we show up with others in ways we don't understand. Examine the labels you give yourself or that others have assigned to you, such as woman, Asian, tall, gay, old, white male, tattooed, Black, obese, Christian, Sikh, trans, smart, stupid. Have you felt judged, or have you judged yourself, because of these labels? The point is not whether you are or are not being judged, but whether you *believe* you are. That belief is what you may be inserting into the dynamic of a relationship, and completely unconsciously.

For example, I've examined how I react to people with tattoos, dyed hair, and body piercings. I've been judgmental and have made up stories about "those people." They must be creative artist types, or rebellious. *Why else would they go against the crowd?* I asked myself. I am now agnostic to people with these physical characteristics. If I were on their team, I might advise them to be mindful in, for example, a job interview. If they expressed concern about their appearance, I might suggest that they not assume that the interviewer will react negatively, positively, or indifferently, for that matter. Remember Momma's Rule #2:

"What others think of you is none of your
business."

I might invite them to look more deeply at their own prejudices and assumptions and suggest they name or identify them.
Probing deeper, I might ask them to tell me, truthfully, why
they really got a tattoo or dyed their hair. My intent is to arrive
at their truth. Remember that often-quoted wisdom from John
8:32 (the New King James Version), "And the truth shall set
you free"? Alcoholics Anonymous meetings begin with folks
introducing themselves: "Hi, my name is Shondra, and I'm an
alcoholic." Saying what is true without judgment is liberating.

Additionally, I have come to appreciate that for many people, coming out of the "closet" is a deeply liberating experience,
even at the risk of judgment, prejudice, estrangement, or violence. My realization that I was judgmental about people with
tattoos and dyed hair freed me to begin seeing them as human
beings. This is what I think Dr. King meant when he spoke of
the content of one's character.

OBSERVATIONS AND MISSED OPPORTUNITIES

As you know by now, I'm an observer of people and a collec-
tor of stories that illustrate lost opportunities that befall folks
because they don't practice or even know about the value of
manners as a way to enhance their professional careers and/or
personal relationships. Here are a few experiences I've had that
highlight this kind of lost opportunity.

AN ENCOUNTER AT THE AIRPORT

While walking to the airport terminal from the parking lot, I
saw a neck pillow on the sidewalk and picked it up to take to

the lost and found. An airline agent suggested I take it to the airport's information desk. As I approached the desk, I noticed the young man, about seventeen to nineteen years old, sitting behind the counter. He had earphones on and was staring at his phone. He didn't look up as I reached the desk. I leaned in slightly and said, "Excuse me, please. I was told I should bring this lost item to you." He looked up with his eyes but kept his head aimed at his phone. He removed his left earbud and looked at me as if to say, "*Excuse me?*" But he said nothing. I repeated my statement. Still seated, he abruptly took the item from me, said, "Okay," put his earbud back in, and resumed looking at whatever was captivating him.

Recall, from the chapter on interviewing, that *we are always interviewing*. This young man had just flunked his interview! For all I know, he was an introverted whiz kid with little stability at home, and this job was his ticket out. The job I could have offered him would have *definitely* been his ticket out. Perhaps he had no one to coach him about the value of good manners. His behavior and attitude told me that he wouldn't be a good bet in my company. As the former-basketball-star-turned-TV-celebrity Charles Barkley once said, "I may be wrong, but I doubt it."

What could he have done differently? How could his behavior have inspired me to want to support him, assuming he wanted my help? For starters, he could have removed his headphones, stood up, smiled, and asked, "How may I help you, sir?" He could have shown even a minimal amount of attention to the job he'd been hired to do and, therefore, noticed me well before I got to the desk. He could have *pretended*, remembering his training, to be eager to help a customer because he genuinely loves helping people. He didn't even have to be like Gabriel, my young science fair friend. After I'd given him the neck pillow, he might have acknowledged that I'd been a good citizen and taken the time to bring it to his department. He could have said, "Thanks so much for bringing this in; I hope we can find its owner."

If he had done even a couple of those things, I may have engaged him further, asking where he's from and about his interests in my attempt to discover any of these characteristics that might make him a good candidate for a job:

- ambition or an interest in learning, growing, and developing
- a dream of something bigger and better than where he is now
- a plan or an intention to come up with a plan
- openness to receive support; eager to seek a mentor

My purpose as a NASA leader was *to give,* and I was always looking for an opportunity, opening, or invitation to do so. (This is still my purpose.) This young man may have lost out because of his deep interest and focus on something other than this old man. Or, he could have been the kind of young person who saw "elder" as an opportunity to learn. He could have assumed I knew something useful and that I would offer it if asked. He could have started a rapport-building conversation with me, indulging me with questions that would open the door of communication between us:

"Where are you headed today?"

"Hawaii."

"Wow, that's nice. What do you do?"

"I'm retired from NASA."

"Really? Cool. What did you do at NASA?"

I could have read this as someone with higher aspirations. I've had this kind of experience several times. But this young man flunked his interview. He wasn't willing to take advantage of meeting a stranger like panning for gold, hoping to find a nugget of advice or wisdom or perhaps a different path to his throne. Too bad. If I sense a genuine, open, curious, or hopeful individual, I'm in. There's nothing more gratifying to me than aligning myself to someone's growth and success journey. This makes me feel as if I'm also on a winning team. Being on a winning team not only brings me joy, but I get to learn and grow, as well. I become a better person. We both win.

DEVICES

I have attended and led many meetings. The advent of laptop computers and smartphones, both nonexistent in the first half of my career, has resulted in their increased presence in meetings. For some, myself included, their presence in meetings is a mixed bag. Our electronic devices can help us use our time more effectively, manage the daily avalanche of emails, quickly research a discussion point, take notes, or schedule another meeting. They can also distract and divert us toward shallow or fragmented human engagement.

I've been in meetings in which someone's cell phone interrupts the conversation, often with an annoying ringtone. To make matters worse, sometimes the owner doesn't hear his phone or thinks it's someone else's. I've watched people desperately searching through their purses, briefcases, and backpacks for the offending phone. Men will do the rapid pocket pat-down, looking for their dang phone. Everyone scurries, fretting that their phone is the culprit.

In some of my staff meetings, I've often had the impression that my staff's computers, iPads, or cell phones were more important than the topic at hand. At best, they could only half-heartedly follow the discussion while deep into their electronic devices.

Note: *However distracting and irritating devices in meetings might be, reacting negatively can backfire. In one meeting,*

I became so annoyed with the prevalence of electronic device use that I stopped my meeting and said (with an attitude), "I see that many of you are on your computers or iPads. Is there something you're doing that's more important than this meeting?" To my embarrassment, a couple of folks replied that they were taking notes, and they even turned their laptops around to show me. Another person said she had her report on her laptop, and when it was her turn, she was prepared to brief the group. I didn't raise this matter again, though I still suspect that others were not just taking notes or getting ready to brief.

But what about all those who aren't taking notes or preparing their report? During one daylong meeting, out of the blue someone blurted, "Oh, Prince just died." This halted our discussion until we could all take a moment to lament the passing of the music legend. Some felt inspired to start singing some of his songs. I had two reactions and a strong feeling. First, I deduced that *this* person hadn't been taking notes on his cell phone, and second, the timing of the blurted announcement seemed disrespectful to us—and to Prince, for that matter. My colleague could have waited until our break to share the news. My strong feeling? This was bad meeting manners.

There's an amusing story that former president Barack Obama and his wife, Michelle, were attending one of their daughter's sporting events. On the sidelines, the First Lady noticed the president glancing at his smartphone. She surreptitiously swatted his device-holding hand. An enterprising reporter caught the incident. The message was clear. Get off your phone and watch your daughter. Okay, the president of the United States has good reasons to check his cell phone. I mean, the missiles could be flying, and he should know, right? Well, no. That's what assistants are for, just like when President Bush's chief of staff interrupted him while he was visiting a class of schoolchildren to inform him of the 9/11 terrorist attacks. We *must* give our children (and anyone we care about) our full attention. Children notice, and intuitively feel, when we're present but not really with them and not "giving" them our complete attention.

My behavior hasn't always matched my standards and preferences regarding electronics. Usually, I notice when my attention drifts away from someone. It's similar to what you learn in a meditation practice regarding "follow your breath," only to discover within seconds of your practice that your mind is wandering all over the place. At this moment, I deploy what I call the "catch and release" strategy. I catch myself on my phone or in mindless wander, then release myself from my dependency on the distraction. I feel liberated by retaking control over both my intention and my attention.

The ultimate violation of cell phone etiquette for me was when I held a funeral for my father in the Philippines before I repatriated his remains. The group of mourners was small— Dad's caregivers, his landlord, and others who knew and supported him. There were many attendees I didn't know, including the priest. The setting was not formal—there were no pews or altar. We were in an anteroom to the church.

We stood around my father's glass-topped casket, facing the priest for the brief service. I was standing in the front, together with his caregivers. At some point, while the priest was saying something in Tagalog, a cell phone rang behind me. I made a quick turn in startled reaction to see a woman I didn't know. That the phone rang in a place of worship was bad enough. To my disgust, the woman then energetically conversed in Tagalog, making no attempt to soften her voice or cover her mouth, let alone leave.

I bit my lip, not sure if this was accepted behavior in the Philippines. Besides, I was grieving the death of my father. Nothing else mattered at that moment. For the record, I never take my cell phone inside any place of worship. I don't need it.

Trust me, if God needs me, She will send someone in to get me. I just hope it won't be a one-way summons.

WHAT TOOK YOU SO LONG?

Occasionally, my commitment to a friendship has been tested. In two similar examples, these friends were experiencing difficult challenges and asked for financial help or help getting a job. In both cases, I was, to be honest, offended. Why? Because in both cases, I hadn't heard from them in a very long time. My thoughts were, *Where have you been? I haven't heard from you in X years, and now you reach out when you need something?* For sure, some friendships are so enduring that time matters little, so this is not black and white. I may not hear from my childhood friend Lino for many years, but if he calls me in need, there's no question I'll help any way I can. Tread carefully with your rush to judgment, and remember Momma's Rule #4:

> "Don't compare your life to others, and don't judge others. You have no idea what their journey is about."

If a friend connects with me once in a blue moon just to say hi and that she's thinking of me, I feel great. She's making a deposit into our friendship bank. She doesn't want anything other than to connect. She's cultivating our friendship. I feel worthy of her time. If a friend that I have not heard from in several years contacts me and, after pleasantries, reveals that she needs my help finding a job, needs money, or wants me to introduce her to someone, then she's attempting to make a withdrawal from a friendship bank that has insufficient funds. Okay, I know this isn't a perfect analogy. It implies that relationships are sustained by keeping value between people in balance. It implies that unconditional love is a myth and that friendships, partnerships, and even love are conditional: I will not help you unless you have helped me.

This is the conundrum. I'm not interested in my friendships being rooted in the cold calculus of "I will only put out what they put in. You don't contact me in five years, and now you do because you want something?" On the other hand, this person may have called because of the type of friends we are. Maybe we are lifelong friends, for which there is no statute of limitations. If this person thought I would be checking our friendship bank's balance, she may not have called.[15] I see no simple strategy for this challenge. I do recommend cultivating your friendships and relationships for no reason at all except that it's worth it. *Give* without expecting anything in return. Don't give just to build your "friendship account" so you can withdraw later. Just give. Do little things for someone in your friend group each day. Call or text a friend for no reason other than to say hi and that you're thinking of them.

This idea of giving careful attention goes beyond friendship. Try picking up a piece of trash on your walk so the person who follows you can experience uncluttered beauty in the park. We know about this already. It's called random acts of kindness. Do them without expecting anything in return. Do a kind act when no one is looking or expecting it. Paradoxically, you will get something back. It may not be exactly what you want, but the universe provides. I believe this, and I experience this often, yet I cannot offer one iota of scientific evidence that it's true. This is just my experience. This is perhaps the pinkest pink suit I recommend you try on. You will need to wear it for a while. As difficult as it may be, you must let go of

---

15. In *Predictably Irrational*, Dan Ariely writes about favors and give-and-take with detailed studies analyzing people's behaviors. www.danariely.com. Stephen R. Covey talks about "emotional bank accounts" in his seminal *The 7 Habits of Highly Effective People*. Covey's son, Stephen M. R. Covey, also discusses building trust accounts in his book, *The Speed of Trust*.

all expectations that you will get *something* in return for your good deeds, except the joy of just doing them.

A MANNERS CONTINUUM

To briefly review some of the key elements of practicing good manners, let's look at these three reminders:

1. There are exceptions and nuances for almost any scenario that requires proper manners. Experience, consulting with your team, and your own intuition will help you best determine how to act in most situations.

2. Being mindful and aware of your engagement with people and how you are showing up to them is always a good strategy. The key is how you react to the signals and responses you receive in a situation. Observe and learn. Don't judge, evaluate, or react right away to what you see. Give yourself time to properly assess the situation so that you don't make conclusions based on incomplete or inaccurate information.

3. Context and time matter. Different cultures, countries, groups, "tribes," and organizations may have different standards and norms for what is and isn't acceptable behavior. We also evolve. Good manners in 1950 may be irrelevant in 2050. I believe the fundamental values that underlie manners remain, though—respect, attitude, integrity, authenticity, caring, and civility. Bind these with deep awareness, openness, and humility while offering your attention. A good sense of humor helps, too.

I've broken the continuum of situational manners into several common experiences to help you navigate the hallways of good manners.

- Engaging in Conversation
- One-on-one
- Groups
- Being Interviewed
- Receiving a Compliment
- Receiving a Gift
- Being a Guest at Someone's Home
- Starting a New Job

CONVERSATION: ONE-ON-ONE

Be a good listener. This means really "hearing and understanding"—*getting* what's being shared. Consider this scale from lowest to highest: hearing > listening > active listening > presence listening. Hearing means you have heard the words and can probably repeat them verbatim. My kids are great at this, even when I accuse them of not listening to me. Listening means you're capturing the person's communication a bit more carefully. Active listening typically means you listen to someone and then paraphrase what they said to make sure you heard correctly. Active listening is helpful in a professional or work environment. Presence listening engages your entire being—your eyes, mind, heart, and body. You are getting the candy bar taste, not just the description. The talker knows they are the only person in the world right now with whom you are connected. Presence listening is best with a partner, a friend, or someone who's profoundly moved to share with you. Presence listening captures the unspoken communication. Observe body language, including your own. What is that person's body telling you? What is your own body telling you? If you can, communicate with the person with your body square to them, face-to-face. Notice if your eyes dart around the room, as if you're looking for someone else or are distracted. Do *not* check your cell phone. In fact, good manners include turning your cell down or off when in deep conversation. Your phone has voice mail capability. Use it.

Talk less about yourself. Ask more about the other person. If you know you have a limited amount of time to talk, and you're being asked for a reply, then just reply, without adding on a story in your reply. When it's time for you to go, cut yourself off, not the person with whom you are speaking. Express gratitude for their time.

CONVERSATION: GROUPS

Try being the observer in a group conversation. Just listen and pay close attention. See what you can learn about the people with whom you are conversing. Communicating with your close friends and buddies is different from your professional colleagues or those in a more formal business or social environment. For the former, just be mindful of your true colors coming forth. Let your moral compass be your guide versus assessing the group's compass and trying to mimic them. For example, if people in the group tell sexist or racist jokes, you don't need to mimic that behavior to feel accepted by the group. Imagine your own personal "manners angel" sitting on your shoulder, watching you. How would your angel view your behavior? In all cases, engage in communication with this intention: What can I learn about those in the group, right now? Is there something that isn't being spoken, yet I sense is present? What value can I bring to anyone in the circle in addition to my full, undivided attention and love?

BEING INTERVIEWED

Interviews vary. For the purposes of this example, let's assume that you're being interviewed by one or more people in person. Note: If you have a choice to be interviewed in person or via phone or video conference, choose in person. Arrive ten to fifteen minutes early. Have a notepad with you and a half-dozen fresh copies of your résumé. Stand when the interviewer enters the room, and extend your hand first.[16] Send a handwritten thank-you note within forty-eight hours after the interview.

If you know you'll be late, contact the person with whom you have the appointment and let them know when you expect to arrive, and then do your very best to arrive five minutes before that time. Acknowledge being late, apologize, and do not offer *a* why-I-am-late story. Never make an excuse if you arrive late, even if the excuse is understandable, such as an accident on the freeway, a last-minute sick child, or a meteorite that hit your car. Take responsibility for being late by acknowledging you're late. If it feels right, just apologize. "I would like to acknowledge that I'm ten minutes late." If the reply is "Oh, don't worry about it" or "That's okay," respond with a thankyou. That's it. Any additional story or excuse around why you're late will sound like BS because it is. You're late. Period. Remember the rain? It is what it is. And let's be honest, there may or may not be consequences to your lateness. Remember

---

16. The COVID-19 pandemic changed many practices, including shaking hands. My view is that even if the virus is mitigated or eliminated, or people are protected from it, people may be continue to be reluctant to shake hands, knowing that it is one of the easiest ways to transmit a virus or other germs. As a manners matter, if you don't feel comfortable shaking someone's hand, you can always place your hand over your heart while telling the person that it is nice to meet them. If the person looks confused or seems mildly offended at your gesture, you can politely let them know that you are minimizing physical contact for health reasons—a true statement. You can also joke that you don't want to give them *your* germs, which is also technically true.

the exercise where you had to be at a certain place at a specific time in order to get millions of dollars? Treat your interview like that. Arrange your universe to ensure prompt arrival with ten to fifteen minutes to spare. At NASA we called this building in a "schedule margin." Every NASA project plan has some schedule margin built in.

When you're asked a question, answer *that* question. If you want to use that question to add a separate point (this is called a pivot or a swerve, a skill perfected by many politicians being interviewed by the news media), that's fine, but answer the question first. Answers should be succinct, without sounding like you memorized your answer. Wait at least one breath before responding to a question. If you aren't sure of your answer, ask to take a minute to collect your thoughts, and use your notebook to construct your response. Be mindful of your eye contact and body language. Notice if your eyes are darting around the room, if you're fidgeting with your hands, or if one leg bounces rapidly. If you're anxious, breathe consciously and completely. Slow your cadence.

Be prepared to ask one or two questions if given the opportunity, but at least one. Remember, the interview starts when you walk in the door or sooner, and it isn't over when you shake the interviewer's hand and thank them for their time. As long as you are in eyeshot or earshot of your interviewer or their colleagues, before or after the formal interview, then you are interviewing. Anything you have done electronically at any time is fair game for an interviewer to have studied. It's your digital tattoo. Know what they can know about you in case you need to address that. Unless you are interviewing to be a stand-up comic, don't joke or try to be funny, though a mild sense of humor is fine. Do not try to be "down" with your interviewer by appropriating anything from what you think your interviewer is like. For example, I, as a Black man walking into an interview and seeing another Black man, would *never* say, "What's goin' on, brotha'?" This is patronizing and suggests that I may be expecting favoritism. This is true even if you know the person and have an informal relationship with them and may use that language at other times.

During an interview I conducted with a Caucasian woman, she volunteered that her boyfriend was Black. I felt offended. My thought bubble was, "Oh, well *that* makes her qualified for the job . . . *not!*" I understand what she was doing. She wanted me to know that she was comfortable with Black men because her boyfriend was Black. She likely hoped that if I knew her boyfriend was Black, then I would like her more, and, as such, would be more inclined to hire her. Again, *Je m'en fiche!* The race of her boyfriend isn't relevant. If you want to establish rapport, ask questions about the interviewer and listen genuinely to their replies. Imagine leaving the interview and your quiz is not about how well you did, but about what you learned about your interviewer and the company. Your goal is *to give* and to learn.

Always send a handwritten thank-you note to your interviewer. *Never* email or text a formal thank-you. Use your best penmanship on professional-looking stationery. If you did not get a business card from your interviewer, be creative to find the correct mailing address. There's no excuse in today's digital environment not to get the address and send the thank-you.

There are many books and resources on the art of interviewing. Study those, too, and practice. Be mindful of the one-size-does-not-fit-all rule. How you handle one interview may differ from the next interview. My way isn't the only way. Specific behaviors and actions may vary, but your foundational manners should be the same.

RECEIVING A COMPLIMENT

If you receive a compliment, say "Thank you" or "I appreciate that." If someone thanks you, respond with "You're welcome." This may seem obvious, but trust me, I've heard many ill-advised responses. For example, some people want to respond to a compliment with a quick return compliment. Resist doing this. Just say "Thank you." Returning a compliment immediately appears to discount the compliment that was given, as if you cannot receive something without feeling obliged to give it back. Accept the compliment as a gift and say "Thank you." If someone thanks you for something you've done, simply respond with "You are welcome," "It was my pleasure," or just "My pleasure." Resist wanting to make light of your original beneficence with "It was no big deal," "No thanks required," or a snippy "Think nothing of it." The goal is to affirm the value and the *gift of the compliment.*

A cousin to this etiquette is the often robotic "Hi, how *are* you?" which is often quickly answered with "Fine, how are you?" Both parties rarely want to know the real, long-story answer. These pleasantries are more a way of acknowledging each other's presence. Consider whether you really want to know how someone is when you ask this question. If you do, you can always ask a follow-up or related question, specific to something you know about that person. If you recall that the last time you spoke to that person, they had a cold, ask about their health. The more specific things you recall from your last encounter, the better. It shows you were really giving attention.

On the other side, if someone asks about you, resist responding quickly with "Fine," then back at them with "How are you?" Take a breath and consider your answer. You know that most people who ask how you are aren't anticipating a long story about your latest health problems or relationship woes. But you can be truthful with a summary—if you're not fine, offer to discuss it later, as in "Thanks for asking. I've had better days physically, and on top of that I have been going through a lot at work. Can I fill you in later? I value your support."

If you're uncomfortable providing details, joke about it. I will use an expression my grandmother used when she wasn't feeling 100 percent: "Oh, I am tolerable." Or I'll say, "Well, I made roll call today." These expressions allow me to speak honestly about my status without divulging details. If the person with whom I am talking presses me, I may offer additional details, but I will offer them in a way that communicates "Not now, please." I usually say, "I don't want to get into it now, but feel free to check with me later"—if you mean that. If not, then an "I'm good" response is enough.

Not paying close attention or being unaware of context has risks. For instance, one night my wife and I were having dinner with a couple. Soon after we sat down, I looked at the woman and asked how she was. I had a sense that something was off. She responded immediately with "Fine." Looking into her eyes and noticing her body language, I didn't get it. In a slow, focused, soft tone, I asked, "Are you really fine?" She paused, then confessed, "No." I nodded. And that was the end of our exchange. I didn't press. The context was that this couple had lost their young adult child to an illness. I have no sense of what it's like to lose a child, and it angers, terrifies, and saddens me to even think about it. Our brief exchange could have been a formality, but it wasn't. Without needing to say more, I felt the depth of her despair to the extent I could imagine. I also understood, at that very moment, that a parent never "gets over" losing a child. I sensed she understood that I understood. I will never forget that moving moment. It happened because we were both aware and authentic.

RECEIVING A GIFT

A gift should be acknowledged with a handwritten note of thanks, mailed within two to four days of receiving it. One exception is a wedding gift. People expect newlyweds to be away after they marry, so it's not reasonable for them to write immediately. I'm pretty sure we opened our wedding gifts after we returned from our honeymoon.

Not all gifts warrant a written acknowledgment. An inexpensive token gift may be acknowledged with a phone call, an email, or an in-person expression of gratitude. Trust your instincts. There are plenty of resources on this matter, so please research them to understand more about proper etiquette. The guidance is to handwrite thank-you notes when you receive a gift, including a dinner party invitation. Don't use email or texting to thank someone unless it's something such as the gift of someone's time. "David, I enjoyed talking to you this morning at Starbucks. Can I call you later this week to chat more about XYZ?"

What is it about handwriting a note? In today's world of electronic instant everything, an elegantly crafted handwritten note says this: *I am grateful for your gift, and I care about you enough to make time to get good stationery, carefully craft my message in my best handwriting, stamp the envelope, and mail it.* In the time it takes to do all that, you could have fired off twenty emails, made a deposit in your bank account, and booked a flight for your next vacation. But you didn't do that—because you're grateful for the gift and the person who gave it to you. The person and their graciousness are worth your valuable time.

My close friend Jamie shared an affirming story about the doctor who did her knee replacement surgery. He not only called to check on her after the surgery, he sent her a legible handwritten thank-you note for the privilege of supporting her health needs. If you think "doctor" and "legible handwritten thank-you note" seem incompatible, join the club. Jamie knew I was writing this book on manners, and she knows Momma's feelings about handwritten thank-you notes. She couldn't wait to share that story with me and tell me how his simple act of gratitude had powerfully impacted her.

BEING A GUEST AT SOMEONE'S HOME

Regardless of what your host says, bring a gift. This can be flowers, something to eat, a recent article or book you liked, or a small souvenir you picked up on a recent trip. You can also insist on buying them dinner one evening. Again, the goal is to affirm the generosity of your hosts, not counter their offer of a room with something of equal value to make yourself feel that your stay is "paid for." While at your host's home, respect their rituals, respect their space, and never assume you are excused from domestic work.

Your goal is to have your hosts feel that your presence added value to their home and that when you leave, they will want you to come back. One "fail" I heard from a friend was her guest who asked, "What's for dinner?" *Never ask this.* At most, say, "I would love to help you make dinner or set the table." Depending on your familiarity with your hosts, do not even ask; just do it. If that bothers your host and they demur, resist a bit and then honor their wishes. When the day comes for you to leave, strip the bed and fold the sheets and pillowcases in a neat stack. Place them on top of the bedspread, or in a laundry bin if they have one. Your bathroom and room should be just as clean, if not cleaner, than when you arrived. Your hosts' guest room is not your dorm, hotel, or campsite. "Make yourself at home" does not mean "make it as your home."

STARTING A NEW JOB

Starting a new job can be both exciting and a source of anxiety. You're excited to do something new or perhaps happy that you have a source of income or a higher income. Perhaps you are hopeful this new job will be better than the last one. You may also wonder if your new colleagues will like you, if you will fit in, and if you're up for the new challenge. How fast will you learn new processes and rules (especially the unwritten ones), or who the real influencers are, as well as who might be difficult?

Research suggests that we begin to draw conclusions about people we meet immediately. One study had students look at videos of a professor giving a lecture. It turns out that within seconds, the students determined if they liked the professor and whether or not they wanted to attend his class. The interesting thing about this experiment was that the sound was off. The students determined this based on body language, physical expressions, and looks alone. The students' assessments strongly correlated with other students' feedback of the professor after they had actually taken his class.

Good manners would dictate that your new boss introduces you to the rest of the team on day one. This doesn't always happen, or at least not on day one. I've started jobs on a day when my boss was traveling, on vacation, or in an all-day meeting. If this is the case, don't wait for your boss to introduce you. Take responsibility to get to know your new teammates. Your goal is to let them know that you're happy to be on their team and you're eager to learn from them. Your goal is *not* to "credential." "Credentialing" is when you roll out your degrees and awards and prior accomplishments, like the star athlete who shows off his parents' scrapbook, containing all his glory. *Never* do this. Resist even if they ask. Assume your new office mates will test or bait you in some way. They may say, "So, I understand you went to Harvard. Wow, you must be really smart." They aren't looking for you to agree with them. What they want to know is, "And do you put your underwear on the same way I do?" Of course, no need to brush off the question, if in fact you get asked a real question. This may be a good time for some self-deprecating humor like "Well, I learned that I wasn't the sharpest tool in the shed." This assures your new colleagues that you know you're no better than they are. You make mistakes, and yes, your poop does stink. Your history is somewhat irrelevant. It's what you plan to do and how you will show up going forward that matters. A bit of humility builds rapport.

GOOD MANNERS—A WAY OF BEING

Mastering any skill requires practice, getting skinned knees, failing several times, learning from mistakes, being coached, struggling, and risking looking foolish. This is true with mastering the art of good manners, especially because manners can be subjective. Context and cultural norms are highly relevant. Our life experiences indelibly shape the dynamics of our responses to others. Offices, groups, teams, and individuals each have histories made up of stories and values that will influence the way their members may respond to each other, and/or to another person or circumstance. The skill of developing good manners is the skill of synthesizing variables that include conflicting data, mixed experiences, and sometimes different or even opposing values. You cannot program good manners the way you might program a robot to execute certain tasks. Good manners are an organic, dynamic, and authentic way of being, with a moral dimension rooted in caring, respect, and love.

I've learned that most people share my conviction that good manners are needed more than ever. They understand that manners are more than just civility, etiquette, or politeness. Though manners encompass a broad range of skills, they are actually more than just skills. Manners are *a way of being* that is rooted in one's essence.

Our society moves at lightning speed. In the rush to get to the next place—whatever that is—we need to pay attention to how we conduct ourselves. If we lose our authenticity along the way or become numb to our humanity, then what exactly are we so busy running toward? Maybe we are running *from* ourselves. We need to have an honest conversation with ourselves about manners and examine the delicate and sensitive aspects, so that we are prepared when we enter a new or vulnerable situation. Manners are complex because human dynamics are complex. One person's assumed good manners are another's perceived slight. Everyone, especially me, has a view about the "right" or best way to be, what defines good behavior, or what is acceptable in the home, school, or workplace. The dynamics of human interaction evolve. Rules, policies, standards, and conventions of what is acceptable in particular situations evolve. What may have been bad manners when I began my career (not wearing a tie to work), may be acceptable now. What might have been tolerated then (jokes with racial or sexual overtones) could be grounds for termination now.

I hope you've enjoyed the stories, experiences, and insights I've shared and have learned from. I hope the anecdotes and messages offer practical wisdom as you navigate your way to and through college, participate in a job interview, anticipate the interviews you don't expect, or journey through your career. Perhaps you found guidance that improves your relationships with friends and family. The more you learn about and practice good manners, the wiser you'll be. It is my hope that this journey has inspired you to view manners as *a way of living gracefully,* with values of respect, kindness, and compassion toward others and yourself. I hope that you've come to that splendid place that Dennis and I did when we became fully aware of the beneficial effects of good manners—more than our brains and more than our money. In these stories, I've merged what my mother taught my brother Dennis and me about the importance of good manners with lessons I've absorbed from my thirty-five-year experience with NASA, as well as my training and studies both inside and outside of NASA. My intent has been to pay it forward and leave you with at least one point, one story, one suggestion, or one idea that will bend the arc of your path toward your rightful throne. How do you get to your throne? I'll let Momma have the last word, as she always did:

Manners will take you where brains and money won't.

ACKNOWLEDGMENTS

This book is first and foremost a tribute to our mother, Muriel Yvonne Gassett James. Without her love, patience, and perseverance, we would not be the men we are. Thank God Momma lived long enough to see us reach orbit and stay there.

I am reminded of the moon program. Yes, you can name the first man on the moon, but can you name the launch director? The wind tunnel test engineer for the Saturn V rocket? Any of the tens of thousands of engineers and administrative people, civil servants, and contractors who contributed to the successful mission? What about the janitors who kept the offices clean, enabling their colleagues to work in an environment that was conducive to ensuring that the greatest feat of human engineering could happen? Without them—no moon landing. As the author of this book, I perch at the tip of the proverbial iceberg of many generous and dedicated people, some who do not even know they contributed. Without them—no book.

THE BETA REVIEWERS

Several brave souls accepted the challenge of being "beta reviewers." They scrutinized the manuscript and offered helpful, detailed and honest feedback. I give gratitude to Karen Bradford, Gil Damon, Dr. Matthew Daniels, Brian Delgado, Scott Delgado, Tony Delgado, Milo Goldstein, Max Grasso,

Sojourner Hunt, Brandon James, Jemma Johnson-Shoucair, Gil Knowles, Taylor Kockenmeister, Chris Ledbetter, Eli Miller, Alexia Narcisse, Brandon Outlaw, Dr. Wendy Okolo, Kim Prillerman, Jacinta Richardson, Ed Shoucair, Noah Shpak, Denise Snow, Matt Sorgenfrei, and Dr. Andrea Struve. Bless you all!

MY EDITOR AND PUBLISHER

There must be a special place in Heaven for editors of first-time authors who think Oprah just can't wait to read their opuses. Patience, tolerance, and commitment don't begin to describe Parthenia Hicks, poet laureate and editor extraordinaire. I am grateful to Rick and Sandy for introducing us, and I am grateful to the gods for fortifying Parthenia with the courage and strength to indulge my novice ways. Thank you, Parthenia, for your wise editorial counsel and diligence swathed in loving support.

Every astronaut knows there are teams of dedicated, professional people whose number-one job is to make sure they reach orbit and bring them back safely. Getting this book into "orbit" professionally and safely was the job of Girl Friday Productions. I am grateful to Sara Addicott, Georgie Hockett, and Michael Trudeau and their teams for their expertise and care that turned this dream into reality.

Special thanks to Joe Haddad and Shawna James, who kindly lent their artistic expertise to my novice eyes to help me think through the emotional and personal decisions required to choose an imprint logo and the cover.

CONGRESSMAN ERIC SWALWELL

When Eric first ran for Congress, he came to my house and asked for my support. In the thirty-eight years I had been eligible to vote, I couldn't recall a time someone running for Congress had come knocking in person. I was impressed with his manner and his passion to represent and serve. I appreciate Eric's willingness to write the foreword, and I am proud to call him my congressman.

MY NASA COLLEAGUES

To my many NASA colleagues, thank you for being my extended family. I appreciate those at NASA's Ames Research Center in Silicon Valley, where I spent most of my career. I am in awe of what you do for the United States and for humanity. The people who deserve special praise are those who worked for me when I became a supervisor. I am grateful for the civil servants and contractors in the Ames Education office for their commitment to inspiring the next generation of explorers and innovators—"as only NASA can." There are engineers and scientists somewhere in this country who owe their careers today to your inspiration of yesterday. Thank you for your service.

I am fortunate to have had many NASA colleagues who also became my friends. One, however, stands out: Lew Braxton. Lew and I became roommates early in our careers and enjoyed many fun social times together. Being typical guys, we argued for years about who Karen H. liked the best after we realized we had both dated her in the past (at different times, of course). There are two moments in my NASA history with Lew that had an indelible impact on my career. The first was when he told me he was going to be the deputy center director at Ames, the first Black person to hold that position. When he shared that news, before it was officially announced, I fought back tears of pride. He had come a long way in NASA from his start as a student intern. This strengthened my resolve for higher aspirations in the agency. On the flip side, Lew once kept me from getting fired by the Center Director for something stupid I did. That story will have to wait for another time.

The highlight of my career was being selected as NASA's associate administrator for education. I am grateful to my headquarters colleagues, who welcomed me, helped me, tolerated me, encouraged me, and even criticized me. I stood on the shoulders of NASA Education leaders before me, especially Frank Owens, Dr. Adena Loston, John Hairston, James Stofan, and Dr. Bernice Alston, who all helped shape my NASA Education manners. There are too many wonderful NASA colleagues to name individually, but I would be remiss if I didn't call out my friend Dwayne Brown, my office mate in 1983 and the first person I went to see when I arrived at NASA HQ in 2014 with this question: "So how do I stay out of the doghouse here?" A special shout-out to Sherri McGee, truly the "oracle" for NASA Education in the early days. I am grateful to my Office of Education front office team of Dr. Roosevelt Johnson, Kevin Metrocavage, and Mea Miller. Any success I enjoyed I owe to all the professionals in the Office of Education, Mission Directorate education leads, and the NASA Centers' Education Directors, who, together with their staff, actually did the work. A special thanks to Mike Kincaid, whose professional path crossed with mine a few times. Mike, you were there at the dawn of my tenure as associate administrator with Cheryl (bless you, Cheryl!) to help me get started, and you graciously accepted the baton and succeeded me upon my retirement. My personal heroes at NASA include Barbara Morgan, who, from the shadows of the 1986 Challenger tragedy, became our second educator astronaut, successfully flying on STS 118, the 119th space shuttle flight. Meeting and supporting Barbara in the aftermath of the Challenger tragedy would change my career trajectory for good. She was the first person to call and congratulate me when I became the associate administrator for education.

I am deeply grateful for Major General Charles F. Bolden Jr., the twelfth administrator of NASA, for taking a chance with hiring me. Many will never fully appreciate the extent of Charlie's stellar character and leadership abilities. It was not lost on me that my NASA Headquarters job meant a personal once-in-a-lifetime occurrence. I had the privilege of working for the first Black (Senate confirmed) NASA administrator who, in turn, worked for the first Black president of the United States. Wow! I am indebted for the able guidance of Robert Lightfoot, Lesa Roe, and Ellen Stofan, all of whom skillfully guided our agency through some challenging times and showed me how to lead with grace. And I really hit the jackpot when Dr. Dava Newman became the deputy administrator. I couldn't have asked for a better mentor and boss. Thank you all for putting up with me.

My predecessor, NASA astronaut Leland Melvin, set the bar too high for anyone to follow. Fortunately, they took away his bar and gave me a different one. Thank goodness! Talk about a rock star. Handsome, charismatic, and extremely intelligent, Leland, as I write, is the only flown astronaut to have previously been a professional NFL football player. I'm always grateful for your encouragement with this project, my brother, and I appreciate all you do to inspire students.

EMILY POST

The twentieth-century writer Emily Post, with her seminal work, *Etiquette* (1922), is still relevant and foundational. I respectfully acknowledge her contributions and those of her descendants at the Emily Post Institute in Vermont. I unabashedly stand on their shoulders. If the reader is inspired to further their manners' work, I strongly recommend reading *The Etiquette Advantage in Business: Personal Skills for Professional Success*, 3rd edition, by Peter Post.

MY FAMILY

To my spiritual hero, friend, cousin, and someone I have loved and admired for as long as I have known her—Dr. Matti Dobbs Mavritte. Bless you, and thank you for your love and guidance in this endeavor and for always believing in me and this project.

To my best friend, collaborator, and brother, Captain Dennis Dobbs James, who patiently, and at times painfully, navigated early drafts of the manuscript. I particularly appreciate Dennis's occasional channeling of our dear mother, complete with pursed lips and utter disdain for my committing some grammatical crime worthy of public humiliation. Surely, without Dennis's corrections, Momma would pack up and tell her angel friends in Heaven, "Excuse me. I'll be back soon. My poor son Donald has lost his mind." I would do anything to have Momma back, even for one more admonishment about my grammatical carelessness.

The rocks of my life are my wife, Tanya, and our children, Brandon and Shawna. I am grateful for their love, support, and patience. They are the core of Team Donald. It is for them that I live. It is from them that I have joy.

ABOUT THE AUTHORS

DONALD G. JAMES

 Donald Gregory James is an executive leader, a manager, a facilitator, a communicator, a mentor, and a friend, father, and husband.

Donald began his thirty-five-year NASA career as a Presidential Management Intern at NASA's Goddard Space Flight Center, Maryland, in 1982. In 1984, he transferred to NASA's Ames Research Center in Mountain View, California, where he served in a variety of roles of increasing responsibility and complexity, including public affairs, government and community relations, and education.

Donald decided to make a career at NASA after the 1986 *Challenger* tragedy. *Challenger* affected him deeply. Asked to support the postaccident speaking tour of backup Teacher in Space Project astronaut Barbara Morgan, Donald was inspired by the overwhelming love and support for America's space program—and education—that he realized NASA was a special place where he could make a difference. His journey of public service would take him from being an intern to the Senior Executive Service as a member of NASA's senior leadership team.

I realized that much of my success came from
the lessons I learned from my mother, especially her insistence on having good manners.
I realized manners were the foundation of my
life. When my mother died five months after
I retired, I decided to share her lessons and
my NASA experiences to help college-bound
students and early-career professionals.

Donald served as Ames's education director from 1999
to 2006. In the fall of 1996, he co-led the record-setting open
house at Ames, which attracted over a quarter of a million visitors in one day. In early 2006, Donald worked on the *Orion*
crew spacecraft at NASA Johnson Space Center, where he
drafted the program's first project plan. Later that year, he was
named project manager for NASA's (successful) bid to host the
International Space University's 2009 Space Studies Program
(ISU-SSP), attracting an ISU-SSP record 136 students from
over thirty-three nations, supported by over fifteen corporate
and nonprofit partners.

In August of 2014, NASA Administrator Charlie Bolden
selected Donald to serve as the agency's associate administrator for education, where he led an enterprise composed of 75
civil servants and over 250 contractors who were organized to
strengthen NASA's and the nation's future technical workforce.
Under his leadership, NASA learner and educator engagement
reached over a million people a year. He retired from NASA on
March 31, 2017.

Donald holds a BA in international relations from the
University of Southern California. He was awarded a three-year
graduate fellowship from the National Science Foundation to
pursue his MA in international economic development from
the American University. He also studied economics and history at Cambridge University and attended Harvard's Senior

Executive Fellows program. He is the recipient of numerous awards and citations for exemplary service.

Donald was inspired by the places he's lived overseas, including Ghana, Thailand, Kenya, and Niger. He's also traveled to Morocco, Uganda, France, Italy, Spain, Germany, Mexico, Canada, China, the Philippines, Hong Kong, the UK, and Japan.

Donald and his wife, Tanya, live in Pleasanton, California. Their children, Brandon and Shawna, are embarking on their careers in business and theater respectively.

DENNIS D. JAMES

Donald's book collaborator, his younger brother Dennis Dobbs James, is a captain with American Airlines. Dennis learned to fly in the US Marine Corps, where he flew the RF-4 *Phantom*. Dennis has been a licensed pilot for thirty-eight years. As a commercial pilot, he has flown several aircraft throughout his career.

In addition to the places he and Donald have lived abroad, Dennis has also traveled extensively internationally and throughout the United States.

Dennis holds a BA in journalism from the University of Southern California and an MBA from the University of California, Irvine. He also mentors young people and early-career professionals. He was the founder of "Young Aces," a nonprofit established to take young, at-risk youth flying to inspire them to consider aviation careers. Dennis is an avid golfer and currently lives in Roseville, California.

MURIEL YVONNE GASSETT JAMES ("MOMMA")

Muriel Yvonne Gassett James (1929–2017) was reared and educated in Atlanta, Georgia, where she attended the First Congregational Church and graduated from Spelman College, a historic Black women's college. She earned a master's degree in French at Middlebury College in Vermont.

At Middlebury, she met and married another student, Charles James. Muriel accompanied Charles when he attended law school at Yale. After his graduation in the early 1950s, the young couple drove across the country to California, settling first in Sacramento and later in Stockton, where Charles established a private law practice.

While in Stockton, Muriel gave birth to three sons. The eldest, Charles Jr., died tragically at three years of age. The family returned to Sacramento in 1962 when Charles Sr. joined the California State Attorney General's office. Two years later, Charles accepted an administrative position with the newly established Peace Corps. "Hi honey, we're moving to Ghana," he announced to his wife. Ever the good trooper, Muriel packed up the family and moved to Accra. Their marriage ended in Africa, and Muriel returned to Sacramento with her two sons to begin her long teaching career.

She taught English and French in junior high and then high school in Sacramento. She loved her students. Over the years, student demographics changed, especially after the Vietnam War. Some students Americanized their names to make them easier for teachers and students to pronounce. But Muriel insisted on learning their birth names and pronouncing them as their parents did.

Muriel was also a stickler for correct English. "You lie down when you are tired, but you lay (something) down." "You rear children and raise chickens." "You have finished a project, but your food is done."

After retirement in 1989, she enjoyed a life of duplicate bridge, socializing with her many friends, spending time with her two "boys," as she called them, enjoying her two grandchildren, and her most recent pastime—"working at the office." The "office" was actually the casino. Muriel loved to gamble—nickel slots only. It is fitting that the day before she died, she had gone to "the office" with her dear friend Marcellet and won.

Muriel was a lifetime member of the NAACP and maintained close contact with her Delta Sigma Theta sorority sisters. But her main occupation and passion in life was her boys, Donald and Dennis. She gave them her time, a solid education, and unconditional love.

Made in the USA
Las Vegas, NV
30 January 2021

16776326R00164